Usurpers, A New Look
at Medieval Kings

Usurpers, A New Look at Medieval Kings

Michele Morrical

PEN & SWORD
HISTORY

First published in Great Britain in 2021 by
Pen & Sword History
An imprint of
Pen & Sword Books Ltd
Yorkshire – Philadelphia

ISBN 978 1 52677 950 2

A CIP catalogue record for this book is
available from the British Library.

Typeset by Mac Style
Printed and bound by CPI Group (UK) Ltd, Croydon, CR0 4YY

Pen & Sword Books Limited incorporates the imprints of Atlas,
Archaeology, Aviation, Discovery, Family History, Fiction, History,
Maritime, Military, Military Classics, Politics, Select, Transport,
True Crime, Air World, Frontline Publishing, Leo Cooper, Remember
When, Seaforth Publishing, The Praetorian Press, Wharncliffe
Local History, Wharncliffe Transport, Wharncliffe True Crime
and White Owl.

For a complete list of Pen & Sword titles please contact

PEN & SWORD BOOKS LIMITED
47 Church Street, Barnsley, South Yorkshire, S70 2AS, England
E-mail: enquiries@pen-and-sword.co.uk
Website: www.pen-and-sword.co.uk

Or

PEN AND SWORD BOOKS
1950 Lawrence Rd, Havertown, PA 19083, USA
E-mail: Uspen-and-sword@casematepublishers.com
Website: www.penandswordbooks.com

Contents

Introduction

In the Middle Ages, England had to contend with a string of usurpers who deposed reigning kings and seized power for their own houses, thereby disrupting the British monarchy and ultimately changing the course of English history. There have been many infamous usurpers to come out of medieval England including William the Conqueror, King Stephen, Henry Bolingbroke, Edward IV, Richard III, and Henry Tudor. But did they really deserve the title of usurper or were they unfairly vilified by biased chroniclers and royal propaganda?

In this book we will examine the lives of six medieval kings, the circumstances that brought each man to power, and whether or not they really usurped their thrones. Along the way readers will hear stories of some of the most fascinating and daring people from medieval Europe, including Empress Matilda, the first woman who nearly succeeded at becoming queen of England; Eleanor of Aquitaine, the queen of both France and England; the cruel reign of Richard II which caused his own family to revolt against him; the struggle between Henry VI, Margaret of Anjou, Richard of York, and Edward IV during the Wars of the Roses; Richard III and his monstrous reputation as a child-killer; and Henry VII, who came out of obscurity and established arguably the most famous royal family of all: the Tudors.

The reader might be surprised to know that not all these kings were really usurpers, at least not in this author's opinion. The purpose of this book is to correct popular misconceptions and long-held beliefs about these six kings who have been traditionally labeled as usurpers. One of the most difficult aspects of doing historical research during this time period is the lack of trustworthy sources, or sometimes the lack of any sources at all. Notably, you have the chroniclers who are clearly biased, perhaps even hired by a king to write the official history of their reign, so it's important to take those accounts with a grain of salt. To unravel the truth, I have relied on a variety of sources, including medieval chroniclers, vintage biographies from the late-nineteenth and early-twentieth centuries, and the newest research by modern-day historians for the most accurate, up-to-date information we have on the lives of these infamous medieval kings of England.

Part I

William the Conqueror (1066–1087)

1

The Anglo-Saxons

Life in early medieval England was often a frightening, brutal experience for its residents. Between the years 410 to 1066, England's inhabitants endured repeated invasions from Continental intruders, resulting in the loss of land, the slaughter of their families, and forced submission to foreign kings.[1] Prior to the centuries of invasions, England had some manner of safety and protection as it was under the rule of the mighty Roman Empire. When the Roman Empire fell in 410 AD, England found itself isolated and unprotected with no overlord to protect it from the threat of foreign invaders. Having no cohesive united defence, such as a standing army or castles to protect its people, England found itself in a power vacuum that many foreign countries were quick to take advantage of. After the fall of Rome, the vulnerable island of Great Britain became an easy target for invasion.

The first large scale foreign invasion came from a group of German and Danish migrants who later became known as the Anglo-Saxons. Their three tribes, the Angles, Saxons, and Jutes, sailed to England shortly after the fall of the Roman Empire and conquered both the eastern and southern territories.[2] They hadn't just come to England to conquer it and return home with their booty: they had come to stay. England had a wealth of natural resources and with no English ruler to oppose them, it was quite easy for them to move in, establish rule over all the occupants, and divide the land up among themselves.

The Anglo-Saxons organised England into seven separate kingdoms: East Anglia, Northumbria, Mercia, Wessex, Sussex, Essex, and Kent. The seven kingdoms of the Anglo-Saxons operated independently from each other, meaning they had their own rulers, their own policies, customs, and even languages. They spent the entirety of the 400-year establishment fighting against each other to expand their territories because more land meant more income from taxes. It was one of the easiest ways to quickly enrich themselves and more money meant more power.

In the 860s, a new, more serious threat emerged: the Vikings. These Nordic warriors had begun terrorising all of Europe with their technologically advanced longships and their superior military skills. By 871 they had successfully overtaken every single Anglo-Saxon kingdom except for Wessex which at that time was ruled by King Alfred. Alfred successfully fought off the Vikings for many years and also held them back by negotiating peace treaties. Alfred was unrelenting in the defence of his kingdom and after fifteen years of conflict, the Vikings finally gave up and the last of the invaders left England. Alfred was the last ruler standing and in 886, he was appointed King of the Anglo-Saxons, having rule over all the seven kingdoms of England.[3]

Over the next thirteen years of his reign, Alfred managed to establish England as a single, unified kingdom. He organised its military defences, established boroughs, and built large fortifications to protect citizens and soldiers. Not only was he a brilliant military strategist, he was also a very educated man. He had personally translated many important religious works into English and encouraged the Anglo-Saxons to adopt English in the vernacular rather than Latin which was a language only the nobility could read.[4] He was a very pious man and felt it his duty to convert his people from the old pagan ways to his newly adopted religion: Christianity.[5]

King Alfred the Great died on 26 October 899 from an unknown abdominal illness or disease that had plagued him throughout his life.[6] He was succeeded by his eldest son, Edward the Elder, and thereafter King Alfred's bloodline ruled England for the next 130 years.[7] These years were marked by a constant state of war against Scandinavian invaders as evidenced by the relatively short reigns of Alfred's descendants. During those 130 years, nine of Alfred's heirs ruled which gives them each an average reign of only fourteen years. It was indeed a dangerous life, not just for the inhabitants of England but especially for the rulers.

The rule of Alfred's descendants ended in 1016 when the king of Denmark, Cnut the Great, took over England and added 'King of England' to his title. Just three years earlier, Cnut's father, King Sweyn Forkbeard had successfully deposed the current reigning English king, Aethelred the Unready, great-great-grandson of King Alfred. Aethelred was a terrible king. He was badly advised and ill-prepared to deal with the Viking invaders who had renewed their invasions early in his reign. He had no military strategy in place to protect the citizens of England and they hated him for leaving them helpless against the Viking raiders. Even Aethelred's own son, Edmund Ironside, revolted against his father's incompetent rule.[8]

Aethelred did have one strategy for dealing with Viking invaders: paying them off. In 991, Aethelred paid £16,000 to King Olaf of Norway for him to abort his invasion of England. When word got out that England was handing out money to invaders, they were hit by even more raiders looking to get their fair share of the king's money. Throughout the remainder of his reign, Aethelred spent at least £250,000 paying the Vikings just to leave, the equivalent of hundreds of millions of pounds today.[9]

It wasn't long before the Vikings decided they wanted more than just money, they wanted to rule this rich kingdom of England themselves. After many more years of relentless war, the kingdom was on the brink of collapse as King Cnut of Norway neared the city of London with his army. Aethelred and his reconciled son, Edmund Ironside, tried to defend London but were defeated and King Aethelred died shortly after the battle. Edmund Ironside inherited the throne and continued fighting off the Vikings but was defeated badly by Cnut at the Battle of Assandun in Essex and was forced to name Cnut as his own heir. Just one month after the agreement was made, Edmund mysteriously died, and Cnut succeeded him. England was now ruled by a Danish king.

One of Cnut's first acts as king of England was tradition in Viking culture: marrying the widow of the defeated enemy, which in this case was Emma. Emma was a Norman princess who had first been married to Aethelred the Unready in 1002 when she was 17 years old. Despite hating each other, Aethelred and Emma managed to produce two male heirs: Edward and Alfred.[10] Emma's second marriage to Cnut also produced a son: Harthacnut. In the Viking tradition, polygamy was totally acceptable, so Cnut kept his first wife, Aelfgifu, and together they had two sons: Swein and Harold Harefoot. This messy family tree triggered a succession crisis when the 40-year-old King Cnut died unexpectedly on 12 November 1035 without officially naming his heir.[11]

To be fair to Cnut, he did have a succession plan in mind, he just never put it in writing. He wanted to divide up his many possessions among his three sons. Swein, his eldest son by his first marriage, was sent to Norway to rule as his regent. Harold Harefoot would be made regent in England. For Hathacnut, his son with second wife Emma, Denmark would be the location of his regency. Since Cnut never made these assignments official, his councillors were forced to select the next king of England. This must have been a nerve-racking task considering the king had no less than three sons competing for their father's inheritance. They believed Harthacnut to be Cnut's true heir, however, Harthacnut was stuck in Denmark fighting off an invasion from King Magnus of Norway. Instead, the council decided to make Harold the temporary regent in England until such time as Harthacnut returned to England from Denmark to begin his official reign.

Harold had different plans. Since he was the only son physically located in England when his father died, he took full advantage of the situation and immediately started manoeuvring to have himself coronated as king of England. Queen Emma tried but failed to raise a resistance against Harold (she instead favoured her own son Harthacnut) but was forced to flee to Flanders. Harold's path to the throne was now clear and he was coronated as Harold I, King of England on 12 November 1035. He was not to be a popular king though. The *Prose Brut Chronicle* disparaged him in the following passage: 'He went astray from the qualities and conduct of his father King Cnut, for he cared not at all for knighthood, for courtesy, or for honour, but only for his own will.'[12] He should have taken more care because he had a lot of brothers waiting in the wings to take his place should he be deposed.

Aside from Cnut's three sons, there were two other young boys who were in the running for king of England: Edward (later known as Edward the Confessor) and his brother Alfred. As sons of the former king of England, Aethelred the Unready, most people considered them to be the true heirs to the throne, not the Danish king's sons. Cnut considered Emma's two sons enough of a threat that he sent them out of the realm, and they were raised with cousins in Normandy. Some chroniclers suggest he meant to have them killed but experienced an emotion rare to him: mercy.[13] Now, their mother Emma was about to toss them into the drama.

In the fall of 1036, Emma wrote to Edward and Alfred in Normandy encouraging them to mount an invasion against King Harold. As sons of King Aethelred, they had more than enough blood-right to rule the kingdom of England. Edward followed his mother's request and mounted a half-hearted attempt at an English invasion but returned to Normandy when he realised his forces would be insufficient to get the job done. His brother Alfred then made an invasion attempt of his own but was captured by Earl Godwin, the most powerful nobleman and land magnate in England who was a close ally of King Harold's. Godwin turned Alfred over to the king's men and he was brutally tortured, blinded, and killed.[14]

2

William the Bastard

The murder of his own wife's son did very little for King Harold's popularity. He was already widely hated throughout England and the cruel execution of Alfred only served to compound the problem.[1] However, there was someone who hated King Harold far more than the citizens of England: his half-brother Harthacnut.

Harthacnut expected to be king of England upon King Cnut's death in 1035, according to his father's verbal wishes, but Harold was in the right place at the right time and took the throne for himself rather than being his brother's regent. In 1039 after finally signing a treaty with King Magnus of Norway, Harthacnut turned his attention to deposing his brother Harold and claiming the throne of England for himself. He had prepared a large invasion fleet in Denmark and his mother Emma was drumming up support for him in Flanders. All the invasion preparations turned out to be quite unnecessary when in March 1040 King Harold died and messengers came to Harthacnut asking him to be the next king of England. Even though he had won back the Crown, his hatred of Harold had not been extinguished. He openly displayed his disgust for his brother by dumping his dead corpse in the River Thames, which was a terribly undignified ending for a king.[2]

If the citizens of England were looking forward to the return of the rightful king after the deposition of the usurping brother, they were about to be utterly disappointed. Harthacnut didn't exactly have a soft touch, he was more of a bull in a china shop, and his reign ended up being an utter failure.[3] As the new king of England, he set about punishing all the people he believed to be involved in his stepbrother Alfred's murder. Next, he quadrupled taxes on his people which caused the people of Worcester to rise up in rebellion against their king. Harthacnut's not-so-subtle response was to lay waste to the town, killing the citizens, and burning down their houses.[4]

With his kingdom seemingly out of control and on the brink of collapse, the unmarried and childless King Harthacnut invited his half-brother, Edward, to come to England and help him hold the kingdom. It was quite possible that Harthacnut knew he had a fatal illness, and having fathered no children, had no heir.[5] It seems that his invitation to Edward was a clear attempt to bring him into the fold of royal government in preparation to take it over himself one day. Harthacnut's decision to bring Edward to England was a prudent choice because just one year later, King Harthacnut dropped dead at a wedding feast on Easter Sunday 1043.

On 3 April 1043 at Winchester Cathedral, Edward the Confessor was crowned King of England and the English monarchy was back in the hands of a descendent of King Alfred the Great. Edward the Confessor reigned for twenty-six years, longer than any other of King Alfred's descendants. While Edward was a much more capable ruler than his half-brothers, he didn't exactly set the world on fire. He was known mostly for his monkish piousness but was also described by some chroniclers as weird and weak.[6] He was likely a somber guy due to the circumstances of his upbringing. He had lived in exile most of his life and his own mother abandoned him to marry his father's enemy, so it's no doubt this affected his personality.

The two main focuses of Edward the Confessor's reign were fighting off Viking invasions and trying to gain the support of the powerful Godwins of England, former allies of the hated King Harthacnut. Earl Godwin had only been in his early twenties when he rose to power as a close companion and adviser to King Cnut, Harthacnut's father. King Cnut often left Godwin in control of England while he was abroad on business. Since Godwin was the most powerful man in England and held virtually all the power in northern England, it was imperative for Edward to win him to his side.

The first order of business in this endeavor was to settle the matter of the murder of Edward's brother, Alfred, which Godwin had been accused of participating in. Edward gave his forgiveness to Godwin and from that point the two sides were reconciled. They sealed their new alliance with a marriage. On 23 January 1045, Edward married Earl Godwin's daughter Edith. But the peace wouldn't last for long. Godwin was an overmighty lord and King Edward struggled to keep in under submission.

Trouble between the men came to a head in the fall of 1051 when Godwin refused King Edward's command to harry the towns of Kent and Dover after their people attacked the king's brother-in-law, Count Eustace of Boulogne, and killed nineteen of his men. After Godwin's refusal, Edward called a special council meeting in London to address the issue, and probably intended to put Godwin on trial but sensing the danger, Godwin was a no-show. As punishment, King Edward stripped the family of all their earldoms, exiled them, and sent his own wife Edith, Earl Godwin's daughter, to a nunnery.

Earl Godwin would not be deterred. He spent his time in exile planning a rebellion against King Edward. In the spring of 1052 Godwin attempted to invade England, however, the English coast was heavily guarded by the king's men and a storm forced Godwin to abort. He was back with another invasion attempt in August 1053 and this time King Edward was forced to reconcile and restore the Godwin's earldoms rather than face a new civil war. Edward also restored his wife Edith and took her back in. Despite this difficulty, Edward and Edith had a seemingly happy marriage and a cordial relationship, although they remained childless. It's no wonder since all the chroniclers of that time wrote about how their relationship had more of a father and daughter dynamic than that of a husband and wife.[7] In all actuality, he was probably too devout to his religion to give his wife a child. Plus, there was a big age difference. Edward was 42 when they were married and Edith was only 20, so it's not surprising that the pious Edward took on a fatherly role towards her.

The combined trouble with Godwin and the lack of children from his marriage with Edith made Edward for the first time seriously consider who he should name as his heir to the throne of England. There were several contenders including Edgar Ætheling, grandson of Edmund Ironside (King Edmund II), but he was a young child and had lived his life in exile. He certainly wouldn't be a strong enough king to ward off the aggression of the powerful Godwins. Then there was a Godwin himself: Harold, son of Earl Godwin. Harold was the earl of Essex and some favoured him since he was English, but Edward found him unacceptable. Then there were two foreigners: King Sweyn of Denmark and King Harald Hardrada of Norway, but no Englishmen wanted to be ruled by Scandinavians. Lastly there was Duke William of Normandy, a cousin of King Edward's, therefore, a contender with royal English blood in his very veins.

Born in 1027 or 1028, William was the illegitimate son of Edward the Confessor's cousin, Duke Robert of Normandy, and Herleva, a local girl in town whose father was a tanner.[8] The pregnancy was probably unintentional as the two were only around 17 years old at the time and had vast distance between their social standings. In fact, shortly after the birth of their son William, Herleva was married off to a modest lord near Paris and with him she bore two sons who would also rise to power: Odo of Bayeux and Robert, Earl of Kent and Count of Mortain. Even though William was technically a bastard, his father Robert had no other sons, so he named William as his successor to the duchy of Normandy. The Normans didn't get hung up on legitimacy as much as the English did when it came to succession and inheritances.

In 1034 Duke Robert shocked his Norman magnates when he announced he would be going to Jerusalem on pilgrimage. The journey to the Holy Lands was fraught with peril and he was also endangering his Norman nobles by withdrawing his personal protection for the next few years. His noblemen were right to be worried: on his journey home from Jerusalem he died from a sudden illness, leaving his 7-year-old son as the new duke of Normandy.

Normandy was a very dangerous and unsettled place, especially now that a child was at the reigns. Fortunately, Robert left William a strong support system to help protect him and help rule during his minority. Unfortunately, these men became the targets of feuding aristocracy families and all died mysteriously or by outright murder in the early years of William's reign. The environment was so dangerous that his uncle Walter slept in his chamber at night and on more than one occasion had to whisk the boy away to safety to avoid assassination attempts.[9] The effect that this must have had on a child's psychology is difficult to understand but it would certainly shape his character and strengthen his resolve to put Normandy in order.

In 1046 William was 18 years old and ready to end his minority, meaning he was ready to take the reins and rule over Normandy in his own right. Later that year he faced his first huge crisis when his own cousin, Guy of Burgundy, rebelled against him and tried to take the duchy of Normandy from him. It was only with the help of his overlord, King Henry I of France, that William was able to put down the rebellion at the Battle of Val-ès-Dunes. However, Guy would spend the next four years taunting William with little skirmishes until finally in 1050 William captured Guy and exiled him from the duchy.

William learned from his experiences with his cousin Guy and determined to rule his duchy proactively instead of reactively. From 1051 on he quickly emerged as a powerful force in Normandy and throughout the whole of France. He launched offensive campaigns to take back control of towns and fortresses that had been captured from him while he was still a young, ineffective ruler. In the autumn of 1051, he entered into a dispute with the count of Anjou which resulted in William capturing the towns of Domfront and Alençon, two vitally important strongholds in southern Normandy. It was from these campaigns that William received his reputation as being a fierce and cruel warrior, laying waste to the towns and unmercifully torturing and killing its inhabitants.[10]

In the fall of 1051, William's newfound reputation as a power player got the attention of King Edward who had recently fallen out with the Godwins. Edward invited his cousin to England for a visit and it was during this visit that King Edward apparently promised to name William as his heir, which would make him king of England upon Edward's death.[11] It really wasn't Edward's throne to give away because in England it was not yet customary for the current king to select a successor. Instead, the decision was made by the Witan or Witenagemot, a group of archbishops, bishops, earls, abbots, and other high officials.[12] Whether Edward really promised William the throne is undocumented and many chroniclers have written that Edward also promised the throne to many others, including King Harald Haldrada of Norway. Nevertheless, William whole-heartedly believed that he would be Edward's heir and would be the next king of England. In fact, for the next fifteen years William went around advertising the fact and let it be known everywhere that Edward had selected him as heir to the English throne.

Back in Normandy William had a lot of other things to worry about rather than the English throne. He faced another major challenge in early 1054 when the king, Henry I of France, formed an alliance with William's enemy, the count of Anjou, thus breaking William's own alliance with France. William must have felt that his very duchy was under the threat of extinction with Henry I's invasion. The new French alliance launched a two-pronged coordinated invasion of Normandy and William responded swiftly. He split his considerable army into two forces, himself leading men west to face the king of France. William sent his most trusted magnates east to battle the French forces led by his own brother, Odo, in what would become known as the Battle of Mortemer. After several hours of intense fighting, the French forces fell into disarray and were soundly slaughtered by the Normans. When news of the French army's defeat at Mortemer reached King Henry I in western France, he simply surrendered and withdrew his troops. But the king wasn't done challenging William just yet. He launched another joint invasion with the count of Anjou in August 1057, but was decimated by William's troops at the Battle of Varaville and forced to surrender.

The importance of William's victories in the early years of his adult reign cannot be understated. Not only did he successfully beat the king of France and save his duchy from French rule, he also cemented his position as a fierce and courageous military commander.[13] Nearly all the Norman magnates flocked to his side at this time. It was wise to hitch your future to a powerful man in charge command of his kingdom and he was evidently rising to this stature in the eyes of Normans. They saw in William a new, powerful ruler who could lead their duchy to great prosperity, wealth, and prestige. In fact, it was probably around this time that William began promising Norman barons substantial lands in England if they supported him. Their backing would be an essential component of his success in the conquest of England in 1066.

By 1060, Normandy was a stabilised duchy with an exciting young leader whose star was on the rise. Now that William had defeated all his challengers, he could turn his attention to building up Normandy as an *elite* French duchy and a prominent European player. Under William, the cities of Rouen and Caen were restored and glorified beyond their previous majesty in the days before the Viking invasions. He continued to expand the feudal system which in turn led to a larger, more organised army because his land magnates could call up their fiefs for required service to the king's Norman army. He was also somewhat responsible for the revival of Roman Catholicism in Normandy. William rebuilt the monasteries that had been torn down by the Vikings and reinstated religious houses across his duchy which he subsequently endowed generously. In addition, he sat on many religious councils and even had the power to pass judgement on matters up for discussion and debate.

William's prestige was further increased in 1051 or 1052 when he married Matilda, daughter of Baldwin V, Count of Flanders. William was well-known as a bastard, but Matilda was highly born with impeccable royal lineage. She was descended from both Charlemagne and King Alfred the Great, plus her grandfather and uncle had been kings of France. There is a legend that Matilda initially spurred William's overtures at marriage and thereafter an enraged William pulled her off her horse and beat her in front of her father. Apparently, Matilda was turned on by this show of strength and she actually then agreed to marry him.[14] This scandalous story is likely untrue, but it is possible the story was based on her deep disappointment at being betrothed to a bastard rather than a man of noble and legitimate birth. In either case, William and Matilda had a long and fruitful marriage. He trusted her to be regent in Normandy when he was away and he was said to be completely faithful to her. Together they had ten children that survived into adulthood, including two future kings of England, William II and Henry I.

No doubt the rising influence of Duke William in Normandy was viewed as a threat by the powerful Godwins of England. The family patriarch, Earl Godwin, had died in 1054 after suffering a stroke at Easter dinner and was succeeded by his son Harold who became the earl of Wessex and the king's lieutenant. The Godwin's did not want William to ascend the throne so they put forth a number of other claimants as Edward's heir but ultimately had to stand down and beg forgiveness from the king for overreaching. However, Harold was ambitious and would not be deterred by this minor setback. By this time, he may have had designs of his own on the throne of England.

In 1064, King Edward sent Harold Godwin to Normandy on a royal mission to treat with Duke William. On Harold's voyage across the English Channel, his ship was blown off course and he was forced to come ashore at

Ponthieu instead of Normandy where he was taken prisoner by Count Guy. William came to his rescue, negotiated for his release, and welcomed him with great pomp and circumstance at Rouen. Harold became William's special guest for several months in which time they became close acquaintances and even friends. William took Harold on campaign in Brittany, promised to give him Dover in England when he became king, and even promised one of his daughters in marriage to Harold. Harold then swore an oath to William to support his right to inherit the kingdom of England on Edward the Confessor's death.[15] Whether or not Harold really took the oath has been debated by historians for many years. It seems most likely that he did pledge fealty to William and it may have been forced to do so in order to be allowed to leave Normandy. The other strong possibility is that the two men hatched a plan in which Harold would rule England as William's regent because he would undoubtedly spend a lot of time in his native Normandy.

Things appeared to be set right with the two men but the turn of event in England would change everything. In the fall of 1065, Harold's superiority in England was seriously diminished when there was a major rebellion in northern England against his brother, Tostig, Earl of Northumbria. Tostig was hated for the usual reasons: high taxes, oppressive rule, cruel treatment, unlawful murder, and jealousy of his great wealth and power. The rebels overcame Tostig's guards, ransacked his treasury, and killed at least 200 of his men, including many of Godwin's supporters in the north. Tostig's inability the thwart the rebellion caused the leaders of Yorkshire to send for help from Morcar, the younger brother of the earl of Mercia, and they quickly elected him the new earl of Northumbria.

Harold met the rebels at Northampton and negotiated on behalf of King Edward but the rebels would not surrender unless the king agreed to exile Tostig. The king refused and both sides were at a stalemate. An armed military conflict was now inevitable but so few men turned up to serve in the king's army that Harold had no choice but to surrender. King Edward's submission to the rebels shortly before Christmas 1065 seriously degraded royal authority. This rebellion also did much to destroy the political stability that England had been experiencing under the reign of King Edward the Confessor.

After the disastrous rebellion, there was a huge event the king was keenly looking forward to: the dedication of the new church at Westminster, one of Edward's building projects, scheduled for 28 December 1065. Even though it was his crowning glory, King Edward did not attend the ceremony because he had fallen seriously ill and taken to his bed. He experienced a quick decline in his health during the preceding months and the northern rebellion had drained him physically, emotionally, and spiritually. He took to his bedchamber on 26 December 1065 and never recovered. He died on 5 January 1066, surrounded by his wife and his closest councillors, including Harold Godwin.

On his deathbed, one would have expected King Edward to confirm William of Normandy as his successor to the English throne, however, he did no such thing. In fact, the words he spoke on his deathbed were interpreted as the selection of Harold Godwin. In the *Vita* chronicle, Edward's last words to Harold were reported to be 'I also commend to you those men who have left their native land for love of me and served me faithfully. Take an oath of fealty from them if they wish, and protect and retain them; or send them with your safe conduct across the Channel to their own homes with all they have acquired in my service.'[16] Nowhere in that statement did Edward say Harold should be king. In contrast, it sounds like he wanted Harold to be regent of England. He's basically asking Harold to protect the English people and take an oath of fealty from them if he felt it was necessary for the purpose of political stability until such time as William of Normandy could arrive in England.

We don't know exactly what transpired on Edward's deathbed and if he did command Harold to be his heir but there is one thing for certain. The Godwins did not want to be ruled by a foreigner and give up any of their power, so Harold took William's vague deathbed statement and ran with it, literally. He immediately went to the Witan and told them Edward had named him as his heir. The Witan then appointed him as the next king of England and he was quickly coronated the next day. If he had been really confident that he was Edward's lawful heir and would be widely accepted instead of Duke William of Normandy, he would not have had such a hasty coronation. Harold Godwin was quite well-liked in England and the citizens probably preferred him to a Norman any day of the week, so they went along with Harold's coronation quite willingly.

It took several days for the news of Edward's death and Harold's coronation to travel from the island of England across the Channel to France and to the duchy of Normandy, home of Duke William. William must have been utterly shocked by this sudden turn of events because he was for so long confident that he would be King Edward's heir. He felt a special sense of betrayal that his new friend Harold pulled off a coup of this magnitude. He had no reason to believe that Harold would usurp the crown from him until this very minute when he received the devastating news.

Within days William fired off an angry letter to Harold demanding that he renounce the throne.[17] Harold flatly refused, arguing that the Witan had lawfully chosen him as the next king of England and William was out of luck. This was an absolute outrage to William. He had quite naively believed that the English citizens would rise up in his favour and supplant King Harold but much to his surprise that didn't happen. William was far too proud a man to back down and play dead to Harold, so he resolved himself to take what he believed was rightly his by force. Within a month, William and his councillors began planning what would become the most important and transformative event in English history – the Norman conquest.

3

The Norman Invasion

William was nothing if not a man of action, so it didn't take him long to come up with a plan. He immediately arranged a war council at Lillebonne Castle and invited all his Norman barons. Their support would be crucial if William were to actually pull off his ambitious plan. At the meeting he announced his intention to sail to England that summer to mount his own invasion and dethrone King Harold.

Such a large-scale venture had never been seen before in Europe, not even during the Viking invasions. It was a crazy idea really. The logistics of moving a huge army and thousands of war horses across the English Channel had never been attempted in these kinds of numbers. Plus, Normans were not known to be the best sailors and in order to cross the Channel they would have to contend with strong headwinds in boats that weren't designed to do that, as opposed to the superior Viking longboats. At first, his barons at first were doubtful, but then his friend William fitz Osbern gave an impassioned speech which persuaded nearly all of them to support William's conquest of England.

William spent the spring and summer of 1066 travelling across Normandy personally overseeing preparations for his English invasion. Of utmost importance was the construction of a fleet to transport the soldiers, horses, and war supplies across the channel. There was an existing Norman fleet of ships but it was insufficient for an operation of this size. William pressed his Norman barons to contribute towards the cost of building up to 1,000 ships which was incredibly expensive and a massive undertaking, especially on such a short time frame.

William also wanted to make sure his duchy of Normandy would be safe while he was away in England so he publicly proclaimed his eldest son Robert as his heir and had the barons pledge fealty to him. Additionally, William set up his wife Matilda and son Robert to rule as regents while he was gone on his quest.

William next turned his attention to building up his army. Although he had a decent-sized army of Norman soldiers, it simply would not be enough to defeat the king's army so he hired foreign mercenaries from Flanders,

Germany, Italy, Denmark, Brittany, and France. He set about training this undisciplined group over the next few months so they would be ready to execute his plan in the fall.

His next step was a masterstroke of genius and without it, his conquest of England would have very likely failed. Religion in medieval Europe was the focal point of life for nearly all its people and their daily routines revolved around it. Most would have attended church services at least once a day and stopped to pray several other times throughout the day. They also strongly believed that God's hand was in everything, from the approval of a king to the destiny of a labouring mother. William was smart enough to know that to get the support of the people, the blessing of the church would be necessary so he quietly sent a small envoy to Rome to plead his case and ask for the pope's support in his conquest. Without hearing Harold's side of the story, Pope Alexander II affirmed William's claims that Harold had unlawfully usurped the crown and he further publicly proclaimed his approval of William's quest to unseat Harold and take the throne for himself.[1]

By Easter 1066, King Harold of England knew he had big trouble on his hands because his spies had reported the massive operation that was now underway in Normandy. In response, Harold called up the men in southern England to man the shores and serve watch for Norman invaders. He must have been seriously scared at the impending invasion by William because he also called in his naval fleet and all 2,000 of his housecarls (the king's bodyguards) to man England's defences. By the time the call-outs were done, King Harold had between 10,000-12,000 soldiers and 300-400 ships. All that summer his troops encamped on the southern shores of England watching the Channel but Duke William and the Norman invasion fleet never materialised.

After eight months of meticulous preparation, William was finally ready to launch the invasion. By 10 August 1066 he had gathered all his soldiers and his considerable fleet of ships in the River Dives just east of the city of Caen in Normandy. All told William had about 10,000 soldiers, 3,000 horses, and as many as 700 ships.[2] Since the victory of the papal proclamation of support, scores of people had flocked to him in Normandy to join his conquest and he would need every single person he could get. He was well aware that King Harold had forces stationed all along the English coast so when William's fleet landed, they would have to go ashore together as one cohesive force and they would have to be ready to fight the minute they stepped on English soil.

In order to pull this off, William had to be very calculated about crossing the English Channel. If he left when the winds were blowing too hard or in the wrong direction, there was a very real chance his fleet would be scattered, maybe even shipwrecked. William could be patient, he was not a hasty man like Harold, so he resolved to wait until the wind changed in his favour. Once the wind conditions were agreeable, he would only have a narrow window of one to two days to lead his army across the channel before the weather was likely to change again.

As William waited to set sail, Harold was dealing with the inability to maintain the army he had stationed on the coast. Apparently after three months of waiting, the English soldiers had used up all the local resources and there was no food left to feed the army. Plus, they technically only owed the king two months of military service each year and they had already surpassed that by six weeks. On 8 September 1066, Harold dispersed his army and returned to London with his housecarls.

King Harold was in London for less than two weeks when he received shocking news that an invasion fleet had landed, but it wasn't the one he had expected from Normandy. This invasion force was led by his own estranged brother, Tostig. Tostig had managed to get King Harald Hardrada of Norway to support his English invasion which immediately made it a very serious threat to King Harold's throne. The rebels landed in northern England on 20 September 1066 and burned the town of Scarborough down to the ground. Next, they marched to the northern stronghold city of York but two northern earls, Mercia and Morcar, raised their own troops against the rebels. After a brief but bloody battle, the city surrendered to Tostig and Hardrada. As part of the conditions of surrender, Tostig and Hardrada demanded hostages from York and the handover was scheduled for 24 September at Stamford Bridge. They anticipated a peaceful changeover, so they did not bother wearing their chainmail, nor did they equip themselves for any type of fighting.[3]

Suddenly out of nowhere came King Harold's royal army. He had been over 300 kilometres away in London on 20 September 1066, when he received news of his brother's invasion and somehow managed to race his army the entire distance in only four days. The royal army immediately engaged in battle with the unprepared invaders who fought bravely in Viking fashion but were no match for the king's army. The Battle of Stamford on 24 September 1066, was the longest battle on English soil at that time, lasting from dawn until dusk. Not only was Tostig's and Hardrada's army decimated, both rebel leaders were slain on the battlefield. In one fell swoop, King Harold had eliminated the rebels in the north and the threat of further Scandinavian invasions.

As Harold and his men recovered from their gruelling battle, there was no way he could have known that another invasion was about to descend on his kingdom, this time in southern England, hundreds of kilometres away from his weary and wounded army. Duke William had been patiently waiting to lead his army across the Channel to challenge Harold for the right to rule England. On the evening of 27 September 1066, the winds suddenly changed and William determined the conditions were as good as they would ever be to make the crossing so his fleet on nearly 1,000 ships set out that night.[4] Foul weather churned up the seas as they made their journey, scattering a few ships, but the vast majority of the fleet made a landing at Pevensey the following morning. At this point, William would have received news that the king had gone north to fight King Harald Hardrada, but he wouldn't have known the outcome at the time he sailed to England, therefore, he did not know which Harold/Harald he would be facing.

As soon as he landed in England, he set his men about quickly building a fortification within Pevensey's town walls. Only a few days later he determined that this small market town would not be enough to support his large number of troops, plus the only route in and out of the town was a marshy road which was not conducive to moving a large army with war horses and various military equipment. William mobilised his troops and marched them to Hastings, a town he probably chose because he knew more about it than any other English town from his friend the Abbot of Fécamp.[5] On their march from Pevensey to Hastings, William's army harried every area they passed through, leaving a massive trail of destruction. They killed nearly half of the inhabitants of Pevensey and levelled four villages on their way to Hastings.[6] William had encouraged his men to cause as much chaos and destruction as possible in order to provoke the king to come fight him and that proved to be a winning strategy. As soon as Harold received news of the Norman landing, he raced south with as much of his army as he could organise quickly.

Just as fast as he had raced north to fight Hardrada and Tostig, King Harold raced south to fight William arriving in London in only four days time. Harold spent one week in London readying himself for the crucial upcoming battle and tried to buy more time to gather his army. It was during this week-long stay in London when he found out about Pope Alexander's confirmation of William and excommunication of himself and his followers. This was truly devastating to Harold. As a pious man, he believed God had ordained him to be king of England but now he felt God was turning against him. He was so shaken that he spent the entirety of the day at Waltham Abbey in spiritual contemplation.[7]

After King Harold recovered from his spiritual crisis, he pulled his advisers together to plan out a strategy to rid themselves of William's army. The most pressing problem was the sorry state of the royal army. The king's forces were seriously depleted due to the loss of life at the Battle of Stamford Bridge and the exhaustive marches they were forced to endure. He needed time to rest his troops and muster more men before he could consider facing off with William's army. To buy time, King Harold dispatched a messenger from London who travelled over 100 kilometres to William at Hastings. The messenger brought this message from King Harold:

> He recalls that King Edward first appointed you as his heir, and he remembers he was himself sent to Normandy to assure you of the succession. But he also knows that the same King, his Lord, bestowed on him the kingdom of England when he was dying. With justice, therefore, he bids you go back to your country with your followers. Otherwise he will break the pact of friendship he made with you in Normandy. And he leaves the choice entirely to you.[8]

William's response was definitive: 'I am ready to submit my case against Harold's for judgement either by the law of Normandy or the law of England, whichever he chooses.' Further messages were exchanged but the two sides were in a stalemate. King Harold was the first to make a move. Although his councillors encouraged the king to wait as long as possible to gather more troops, Harold wanted to strike quickly before the news of the pope's decree spread throughout his kingdom.

Against the advice of his councillors, Harold led his small army out of London on the morning of 12 October 1066 and marched them nearly 100 kilometres to Hastings in less than two days. The exhausted army encamped the evening of 13 October on a high ridge near Caldbec Hill, just north of Hastings. This location was chosen because of its defensive nature and because it blocked the two main roads to London. As soon as Harold's army came into view, William called his men together and ordered them to prepare for battle the following morning. William's army was made up of 7,000-8,000 men and King Harold's army was only slightly larger.[9] Although the numbers were fairly equal, William had an advantage over Harold in that approximately 3,000 of his men were on horseback whereas Harold's disorganised army was comprised of men on foot who were not experienced in the art of warfare. William's army was also much better equipped and trained than the king's forces.

In the early morning hours of 14 October 1066, William's army marched toward the ridge upon which King Harold's army was lined up in battle array. William commenced the Battle of Hastings by sending in his archers who found themselves unable to cause much damage because they had to shoot up the hill. The king deployed his own archers who rained down arrows upon William's front line. To help the archers, William sent in his knights and they engaged the king's men in fierce hand-to-hand combat for several hours, but the Normans struggled to make any ground against Harold who had the advantageous spot high on the ridge.

Having made no progress in breaking the king's lines, William recalled his troops off the hill so they could regroup. Harold's army watched the Normans withdraw down the hill and mistakenly believed they were fleeing the battlefield, so they went running down the hill to ambush William's retreating army. Now that they were on common ground, William's mounted knights swung their lines around and charged on the English foot soldiers, cutting them down easily. Seeing how effective this faux retreat had been in luring Harold's men off the ridge, William tried the new tactic again. He ordered a line of his soldiers to feign retreat and the Englishmen came running down the hill yet again. William's knights quickly cut down the front lines while William's archers finished the job by unloosing a barrage of arrows with devastating effect. This manoeuver was repeated several times and the fighting went on until sunset that evening.

Finally, the archers found their true marks. King Harold, along with his brothers Gyrth and Leofwine, were killed on the battlefield the unrelenting Norman arrows. Harold was shot through the eye and the arrow penetrated his brain.[10] Upon seeing their leader slain, the English soldiers fled the battlefield in fear of their lives. The decisive Battle of Hastings had been won by the Norman invader. A vengeful William ordered his slain Norman soldiers to be buried but left the English corpses to rot on the battlefield. William had lost approximately 3,000 soldiers while the English dead numbered 5,000, including included many members of the nobility. A spiteful William refused to hand over the deceased King Harold's body to his mother despite her promises of a vast amount of gold in exchange. To this day, no one knows exactly where King Harold's body is buried.[11]

Although William had decisively won the showdown battle with the king, the England was not yet his. Next, he would have to get control of London which would be no easy feat. The citizens of London were not likely to welcome a foreign invader with open arms unless they hated their existing king and by all accounts Harold was a very well-liked ruler. So as William rested his troops overnight in Hastings, word reached London of the king's demise and his councillors took swift action by recognising the young Edgar Ætheling as Harold's heir.[12] However, they did not enact a hasty coronation for Edgar as they had done for Harold. Perhaps they doubted this move in light of the pope's declaration that William was the rightful king of England.

After five days of rest, William gathered his army and started marching towards London, capturing and harrying town after town along the way. He manoeuvered his troops around London until they encircled the entire city. With no royal army left to defend them, Londoners were helpless against the fierce Norman army. It was at this point that William received his first submission of fealty pledged by Edith, widow of Edward the Confessor. Next, Edgar Ætheling, Harold's heir, and Stigand, Archbishop of Canterbury, submitted to William and pledged oaths of fealty. With the support of the archbishop of Canterbury whose job is was to coronate kings, everything else fell into place for William. He was not forced to attack the city. Instead, the Witan invited him to become the next king of England.[13]

A few days before Christmas 1066, William and his most loyal retainers made their official entry into the city of London. He was coronated as King of England on Christmas Day 1066. Shortly thereafter he held many meetings with many English noblemen and demanded that they each pledge oaths of fealty to him. Then his builders began constructing the White Tower within the grounds of the Tower of London in order to provide a defensible base in the heart of the city. In Normandy it was much more common to have castles and fortifications in each large town and William was responsible for bringing this innovation to England. In fact, throughout his reign as king, he built nearly 100 castles throughout England, a monumental achievement even by modern-day standards.

By March 1067, William felt England was under control enough for him to return to Normandy and celebrate his monumental victory over King Harold. He left his trustiest Norman magnates back in England to run things in his absence, primarily his brother Odo of Bayeux and his steward William Fitz Osbern. In Normandy he received a hero's welcome and he put on a dazzling display for all the people to see, showing off the riches he had acquired in England, including lavish clothes made of cloth of gold. He spent the next few months on progress in Normandy, showing himself to the people and exhibiting his magnificence. Nevertheless, he was forced to return to England in 1067 when the first serious threat of rebellion arose.

4

The Subjugation of England and Normandy

Although William had won the crown of England in a single battle, the fight to gain control over England itself had only just begun. King William I would spend the first ten years of his reign fighting off foreign invaders and internal rebellions.

During the first full year of his reign, he faced no less than four rebellions. The first rebellion was instigated by English magnate Edric the Wild who called on Welshmen to raise a rebellion in Herefordshire. That rebellion fizzled out as did the second rebellion in Kent. There the citizens asked Count Eustace of Boulogne to come to England and help them overthrow William. The Kentish rebels attempted to take Dover Castle but failed and Eustace fled back across the Channel. The third rebellion was in the summer of 1067 when three illegitimate sons of King Harold invaded from Ireland but they were fought off by the citizens of Bristol.

There was a fourth, more serious threat from King Sweyn II of Denmark that caused William to leave Normandy to deal with the problem personally. But when William landed in England, he discovered another huge problem: the citizens of Exeter were about to launch a rebellion against him. William immediately marched his army of mercenaries to Exeter and besieged the town for eighteen days until they finally surrendered. Thereafter, most surrounding counties submitted in obedience, including Gloucester and Bristol.

By the spring of 1068, William had much to celebrate. He had conquered England against all odds and had survived his first year as king despite numerous rebellions. He celebrated Easter 1068 in London and held a great court at Westminster with his new English magnates and the Norman magnates who had been granted English estates. He must have been feeling secure at this point because he chose this time to bring his wife Matilda to England for the very first time. Along with Matilda on the voyage from Normandy to London were their three sons Robert, Richard, and William.

William's victory celebration turned out to be a little premature as there were still pockets of simmering unrest throughout his new kingdom which would have to be dealt with decisively if he hoped to hold onto his crown.

That became apparent shortly after Easter 1068 when Edgar Ætheling deserted William's court and was harbored by King Malcolm of Scotland. The two men were undoubtedly working together on a plan to supplant William and place Edgar on the throne. Back in England, William's earls in the north, Edwin and Morcar, conspired with the Scotland and King Sweyn II of Denmark to overthrow the king. King William rode north to York, caused the local magnates to submit to him, and negotiated a truce with Scotland.

The year 1069 was no less eventful in terms of uprisings and rebellions. In January 1069, one of William's Norman earls was murdered in the streets of Durham, leading to civil unrest that quickly spread to York. A few months later, Edgar and King Sweyn II launched their joint invasion of York. When the people of York put up a resistance, Edgar and Sweyn burned down their town. The city submitted to Edgar on 20 September 1069.[1]

The fall of York stirred many other rebellions in the north, including revolts in Dorset and Somerset. King William acted swiftly to these latest threats, riding north with his army and putting down rebellions in each town he passed through. Once he neared York, he ordered his troops to harry all the surrounding areas, killing all the animals and burning the crops, so the rebels inhabiting York Castle would have no means of sustenance. William's slash and burn campaign against York was particularly barbaric and the destruction he caused left the city in desolation for an entire generation.[2] So fearful was William's reputation after the harrying of York that even King Sweyn II decided to take his soldiers and ships back home to Denmark. It probably didn't hurt that William offered him a cash bribe to leave.

In the spring of 1070, King Sweyn II came back to England for more, launching an invasion in concert with a Lincolnshire nobleman named Hereward. By June they had ransacked Peterborough Abbey in Cambridgeshire, about 150 kilometres north of London, and burned the cathedral down. Once again, Sweyn was persuaded to leave England with the help of a cash bribe. His partner Hereward wasn't ready to give up yet, so he allied with the troublesome northern earl Morcar in their own rebellion. William led an army against them and captured Morcar but Hereward disappeared and was never heard from again.

While William was in England dealing with unrest there, some of his unruly Norman barons were fostering rebellions of their own. Count Geoffrey of Mayenne instigated a rebellion in the city of Le Mans, Maine in 1069 and then again in the spring of 1070. Further danger emerged in the spring of February 1071 when Baldwin VI, Count of Flanders, passed away and his wife Richildis took control of the duchy on behalf of her son.

William had been too busy putting down rebellions in England to attend to the troubles in Normandy until the winter of 1071 at which time he held court with his leading councillors and left his half-brother Odo of Bayeux in charge of Normandy so he could sail back to England and deal with a new Scandinavian invasion.

William quickly realised that he could not personally deal with all the rebellions on the island of England and the duchy of Normandy at the same time so he devised a plan to deal with Scotland once and for all. In the summer of 1072 he led an offensive army into the heart of Scotland to put down King Malcolm. Malcolm was so frightened by William's huge army that he immediately negotiated a truce and pledged to be his man from that point forward. Additionally, William made him promise not to aid English rebels and made him expel Edgar Ætheling from Scotland.

In early 1073, King William boarded a ship and sailed back to his home duchy of Normandy, intent on subduing the unrest there once and for all. First, he set his sights on gaining back control of Maine, which had fallen under the control of Fulk le Rechin, Count of Anjou, in 1072. William led his army to the capital city of Le Mans and it surrendered to him on 30 March 1073.

At this point Normandy fell under even more danger when the king of France, Philip I, joined with the leading rebels to remove William from Normandy in order to bring the independently ruled Normandy under France's rule. In 1074 Philip conspired with Edgar Ætheling to overthrow the king but William was able to negotiate with Edgar and bring him back to his English court. William knew it would be better to have him close so he could keep an eye on him rather than let him roam England (and Scotland) gathering supporters to his cause.

Next William faced a rebellion in 1075 by Ralph de Gael who held lands in Normandy and the earldom of Norfolk in England. Ralph managed to get several other Breton and English magnates to join his rebellion, including Roger, Earl of Hereford, and Waltheof, Earl of Huntingdon.[3] Ralph also managed to convince King Cnut of Denmark, son of King Sweyn II, to join his rebellion. Ralph's plan was to lead his army to Norwich and meet up with Cnut's huge fleet of warships. However, William's adherents in England, including his brother Odo, quickly dispersed Ralph's army so that when Cnut arrived, Ralph was already gone. Cnut pillaged some border lands but then headed back home to Scotland. William dealt with the rebels harshly, imprisoning them for several months before having them unceremoniously beheaded.

Since the most recent rebellion in 1075 had been instigated by Brittany, William also planned to punish that duchy by bringing war upon them. In September 1076, William led his troops to Dol in Brittany and besieged the city. King Philip of France threw in his support with the besieged Bretons, sending in supplies and reinforcements, successfully fighting off William's army and causing them to retreat. This was the first serious loss in William's recent history and it had the effect of encouraging even more magnates to challenge his authority. But the next person to cause him serious trouble was his very own son and heir, Robert Curthose.

5

Family Betrayal

Robert Curthose was raised in Normandy and received the education and training typical at that time for a child of noble birth. Of utmost importance was learning to fight and yield weapons so he could grow up to be a great warrior like his father. As William the Conqueror (King William I of England)'s eldest son and presumed heir, Robert was expected to inherit all his father's holdings in France, plus the kingdom of England, which resulted in a very big ego.

In 1063 when he was 12 years old, William made Robert the count of Maine which was at that time under Norman rule. In 1067, after William had conquered England, he gave Robert considerable control and responsibilities in the governance of the whole of Normandy. Apparently, this wasn't enough for Robert and his closest companions encouraged him to take what was owed to him by force, essentially encouraging Robert to rebel against his own father.[1]

In the winter of 1077, the high and mighty Robert demanded that William grant him the entire duchy of Normandy and allow him to rule it independently. Robert had always been a loyal son so it came as a shock to William when his son abruptly withdrew himself from the king's court and subsequently launched an attack on Rouen, intent on taking it out of his father's control. It was a fool-hardy mission, one that was doomed to fail, and one that was typical of Robert's hastiness. William ordered the immediate arrest of Robert and the other rebels, so they fled Normandy and established a new power base in Flanders.

Robert became a magnet for all the disaffected nobility in France, including King Philip and many leading magnates in Brittany, Maine, and Anjou. He was a very likable character, but he was also easily bent. The ambitious people in his circle saw in Robert the opportunity to raise their own status if they could put him in control. Things between Robert and King William came to blows in the winter of 1078 when Robert launched his own invasion. His army was besieged by William at Gerberoi Castle and held out for three weeks before deciding to come out and fight. Surprisingly, Robert won the day and William retreated after being unhorsed and stabbed in the arm, possibly by his own son.[2] It was a humiliating loss for William and he decided it was better to give in to his son's demands than risk further war and indignity. By spring 1080 the two sides had come to an agreement which included a promise that Robert would get the duchy of Normandy to run on his own soon.

The trouble in England had not subsided while William was engaged against his son in Normandy. King Malcolm once again menaced William from the English-Scottish border, raiding and harrying English towns. After William's and Robert's reconciliation, the king sent his son north to deal with Scotland while he stayed in Normandy to deal with a new rebellion from the count of Anjou. Additionally, northern England was rising up again and the king sent his half-brother Odo to deal with that trouble.

With the vast amount of territory under his control, it was clear William couldn't oversee it all himself so he entrusted Odo to hold England while he dealt with unrest in Normandy. Serious problems with the arrangement arose in 1082 and William had to sail back to England to deal with what he considered an act of betrayal by Odo. William had discovered that Odo was gathering William's adherents to accompany him to Italy in his venture to win the open papacy. William needed all the men he could get to defend England and it offended him that Odo was focusing their vital resources on his own personal mission. William wasted no time in having Odo arrested and imprisoned in Normandy for the remainder of his life.[3]

No doubt the betrayal of his half-brother Odo was distressing for William and he was soon dealt a further blow when his wife Matilda died from an unrecorded illness on 2 November 1083.[4] William was devastated to lose his wife of thirty-two years, mother of his nine children, and trusty regent in his government. The list of family members he could count on became shorter and shorter. He certainly couldn't trust his son Robert who continued to rebel against his father, in concert with the king of France, for the next four years of William's reign.

6

The Domesday Book

The last few years of William's reign unfolded much the same as the previous years, with constant rebellions and military confrontations in both Normandy and England. He did, however, finally find time to work on the administration of his government in England and the result was the astonishing accomplishment known as the Domesday Book. This book held the results of a nationwide survey in which every plot of land in England was accounted for, as well as the number of citizens, the value of their possessions, and even how many animals they owned. The purpose was to ascertain their taxability for the king so he could collect more taxes from the richest areas of England. Being a Norman, he was unfamiliar with much of England so this census gave him the most accurate accounting of the land and inhabitants of England than was ever attempted before.

The speed at which the survey was undertaken is beyond impressive. William first conceived of the idea of this national census at Christmas 1085 in Gloucester.[1] He spent winter planning out the process in which the survey would be conducted and by spring he had sent men across the kingdom to begin recording the required information from each county, city, and shire. By August 1086, the survey had been completed. It only took the king's appointees a mere six months to gather the information for 30,000 manors and 13,000 other places of note.[2] The king's commissioners had managed to record all the vital census information about England in only six months. After the completion of the book, King William called all his English magnates to Salisbury and made them swear a public oath of fealty to him.

With the Domesday Book complete and the fresh oath of loyalty taken from his magnates, William felt comfortable enough to return to his homeland in Normandy in late 1086. By this time William was nearing 60 years old and not surprisingly he was very tired and worn down from the past twenty years of constant fighting. He was extremely overweight, and he was also suffering with serious stomach or intestinal issues.[3] All these factors combined caused William to enter the first inactive phase of his long career, one in which he rested peacefully in Rouen so he could try to recover from his various maladies. He did rally from his bed once in July 1087 to fight

King Philip of France who was attempting to seize the city of Mantes near Normandy. William employed his usual burn and destroy tactics upon the city, during which he was either injured by fire or collapsed from the heat of the flames.[4]

King William was transported back to his home in Rouen and took to his deathbed surrounded by his sons Henry and William as well as his closest adherents. His son Robert was not present. A priest was called so he could make his final confession and he ordered that all his prisoners should be released upon his death. Then he formally declared his eldest son, Robert Curthose, as heir to the duchy of Normandy, but not to England. He designated the next king of England to be his second son, William Rufus. King William ordered his son William to sail immediately to England and find the archbishop of Canterbury who was the only man who could coronate kings in England. On 26 September 1087, William Rufus was crowned William II at Westminster Abbey in England.

7

Was William the Conqueror a Usurper?

William the Conqueror's arrival in England and his victory at the Battle of Hastings is perhaps the most influential event in British history. Although the English were accustomed to fighting and being ruled by foreign invaders, William would prove to be a different breed of ruler. When he stormed England, he brought with him the Norman way of doing things which was much more sophisticated than the English had ever seen. He set about building a foundation for the fledgling new kingdom of England and much of his work can still be seen and felt in England today. William is credited with ordering the construction of at least 600 castles in England in order to provide protection from enemies and to awe the commoners with the majesty of the buildings.[1] Historian Marc Morris explains, 'Not only did the Normans bring with them new forms of architecture and fortification, new military techniques, a new ruling elite and a new language of government; they also imported a new set of attitudes and morals, which impinged on everything from warfare to politics to religion to law, and even the status of peasantry.'[2]

William the Conqueror was an extremely effective ruler for England and managed to hold on to his crown despite constant invasions and rebellions throughout his twenty-one-year reign. His success was surely based on his early experiences in Normandy where he learned to rule the duchy of Normandy, which he inherited from his father when he was only 7 years old. He escaped several assassination attempts in his youth and eventually learned how to handle the unruly nobles in Normandy who constantly rebelled against his rule.[3] It was in Normandy in the 1050's that William earned his reputation as a ruthless but able leader. He earned a prestigious international reputation when he defeated King Henry I of France not once but twice, first at the Battle of Mortemer in 1054 and again at the Battle of Varaville in 1057. After his decisive victories, his Norman subjects rallied to his side and were instrumental in helping him win the victory at the Battle of Hastings in 1066.

William the Conqueror is known as one of the most famous usurpers in British history, but does he really deserve that title? If Edward the Confessor had promised William the throne as he insisted, why is he labeled a usurper for taking the throne from Harold? Wasn't King Harold the usurper in this situation? The definition of the word usurp is 'to seize and hold (a position, office, power, etc.) by force or without legal right'.[4] Before we can determine if William or Harold were usurpers, we first must determine the law of England at that time in regard to succession.

From the seventh century to the eleventh century, Anglo-Saxon England had in place a council named the Witenaġemot, or Witan for short.[5] The Witan was made up of a group of noblemen and clergy whose job it was to counsel the king in all governmental matters. The Witan also had a very special responsibility: the selection of new kings. It was customary (and lawful) in Anglo-Saxon England for the reigning king to voice his preference towards a particular candidate to succeed him but ultimately the final decision was up to the Witan.

When Edward the Confessor died in 1066, he did not name a successor because it wasn't his place to do so, it would have been up to the Witan. Edward probably did tell Duke William back in 1051 that he wanted him to be his successor, however, the decision was out of his hands. So, when King Edward died with Harold Godwin at his bedside, everyone looked to Harold as the next natural leader of England. They in no way wanted to invite the Norman foreigner Duke William to be king of the English. It was an easy choice for the Witan and Harold hastily had himself coronated before anyone could change their minds.

Therefore, since Harold was selected by the Witan as the next king of England, he was not a usurper. William the Conqueror, on the other hand, was most definitely a usurper. Not only did he take the throne of England illegally by defying the Witan, he also took it by force via the Battle of Hastings and the murder of King Harold of England.

Part II

King Stephen (1135–1154)

8

The Empress Matilda

The story of King Stephen is really the story of Empress Matilda, the woman who was very nearly crowned as the first ruling queen of England. Matilda was the only legitimate living child of King Henry I and although he had proclaimed her as his heir to England and Normandy, there was a monumental struggle over the crown after Henry's death in 1087, causing an eighteen-year civil war known as the Anarchy.

King Henry I was the youngest son of William the Conqueror. Having had three older brothers, Henry never expected that he himself would one day become king of England. Henry's eldest brother, Robert Curthose, had always been expected to be William's heir, however, King William had a change of heart on his deathbed. Robert Curthose was a difficult son. He complained bitterly about sharing his father's titles and lands with his brothers. On several occasions he led rebellions against his father and even recruited the help of foreign monarchs.[1] William feared Robert would lead the kingdom into chaos, so he took the bold move of excluding Robert from the line of succession and granting him the duchy of Normandy instead.

William the Conqueror's next eldest son was Richard of Normandy. Richard died in 1075 during a hunting accident in the New Forest during his teenage years.[2] William's next eldest son, William Rufus, is who he chose to be heir to the throne of England. William Rufus and his little brother Henry were present at their father's deathbed in Rouen, Normandy on 9 September 1087, while their brother Robert Curthose was away with his army leading a campaign against their dying father. As he lay dying, William the Conqueror named William Rufus as his heir and gave him detailed instructions for the succession. William was to depart immediately for London to claim the throne before his riotous brother Robert could try to interfere. King William sent his son with a letter to give to Archbishop Lanfranc in England confirming the king's selection of William Rufus as heir to the throne. Then with little trouble, William Rufus was crowned King William II at Westminster Abbey by the archbishop of Canterbury on 26 September 1087.[3] Unsurprisingly, when Robert Curthose found out that his brother William ascended the throne, he was outraged. In retaliation,

Robert attempted to launch several invasions against his brother William, all of which ultimately failed.

With William on the throne and Robert as duke of Normandy, there wasn't much left for the youngest son Henry to inherit. He was given nothing of substance, only the promise that he might receive his mother's English land holdings one day, which never actually happened.[4] Chronicler Order Vitalis recorded Henry as asking, 'And what, Father, do you give to me?' to which the king responded, 'I give you five thousand pounds of silver from my treasure', Henry snidely pointed out to his father 'What shall I do with treasure if I have no place to make my home?'[5] No doubt Henry was disappointed that his brothers had received so much and he so little.

William II's reign was not nearly as successful as his father's as he was not very well liked by his subjects or the nobility. He was vain, unscrupulous, and worst of all, he had made enemies of the clergy, an essential group to have on your side if you wanted to hold on to the throne.[6] He was also widely disliked because of his shockingly promiscuous behaviour at court. Orderic Vitalis wrote that William II 'never took a lawful wife, but gave himself up insatiably to obscene fornications and repeated adulteries'.[7] William hadn't taken a wife because he preferred homosexual relationships and surrounded himself with men of similar mind who would dress and behave more like girls than men.[8]

After reigning as the king of England for only thirteen years, William II died in a hunting accident in the New Forest on 2 August 1100. This was the same location and manner of death that his brother Richard had suffered nearly thirty years earlier. It was said that King William II was stricken in the chest by a stray arrow loosed by a companion in his hunting party.[9] In fact, the death of King William seemed a little too convenient to some, especially after his younger brother Henry, who was present at the hunt, immediately sped off to claim the throne for himself before Robert Curthose could find out. After William's death, Henry first raced to Winchester, the location of the royal treasury, and took possession of it. Then he called together as many magnates as he could gather and had himself 'elected' as their successor. Next, Henry travelled over 100 kilometres to Westminster and was coronated as King Henry I of England on 5 August 1100.[10]

As expected, Henry's brother Robert Curthose was irate at Henry's actions and mounted an invasion the next summer to fight for the throne of England. King Henry's army marched out to meet Robert's army but instead of fighting, the brothers negotiated a deal. Robert agreed to give up his claim to the throne of England in exchange for 3,000 marks per year and a share of Henry's land holdings in Normandy. This agreement, known as the Treaty of Alton was ratified on 2 August 1101, the anniversary of King William II's death, but the peace between brothers would not last long. Many of Henry's leading magnates held land in both England and Normandy, therefore a schism developed among the barons as to which liege to follow: King Henry or Duke Robert. For the next several years, Normandy descended into chaos until the definitive Battle of Tinchebray on 28 September 1106 in which Henry was victorious and Robert was taken prisoner.[11] Clearly there would be no reconciliation this time. Henry imprisoned his brother Robert for the next thirty years until he died in his early eighties.

King Henry I had proven himself a much more able leader than any of his brothers in his dealings with Robert Curthose and the ongoing civil unrest in Normandy. Not only was he turning out to be a great warrior king, he was also considered an intellectual for his time. Previous kings had not been educated on much besides how to rule and how to fight, so a king like Henry who was an avid reader and collector of books was quite revolutionary for England.

Shortly after his coronation in 1100, Henry made an advantageous marriage to Edith of Scotland (later nicknamed Matilda), who was the daughter of King Malcolm of Scotland. Not only would the marriage bring about peace with Scotland, it also elevated Henry's own status by marrying such a high-born lady who was directly descended from Edward the Confessor, Edmund Ironside, and Alfred the Great. This would ensure that the king's children were from Norman royalty and Old English blood. Over their eighteen-year marriage, Henry and Edith only managed to have two children: daughter Matilda was born in 1102 and son William Adelin was born in 1103. In addition, Henry set the record for illegitimate children born to a king of England with at least twenty bastards that we know of through a multitude of mistresses.[12]

King Henry's first-born child, Matilda, was not the male heir he wished for, however, she could still be a valuable asset to him. Such a high-born daughter would bring a prestigious foreign marriage, one that would help King Henry build valuable alliances for England. Henry considered many suitors carefully and then chose Henry V, the most powerful ruler in Europe, who was to become both the king of Germany and the Holy Roman Emperor. At the age of only 8 years old, Matilda was escorted to Germany where she was to spend the next sixteen years as 'Queen of the Romans'.

Although Matilda was the eldest born child of King Henry I, it was usually the eldest born son who inherited, not the daughter.[13] William Adelin was King Henry's only legitimate son, therefore, the king took special efforts to secure his son's future succession. In 1113 when William was only 9 years old, King Henry arranged his betrothal to the daughter of Fulk V of Anjou which would strengthen England's position in France. At the Christmas court of 1114, King Henry gathered his Norman nobles and made them swear fealty to his son William Adelin and promise to uphold him as the rightful heir to England and Normandy.[14]

Henry I achieved a huge diplomatic victory in mid-1120 when he negotiated a Franco-Norman peace treaty, which put an end to years of fighting between the two kingdoms, but it came at a huge price. In the agreement, King Louis of France acknowledged William Adelin as the rightful duke of Normandy and in return William did homage to Louis.[15] After the conclusion of the peace negotiations, the English delegation was in the mood to celebrate. Henry, William, and hundreds of English noblemen who had accompanied them to France gathered at the port of Barfleur on 25 November 1120 to make their triumphant return to England. King Henry's fleet set sail first, followed by 18-year-old William Adelin, who was travelling in the newly outfitted *White Ship*. There was apparently riotous partying in celebration of their victory in France, not only by the passengers of the *White Ship* but also by the crew.[16] The inebriated partygoers urged the drunken rowers to go as fast as possible so they could catch up with King Henry's ship but in their carelessness, they hit a large rock and capsized. The *White Ship* sank that night and with it, so did Henry I's plans for the future. His heir, William Adelin, was dead and the peace treaty with France would be declared void because the marriage contract could not be fulfilled. Most importantly, Henry now had no heir to England and Normandy.

Although Henry had many illegitimate children, it was not customary in England for bastards to inherit from their royal fathers. Henry now had an urgent need for a new male heir but his first wife, Edith, had died two years prior to the *White Ship* disaster. Henry moved swiftly to negotiate a new marriage to Adeliza, the daughter of the count of Louvain. They were married in January 1121, just two months after the death of William Adelin. After several years of marriage, the royal couple failed to produce any children. Although he still held out hope that they would eventually conceive a male heir, he had to come up with a backup plan.

Henry's ambitious backup plan for his succession began to take shape in the summer of 1125 when the Holy Roman Emperor Henry V died, leaving his daughter Matilda a young widow. Henry I recalled his daughter from Germany to join him back in Normandy. They had not seen each other in sixteen years and Henry spent a considerable amount of time sizing her up, seeing what she had learned about ruling Germany and the Holy Roman Empire. In the autumn of 1126 Henry called together his most trusted advisors to debate and decide upon Henry's heir. By Christmas 1126 Henry had made up his mind to try something quite extraordinary: he declared his daughter Matilda as his heir to England and Normandy.[17]

Why was this a problem? There had never been a female monarch in England, much less Europe at this point in history. There was no law or rule established at that time stating that women could not rule but they were widely considered to be the weaker sex and did not have the strong constitution needed to rule a kingdom.[18] Plus, medieval kings had to continually fight off enemies and lead armies, something a woman had never done.

Henry did have three other royal male relatives that he could have chosen as his heir. His sister Adela had two sons, Theobald, Count of Blois, and Stephen of Blois, Count of Boulogne. Stephen had grown up in Henry's court and was said to be Henry's favourite nephew so he would have been a logical choice.[19] Then there was William Clito, the son of Henry's wayward brother Robert Curthose. Clito was the last living legitimate grandson of William the Conqueror and many considered his hereditary claim to be above that of Henry I's.[20] With his father Robert Curthose still in prison, William Clito became the new figurehead of the resistance against King Henry. All those disaffected with the imprisonment of Curthose now flocked to Clito, including the kings of France and the dukes of Anjou and Flanders. William Clito did have the best hereditary claim to the throne but he was Henry's last choice because of the rebellious behaviour of his imprisoned father.

A fourth male option existed with Henry's illegitimate son Robert of Gloucester. Robert would have made an excellent king. He was well respected, trustworthy, a great warrior, extremely rich, and hugely influential in both Normandy and England. However, bastards were rarely chosen to lead kingdoms, although there had been instances when a bastard conquered a kingdom, including Robert's own grandfather, William the Conqueror.

With his mind made up, King Henry called all his magnates together at Windsor for Christmas 1126 and told them of his decision. On 1 January 1127, the king held a glittering ceremony at Westminster Abbey to officially declare Matilda as his heir and to collect oaths of fealty from his bishops and barons. Each man was called out by name individually and had to promise to uphold Matilda's claim upon the king's death. Henry intentionally did this one by one so in the future none in attendance could claim that they had been silent and not taken the oath.[21] Not everyone would uphold their promise though, especially Stephen of Blois who was present at the oath-taking ceremony but would soon have a change of heart.

After the public oath-taking, King Henry then set about to find his widowed daughter a new husband. For a high-born woman such as herself who was the daughter of a king and a former queen consort of the Holy Roman Emperor, she expected her father to arrange a marriage to a high-ranking nobleman, perhaps to a foreign king or prince. What she got instead was 13-year-old Geoffrey of Anjou, the son of Count Fulk V of Anjou. Matilda was greatly offended by this marriage prospect as she felt herself much above his status, not to mention their eleven-year age difference.[22] Her father Henry had chosen Geoffrey in order to make peace between Normandy and Anjou. She knew that to strengthen her position as future queen of England, she must have a husband, but this was far too low below her station and at first she protested. Eventually, she gave in to her father and agreed to marry Geoffrey.

The marriage between Matilda and Geoffrey of Anjou took place at Le Mans on 17 June 1128. The honeymoon, if there ever was one, was over quickly. Geoffrey was young, brash, and overly confident. Matilda was head-strong, independent, and refused to call herself the Countess of Anjou. Instead, she preferred to be addressed as Empress Matilda.[23] The marriage was so rocky that they split up only a year after the wedding. Matilda moved back to Normandy to be near her father and it was three years later that King Henry finally convinced her to return to her husband and reconcile for the good of Normandy and England. To drive home the point, Henry held a great council at Northampton in September 1131 in which the king's vassals decided she must be sent back to her husband and in turn those in attendance repeated their pledges of fealty to Matilda.

Somehow Matilda and Geoffrey managed to make their marriage work. They apparently found some common ground because shortly after their reunion, Matilda became pregnant. She gave birth to her first child, a son, in March 1133 in Le Mans. She named him Henry after his grandfather. Fourteen months later, Matilda gave birth to their second son, named Geoffrey for his father. The birth did not go well and Matilda was deathly sick afterwards, so much so that she planned for her burial. But luckily for the new Plantagenet dynasty, she recovered completely.

Emboldened by the birth of their sons and future heirs, Matilda and Geoffrey began pressing their claims in Normandy. As part of her dowry, Henry agreed to grant Geoffrey and Matilda several Norman castles near the border of Anjou, including Argentan, Exmes, and Domfront. Yet, after more than five years of marriage, King Henry still refused to turn over the castles, not trusting his son-in-law. He was worried that Geoffrey might try to overpower him and take control of the whole of Normandy. In 1134 or 1135, Geoffrey angrily confronted the king and demanded he hand over the castles at once. Henry doggedly refused. From that point until King

Henry's death, the relationship was strained to say the least, as they disputed back and forth, neither side willing to give an inch. It's unfortunate because unbeknownst to them, there was little time left for a reconciliation.

On the evening of 1 December 1135, King Henry I died at the castle of Lyons-la-Forêt in Normandy after taking to his bed the week before with a sudden illness. Chronicler Henry of Huntingdon, who tends to be rather imaginative, says the king died after eating too many lampreys (eels).[24] No other chronicler mentions the lampreys so Henry of Huntingdon may have embellished that part of the story. We do know that the illness lingered for a week, enough time to gather his leading magnates and clergymen to his bedside. William of Malmesbury wrote that the king 'assigned all lands on both sides of the sea to his daughter in lawful and lasting succession'.[25] But that's not what ended up happening. As soon as the news of Henry's death got out, all hell broke loose, and disorder once again descended upon the kingdom of England.

9

Stolen Crown

On Wednesday, 4 December 1135, Stephen of Blois received urgent news from a messenger who had ridden nearly non-stop on the 200 kilometre journey from Lyons-la-Forêt to report the king's death.[1] One might think Stephen would have been devastated to hear the news that his dear uncle, King Henry I, was dead. One might also think Stephen would come together with his kinsmen to support his cousin Matilda as heir to the throne. Stephen himself had sworn to do so at the oath-taking ceremony at Westminster in 1127, but he did nothing of the sort. He did exactly the opposite.

Only one day after receiving the news of the king's death, Stephen sailed to England. Luckily for him, he was at Wissant in Pas-de-Calais when he received news of the king's death, which allowed him to cross the English Channel at the shortest distance to England and land in Dover just one day later. Stephen and a small retinue of knights rode to London, arriving on Sunday, 8 December 1135, and were heartily welcomed by the citizens as their new leader.[2]

Why would Londoners so easily accept Stephen as their new king when it was widely known that Matilda was King Henry's choice of heir? First of all, Londoners knew Stephen from King Henry's court and he had a reputation as one of the most honourable and knightly of all King Henry's nobles.[3] In contrast, most Londoners had never even seen the foreign-born Matilda. The only time she had ever come to England was for her father's Christmas court of 1126. The citizens of London simply knew and liked Stephen so he seemed the logical choice. Londoners didn't know Matilda, nor did they have any desire to be ruled by a woman.

After securing the support of London, Stephen rode straight to Winchester, the centre of the royal administration, and home of the royal treasury. Stephen had an ally at Winchester in his brother Henry who happened to be the bishop of Winchester. With Henry's help, as well as help from Roger, Bishop of Salisbury, Stephen secured the support of the clergy, which was essential if he was to wear the crown. In order to secure their support, he had to sign an agreement in which he agreed to give the church more power in government, including the right to elect its own candidates as bishops and abbots. By early 1139, Stephen had already broken the promise by arresting the son of Bishop Roger of Salisbury and replacing him as chancellor by one of his own picks.[4]

Stephen did not have the backing of all the high clergymen. Archbishop William of Corbeil challenged Stephen's claim to the throne, asserting that the clergy and nobles had all sworn oaths to Henry I to uphold his daughter Matilda as his heir. Stephen and his backers asserted that those oaths were invalid because they were made under duress. Further, Stephen asserted that Henry had a change of heart on his deathbed and named Stephen as his successor. Stephen's claim was backed up by a rather untrustworthy baron named Hugh Bigod who claimed to hear Henry speak those words to Stephen on his deathbed.[5] We do know that Henry was in dispute with Matilda and Geoffrey at the time of his death, however, it is very unlikely that Henry would have abandoned the plan he had laid out seven years prior for the succession. Henry was very calculated and thoughtful about his plans for the future. He was not the type to make impulsive and reckless decisions based on his emotions. Even so, the clergy and nobility accepted Stephen's story, albeit somewhat hesitantly, and thus handed over the keys to the treasury to him.

The next step in Stephen's takeover of England was to have himself crowned king as quickly as possible. In a hastily arranged and sparsely attended ceremony, Stephen was anointed as King of England by the archbishop of Canterbury at Westminster Abbey on 22 December 1135. The speed in which Stephen was coronated meant the ceremony was poorly attended by the nobility. Many of England's noblemen were still back in Normandy, sworn to remain with King Henry I's corpse until his burial.

What was Matilda doing during Stephen's coup? At the time of her father's death, Matilda was living in Anjou, over 600 kilometres away from Lyons-la-foret.[6] She wouldn't have even received the news of her father's death until Stephen had secured the crown in England. To complicate her position further, she was in the early stages of her third pregnancy and may have been too unwell to travel such distance and across the English Channel to get to London. She was well enough, however, to travel through Normandy with Geoffrey to the disputed border castles that had been part of her dowry and took them unto her possession. They were also given possession of a number of other castles, including Ambrières, Gorron, and Châtillon-sur-Colmont in Maine.[7]

Obviously the first and foremost concern for Geoffrey and Matilda was securing Normandy before the rebellious barons could stir up trouble.

They made no immediate moves to secure Matilda's inheritance across the Channel. In the case of England, Matilda quite naively believed that her father's barons, having sworn an oath to uphold her rights, would soon come to her rescue. In this she seriously miscalculated. They had all been swept up in Stephen's usurpation and the lack of opposition from Matilda's party. Their priority was to secure their own positions, lands, and titles and in order to do this, most thought it would be easier to go with the flow and make friends with their newly anointed king.

The only person who did take action on her behalf was her uncle David, King of Scotland. In January 1136, he launched border raids with England and overtook several castles, including Norham, Alnwick, Wark, Carlisle, and Newcastle. Stephen took decisive action and led the royal army north to deal with the Scottish rebel. Rather than fight, Stephen paid him off to leave. It was a tactic used for hundreds of years to keep the Vikings out, and it was successful for a short time in keeping Scotland at bay. The two kings signed the Treaty of Durham on 5 February 1136.[8]

Just two months later, Stephen was back in England playing the part of king by hosting a large court at Oxford for the Easter celebrations of 1136 'which was more splendid for its throng and size, for gold, silver, jewels, robes, and every kind of sumptuousness, than any that had ever been held in England'.[9] In a perfect stroke of timing, Stephen happened to have with him a letter from Pope Innocent II endorsing his accession to the throne. If the pope had not endorsed his claim, Stephen and anyone who followed him would have been excommunicated from the church. With full approval from the pope, Stephen the final ammunition he needed to secure his position as king of England.

Most of England's barons were present at Stephen's Easter court in Oxford and gave their pledges of fealty to the new king. One person reluctant to do so was Robert, Duke of Gloucester. Robert was the illegitimate son of Henry I and therefore Matilda's half-brother. If Robert would have been born legitimately, he would have undoubtedly been Henry I's heir and he would have made an outstanding king. Although he was a bastard, Robert was well-educated and extremely wealthy by way of his duchy of Gloucester. He was also said to have been very charismatic and was a well-respected knight and military strategist.[10] But for now, it seems Robert found himself stuck in an untenable position. Was he to support his own sister, thus honouring his father's will, or play the part of willing accomplice to Stephen's usurpation?

Stephen had summoned Robert to London several times after his coronation but Robert had made excuses not to come. Robert did not want to take an oath to Stephen because he knew he could not keep it and he didn't want to break the oath he had made to his father. Finally, he could resist Stephen no longer without placing himself in immediate danger, so he came late to Stephen's Easter court and reluctantly pledged his allegiance to the new king.[11]

Unrest in England and abroad would occupy Stephen for the early years of his reign. The first baron to rebel was Baldwin de Redvers, the earl of Devon. He was one of the few magnates who refused to attend the Easter celebrations to swear fealty to Stephen. In the summer of 1136, Baldwin garrisoned the royal castle of Exeter with his own men and held out against King Stephen's siege for several months but then had to surrender because they had run out of food and water. Stephen made his first serious misstep as a king by allowing the rebels at Exeter to leave unpunished. Baldwin went on to stir up further rebellions and then left England to join Matilda's party in Normandy.[12] She was happy to be a magnet for disaffected nobles and gladly welcomed them to her side. Also that summer, she was safely delivered of her third and final son whom she named William after her grandfather William the Conqueror.

Matilda and Geoffrey still had no plans at this time to go to England to stake her claim to the throne. They were far too busy putting down rebellions in Anjou and fighting to take away Normandy from King Stephen's possession. In the fall of 1136, Geoffrey launched a major invasion into Normandy which was countered by Stephen's man Waleran of Meulan. Although he made some initial gains, Geoffrey lost ground and had to send for Matilda to bring him fresh troops in October for the siege of Le Sap. Geoffrey had to retreat shortly thereafter when he was wounded in the foot and his troops were ill with dysentery.[13]

When the next spring rolled around, Stephen felt secure enough in his position to travel to Normandy. There were several important items on his itinerary: show himself to the people he now ruled, gain Norman allies, create a partnership with King Louis of France, and make amends with his brother Theobald, Count of Blois. Stephen sailed to Normandy in March 1137 and progressed through Normandy, arriving at the capital city of Rouen, where he met his brother. Theobald was much aggrieved that his younger brother, Stephen, had taken the throne right from under him. If their branch of the family tree was to carry on the royal line, surely Theobald would be the first heir since he was the oldest brother. He was satisfied, however, with Stephen's offer to pay him 2,000 marks a year, a huge amount, as restitution. Next, Stephen met with King Louis VI of France and made a pact to support each other, with Louis recognising Stephen's right to Normandy and Stephen accepting Louis as his liege.[14]

During Stephen's short time in Normandy, Geoffrey and Matilda worked to stir up trouble and draw him into an armed conflict on their home base. In May 1137, Geoffrey launched a new invasion of Normandy, this time with a very large army, including up to 400 knights, which caused widespread damage as it moved through Normandy. King Stephen and his Flemish commander William of Ypres took the royal army to Lisieux to confront the Angevins. His army was so unruly and disorganised that internal fighting tore it at apart and caused mass desertions. Humiliatingly, Stephen had to come to terms with Geoffrey and Matilda, agreeing to a three-year truce and annual payments of 2,000 marks.[15]

By the winter of 1137, Stephen had sailed back to England to deal with new threats of rebellions. At Christmas he was leading his army north to deal with a new insurgence of Scots as their peace treaty had just expired. Along the way north, Stephen stopped at the town of Bedford to settle a dispute over the castle there. Miles de Beauchamp held the castle for Stephen but now refused to hand it over so the king besieged the castle. The castle did not fall as quickly as he expected, therefore he left a small garrison of men there and headed north to confront the Scottish invaders. Stephen arrived in Northumbria on 2 February 1138 with an enormous army. Instead of engaging the Scottish army in a pitched battle, he bypassed them and travelled into Scottish territory, laying waste to the land. King David knew he could not win against the king's army and so he withdrew his forces back into Scotland for the time being. Next Stephen went west to Hereford castle where rebels were setting up fortifications against him. The king laid siege to the castle and the inhabitants surrendered in three weeks. Just as he had at Exeter, he allowed the rebels to leave unharmed and unpunished.

Stephen may have felt that he was doing a reasonable job putting out the flames of rebellion across his dominions but in May 1138 he was confronted with something wholly different: the defection of one of the leading magnates in England and Normandy, Robert of Gloucester. Robert sent messengers to Stephen declaring his change of allegiance to his sister Matilda and claimed Stephen was plotting to assassinate him.[16] In retaliation, King Stephen attempted to confiscate all of Robert's castles in England, including his stronghold of Bristol, but his siege was unsuccessful against Robert's strong garrison. With the mighty Robert of Gloucester now on her side, Matilda saw a sudden surge in support for her cause. Many of Stephen's discontented vassals followed Robert, bringing with them soldiers and lots of money. With this sudden turn of fortune, Matilda decided the time was right to make her big move.

By fall 1138, Matilda joined her brother Robert in Normandy and they began planning an invasion of England. Aside from allocating ships, weapons, food, soldiers, and all the other supplies needed for a large army, Matilda also took the formal step of issuing a complaint to the pope accusing Stephen of usurping her crown.[17] The matter was heard during the second Lateran Council in Rome which began on 4 April 1139, but Pope Innocent would not overturn his previous decision to support Stephen's right to the throne. Undeterred, Matilda and Robert continued war preparations, hoping that the next pope could be persuaded to see her side.

10

Almost Queen of England

The year 1139 was monumental for Matilda and proved to be the turning point in her bid to win the throne of England. By the summer of that year, rumours began spreading all over England that Robert of Gloucester and Empress Matilda would land an invasion at any moment. Stephen was already on edge and the rumours fueled his paranoid suspicions of those around him, fearing they may betray him and flip to Matilda. Stephen was suspicious of three bishops in particular: Roger of Salisbury and his nephews Alexander of Lincoln and Nigel of Ely. Stephen called them to Oxford in June 1139 based on a trumped-up excuse to account for a skirmish between their men. Stephen's real intent was to arrest them and confiscate their castles, which is exactly what he did. The arrest of the bishops was shocking to everyone in England but especially to the members of the clergy. In fact, after the Oxford incident, Stephen's own brother Henry, Bishop of Winchester, turned his back on the king. Chronicler William of Malmesbury reported that Bishop Henry and other prominent men in England then wrote to Matilda inviting her to invade England and depose King Stephen.[1]

Two months after the Oxford debacle, Matilda and her supporters had completed their invasion plans and were now on their way to England. They sent Baldwin de Redvers on the first ship and he succeeded at gaining possession of Corfe Castle, their planned garrison stronghold in southwest England. Shortly thereafter, on 30 September 1139 Matilda, Robert, and 3,000 soldiers landed in Arundel, about 144 kilometres east of Corfe.[2] The selection of Arundel was not coincidental: it was the castle of Matilda's stepmother, Adeliza. The two women had been in communication before Matilda's invasion and Adeliza was willing to help her stepdaughter by providing safe harbor, even though it did put her at risk of retaliation from Stephen. After delivering Matilda to Adeliza, Robert set out with their army to his stronghold of Bristol Castle which was 225 kilometres away.

Stephen had been en route to deal with Baldwin de Redvers when he suddenly changed course after receiving the news of Matilda's and Robert's landing in Arundel. He arrived at Arundel Castle one week after Matilda's arrival and considered laying a siege but decided to negotiate instead. He made a generous offer to allow Matilda safe conduct to Bristol if she agreed to leave Arundel.[3] Stephen's purpose was to put his two biggest enemies together in one location where he could fight them with all his strength. But ultimately this decision would backfire. If he would have captured Matilda rather than let her go free, it is very possible her support would have fizzled out quickly and Stephen could have avoided years of civil war.

By mid-October 1139, Matilda had arrived in Bristol and was reunited with her brother Robert, plus other prominent English barons, including Miles of Gloucester and Brian fitzCount. Miles was the sheriff of Gloucester County and had opposed Stephen's assumption of the throne. Brian fitzCount was an old friend of Matilda's having grown up together as children at Henry I's court in Normandy. Henry had arranged an advantageous marriage for Brian to Matilda of Wallingford, which made Brian the lord of Wallingford.[4] Wallingford was strategically important because it was the castle closest to London that was in possession of Matilda's supporters. That is precisely why King Stephen chose Wallingford, to force the rebels into an armed confrontation by laying siege to the castle shortly after Matilda's arrival at Bristol. Miles of Gloucester led a rescue mission to Wallingford, broke the king's siege engines, and attacked Stephen's soldiers, causing them to flee and give up the siege.[5]

The Battle of Wallingford was a huge victory for Matilda and gave more legitimacy to her cause. To set herself apart from her brother, she moved from Bristol Castle to the royal castle of Gloucester and established her own household. She then made the bold step of having her own coins minted which gave a legal significance to her claim. By December 1139, support for her cause was growing and she now had her uncle, King David of Scotland, on board. She also received a valuable defection at this time: Nigel, the bishop of Ely, whom Stephen had arrested six months earlier. Although Matilda's support was growing more and more by the day, it was not yet large enough to mount a major offensive against the royal army. Instead, she and her allies spent the entire year of 1140 deployed in guerrilla warfare, besieging and sacking castles all over England. Events in the upcoming new year would finally bring her within grasp of the throne.

In January 1141, trouble at Lincoln Castle would again draw the two sides together into an armed confrontation. Sometime in 1140, King Stephen verbally promised the earldom of Lincoln to William de Roumare.[6] When the existing holder, William d'Aubigny, refused to hand it over, Roumare and his half-brother Ranulf, Earl of Chester, decided to take it by force. They captured Lincoln Castle, expelled its inhabitants, and barred the town gates.

King Stephen was at Windsor celebrating Christmas when he received the news of the situation at Lincoln. He swiftly gathered his army and traveled over 200 kilometres to Lincoln in a matter of days.[7] Although King Stephen besieged Lincoln Castle, Ranulf managed to escape and send an urgent plea for help to his father-in-law, Robert of Gloucester. This was the justification Robert and Matilda needed to show how King Stephen was incapable of controlling his unruly barons.

When Robert received Ranulf's plea for help, he gathered up a large group of soldiers and immediately set out for Lincoln, not only with the purpose of relieving King Stephen's siege but also because he saw an opportunity to take out King Stephen. The first pitched battle of civil war known as the Anarchy took place on 2 February 1141 at the Battle of Lincoln. The royal army was prepared for a siege, not a battle, and were quickly overtaken on the battlefield by Robert's men. Stephen himself fought until the end, until he was hit in the head with a rock and knocked unconscious.[8] He was taken prisoner and held at Robert's Bristol Castle, at first honourably but then after some misbehaviour, he was confined to shackles.[9]

Matilda was thrilled when she learned King Stephen was now her prisoner. She finally gained the upper hand and knew she had to make a calculated choice what to do next to move herself closer to the throne. She certainly needed the support of the church if she were to have any chance of winning her throne so she started there first. Matilda convinced Bishop Henry of Winchester, the papal legate for England and brother of King Stephen, to meet with her at Wherwell near Winchester on 2 March 1141. There she convinced him to flip to her side and work on her behalf to overturn the pope's decision and get support from the leading land barons in England.[10]

On 7 April 1141, Bishop Henry convened a council meeting at Winchester to put forth his argument for setting aside Stephen and making Matilda the new ruler of England. He reminded them of the oaths they had sworn to King Henry I, how Stephen had failed to establish law and order, and how Stephen had broken every promise he had made to the clergy. They were all in agreeance. The decision was made to formally accept Empress Matilda as the rightful heir to the throne, proclaiming her 'Lady of the English' and the royal treasury was put into her possession.[11] The path to her coronation was almost cleared. There was just one last hurdle in the way.

Matilda's final challenge was the most difficult: she would have to get the support of Londoners if she were to wear the crown. The population of London at that time numbered around 30,000 and the citizens had their own militia ready at any moment to defend themselves. Due to their potential military strength, Matilda would have been wise to approach them gently and cordially in order to win them over to her side. Instead, as soon as she arrived in London she began alienating the citizens with her haughty and dismissive nature. Adding insult to injury, she demanded that Londoners pay an extra tax to support her. When they responded that they had no money left because it had all gone to support Stephen, she flew into a fury.[12]

Matilda was so confident in her position that she underestimated the activities of Queen Matilda, Stephen's wife. Along with Stephen's main military commander, William of Ypres, Queen Matilda had been keeping Stephen's cause alive by raising an army in his defence. Just days before Empress Matilda's coronation, Queen Matilda's army was outside of London harrying the countryside and Empress Matilda did nothing to stop them.

On 24 June 1141, the evening prior to her scheduled coronation, Empress Matilda was sitting down to dinner with her leading barons when bells began ringing throughout the city. Then all hell broke loose. The bells were a signal to Londoners that they were being invaded and they should take up arms to defend the city. Londoners opened the outside gates and let Queen Matilda's army in, allowing them to take complete control of the city. Empress Matilda had to flee the city immediately. When the London mob broke into her quarters, it was reported that her food was still lukewarm. She and her party made it to the safety of Oxford but her army somehow broke up and became scattered.[13] Matilda was devastated that she was so close to her goal of being queen but then had it snatched out of her hands. She may have been temporarily disheartened, but she was in no way ready to give up her claim to the throne of England.

11

The Anarchy Continues

After the failed coronation attempt in London, Empress Matilda suffered further devastating losses that would threaten her entire endeavor. In July 1141, she set up her new base at the royal castle in Winchester. She called her ally Bishop Henry to come meet with her several times but he seemed to avoid her. The two had recently been in dispute over Matilda's refusal to recognise the rights of Stephen's 12-year-old son, Eustace. Bishop Henry wanted her to grant the counties of Boulogne and Mortain to Eustace, but she refused to give such power to a possible rival to the throne.[1] It was around this time that Bishop Henry began secretly negotiating with King Stephen's wife, Queen Matilda, to flip back to Stephen's side and take the English nobles with him. When Matilda learned of the bishop's betrayal, she gathered the royal army and headed for Winchester where she planned to confront the turncoat bishop.

On 31 July 1141, Matilda, Robert of Gloucester, and King David of Scotland brought their armies to Wolvesy Castle in Winchester to confront Bishop Henry. When they arrived, they found Bishop Henry was nowhere to be seen and the castle had been left garrisoned against them.[2] Empress Matilda's army quickly overran the city and laid siege to the castle. The townspeople within the castle walls threw flaming objects of every kind at their attackers and ended up burning down almost the entire town of Winchester.[3] This was very bad news for Matilda because there would be no food or shelter for her army to exist on during the siege. Since she couldn't get food and supplies in Winchester, she had to establish a new supply route so she sent a contingent of her army to Wherwell Abbey to guard the road.

In the meantime, Bishop Henry had fled to Farnham and sent an urgent plea of help to Queen Matilda. Since King Stephen was still imprisoned, his wife Queen Matilda took charge of the royal response. She and Stephen's favourite commander, William of Ypres, led an army to Winchester to confront the rebels. The royal army surrounded Empress Matilda's army, essentially trapping them within the city walls and blocking all supply routes. Then William of Ypres led a force to Wherwall where he captured Queen Matilda's men, locked them in the abbey, and set fire to the church.[4]

After a month into the siege, Empress Matilda and her leading nobles were at the point of desperation. Food and drink were mostly gone, all their supply routes had been cut off, and there was no hope of rescue. Rather than raise the white flag of surrender, Empress Matilda and her councillors came up with an escape plan. On the morning of 14 September 1141, Matilda's men opened the city gates, lined up in close formation, and began marching out of the city with Matilda at the front of the vanguard for protection. Queen Matilda's army gave chase and Empress Matilda's frantic entourage were on the run for twelve kilometres before Robert of Gloucester and his rearguard made a stand at Stockbridge, allowing time and space for Empress Matilda to make an escape. She and what was left of her army rode as fast as they could to the nearest friendly castle which was thirty kilometres away at Ludgershall. Then Matilda travelled to Devizes and finally Gloucester where her men planned to regroup.[5] The outcome was so disastrous for Matilda's side that it became known as the 'Rout of Winchester'.

At Gloucester, Empress Matilda observed the arrival each day of her scattered men, always on the look-out for one particular man who had so far been missing: Robert of Gloucester. She soon learned that Robert had been captured by Queen Matilda's army at Stockbridge and was now being held prisoner. Matilda knew that her cause would be thoroughly doomed without the assistance of her brother Robert, especially with the recent loss of support from London, the church, and the treasury. In another desperate move, she decided to negotiate the release of her brother Robert in exchange for the release of King Stephen. This shocking move made it clear she was desperate. Empress Matilda obviously felt that Robert was her only chance at being crowned queen.

At this point, Empress Matilda wasn't just fighting for her own right to the throne but also for the rights of her three sons. If she were to fail in her quest to dethrone King Stephen, the future of her sons would be made difficult and they would probably be punished for being the sons of a traitor. However, if she were to win the throne, her sons' futures would be limitless. They would be the highest-ranking nobles in the entire kingdom and at least one of them would day inherit the throne from their mother.

Negotiations for the exchange of prisoners between Empress Matilda and Queen Matilda dragged on for weeks until they finally came to an agreement in late October 1141. On 1 November, King Stephen was released from Bristol Castle and escorted to Winchester Castle where Robert had been kept captive. After Stephen arrived there safely on 3 November, Robert of Gloucester was released from custody and returned to his sister at Bristol. Upon his release, King Stephen began rebuilding his authority as king, summoning a council meeting at Westminster for 7 December 1141. The main purpose of the meeting was to overturn all the agreements made at the spring council meeting in Winchester when Bishop Henry had support Empress Matilda. During the December meeting, Stephen greatly chastised his brother Henry for assisting the enemy and even read out loud a letter from the pope rebuking Bishop Henry's recent behaviour. To add to the humiliation, Empress Matilda had representatives at the meeting who made it known Bishop Henry was the one who invited Matilda to invade England the previous summer.[6] But in the end, Stephen forgave his brother Henry. On Christmas Day 1141, Stephen held a grand, new coronation ceremony to show he was clearly back in charge of his kingdom.

Matilda held her Christmas court at Oxford with the leading magnates who had stayed loyal to her. A few had been forced to go back to Stephen's side in order to safekeep their own lives. Matilda's main concern was raising an army and having experienced military commanders. In the spring of 1142, Matilda wrote to her husband Geoffrey asking for his assistance. He wrote back saying he first needed Robert of Gloucester's assistance in Normandy and Anjou before he could consider bringing his troops across the Channel to England. Hesitantly, Robert agreed and sailed to Normandy. He was worried for Matilda's safety in his absence, but they had no other choice at this point than to first meet Geoffrey's demands to gain his assistance.

Geoffrey occupied Robert's time in Normandy with battles and sieges against the rebellious Norman and Angevin nobles. Throughout the summer and fall of 1142, Geoffrey and Robert were successful in capturing at least ten castles.[7] They were still campaigning in October 1142 when news reached Robert that Matilda was under siege at Oxford by none other than King Stephen.

When Stephen received the news that Matilda had been left alone at Oxford Castle without the protection of her brother Robert, he set about to take her down once and for all. To kill the daughter of a former king of England would have been indefensible. Instead, he laid plans to capture her, just as her men had captured him. Rather than attacking her directly, he stationed his troops around the city of Oxford, encircled the town, and cut off Matilda's supply lines. Then on 26 September 1142, King Stephen approached Oxford Castle with a very large army. Matilda's soldiers rushed out of the castle to engage them but were quickly overpowered and the king's army was able to penetrate the castle gates. The royal army was not able to gain complete access to the castle so they set up large siege works and continually pounded the castle walls. They also set fire to everything that would burn, levelling much of the surrounding houses, reducing the entire area to smoking rubble.

Matilda was holed up in the castle doing her best just to survive. Things were desperate as they reached the two-month mark of the siege. At that point they were out of food and water, and had no indication that help was on the way. It was probably impossible for Robert to get messages to Matilda that he was indeed working on a rescue mission. As soon as he received word of her besiegement at Oxford in October, he immediately set sail home from Normandy. He had an enormous entourage with him: fifty-two ships, 300–400 knights, and various other soldiers and mercenaries. He also had with him Matilda's eldest son, 9-year-old Henry.[8] The young boy would get to witness firsthand how a great leader like his uncle would handle a situation such as this. Robert mustered all of Matilda's supporters at Cirencester and prepared to lead them to Oxford to rescue Matilda.

After surviving three months of the siege, Matilda decided she could wait no longer. Unaware of her brother Robert's sailing, she orchestrated her own daring escape in mid-December 1142. She and a few companions snuck out a side door in the middle of the night and fled across the snow-blanketed grounds, undetected in their white clothing. To her benefit, the weather was so cold that the Thames was frozen solid, allowing Matilda and her party to cross on foot. After crossing the river, they walked through deep snow for ten kilometres before reaching Abingdon where they were given horses to take them to the safety of Wallingford Castle. There she met her trusty friend Brian fitzCount and they moved on to her stronghold castle of Devizes.

Robert had been on his way to Oxford when he learned of Matilda's courageous escape. He immediately changed course and rode to Devizes to be reunited with her. The joy at the reunion was multiplied when Matilda saw her son Henry, whom she had not seen in several years. Around this time Matilda was coming to accept that she had very little chance of being crowned Queen of England, but now with her eldest son standing before her, she decided to set aside her claim to the throne. Instead, she would fight to depose King Stephen in the name of her son Henry, the closest living male heir to her father, King Henry I. She wisely sent Henry to spend the next couple of years under the tutelage of his uncle Robert. With Robert he would learn everything he needed to know about being a successful ruler.[9]

When the spring campaigning season of 1144 rolled around, both sides were actively besieging each other's castles all across England. During the summer, Stephen captured Wareham from Robert, then headed to Wilton Abbey to set up a base in which to launch a siege in nearby Salisbury. Robert was hot on his heels and arrived at Wilton with his huge army on 1 July 1143. Although darkness was nearing, Robert ordered his army to attack which took Stephen's troops by surprise.

The Battle of Wilton was the third pitched battle of the Anarchy. The royal troops, as did their leaders, gave little fight before fleeing to save their own lives. Robert and his troops razed the entire town.[10] Once again, Stephen proved he did not have the ability to keep his citizens safe, which was a key tenet of kingship. For the next five years, the two sides would continually menace each other with castle sieges and minor skirmishes. Throughout this time the pendulum of power swung back and forth, with each side making gains but then suffering setbacks.

In March 1147, 15-year old Henry, eldest son of Empress Matilda and Geoffrey of Anjou, attempted to insert himself into matters by sailing to England with a small retinue and besieging several small castles. His main target was Cricklade which currently belonged to his cousin Philip, son of Robert of Gloucester. Philip had recently betrayed his family by flipping to Stephen's side and Henry meant to make him pay for it. But the young, naïve Henry didn't have nearly enough men to seriously consider overtaking the castles. He wisely cut his losses when he ran out of money and had no way to get back home to Normandy. He first begged his mother Matilda for money but she refused him. Next, he asked his uncle Robert for help, but he too denied him. It seems they were resolved to give Henry a dose of tough love and let him figure out how to get out of his current situation by himself. In the end, Henry requested Stephen's support and the king was all too happy to oblige in so he could remove this threatening young man from his realm.[11]

The most devastating loss of all to Matilda's cause was yet to come. In the fall of 1147, her brother Robert fell ill with a fever and suddenly died on 31 October 1147. Robert had been her most loyal supporter over the past ten years and she couldn't imagine going on without him. She knew she couldn't accomplish her goal of becoming queen without Robert so instead she decided it was time for a change in tactics. It was time for the next generation to take over the fight.

12

Changing of the Guard

In early 1148, Matilda sailed back to Normandy, never to return to England again. She was 46 years old and weary from thirteen years of constant campaigning against Stephen. When she arrived back in Normandy, she travelled to the capital city of Rouen. There she reunited with her two younger sons who she had not seen in nine years.[1] Together with her eldest son Henry and her husband Geoffrey, the family spent the majority of 1148 regrouping and planning their next steps.

By spring 1149 Matilda felt sufficiently prepared to launch her next offensive campaign. Around Easter, Henry sailed to England, this time not with the intention of battling Stephen but to win the support of the most powerful men in England. As soon as he landed in England, he started to assert his rights as the rightful king of England against Stephen's usurpation. He went to his mother's stronghold of Devizes and received pledges of fealty from the men there. In May 1149, Henry travelled to Carlisle and was knighted by King David, who was now in his sixties. At the knighting ceremony, Henry also received homage from the northern barons.

On his way back south from Carlisle, Henry survived no less than three attempts at capture by Stephen's men.[2] Henry also found that while he was in the north at Carlisle, Stephen's son Eustace had besieged Empress Matilda's castle in Devizes. Henry's forces were just robust enough to break the siege and send Eustace into a retreat. Henry then wisely realised that his army would not be sufficient to contend with the full force of the royal army so he sailed back to Normandy by the end of 1149.

Matilda may not have been active in England but she did not spend her time idly in Normandy. In fact, she spent the better parts of 1150 and 1151 negotiating with King Louis VII of France to support her son Henry as the rightful king of England. Louis was at first hesitant to desert his brother-in-law Stephen, but when Geoffrey and Henry came to him in Paris and offered to give him the Norman county of Vexin, he quickly acquiesced.[3] On their way home from Paris in September 1151, Henry's father Geoffrey of Anjou caught a fever and died at the castle of St Germain-en-Laye. Eighteen-year-old Henry was now the duke of Normandy and the sole leader of his faction in England.

Henry's alliance with King Louis was short-lived due to a serious rift that developed between the two kings. In March 1152, Louis divorced his wife, Eleanor of Aquitaine, on grounds of consanguinity, but the real reason was lack of male heirs. The couple had been married for fifteen years and only had two daughters to show for it. King Louis had to have a male heir and he believed his wife Eleanor was incapable of providing one so he divorced her. Newly single Eleanor was a very valuable marriage prize because she controlled the huge, wealthy duchy of Aquitaine in her own right. Any man married to her would thus receive control of Aquitaine and become the ruling duke. Young Henry realised the potential in the marriage and he himself took the wealthy heiress for his own wife, marrying her only two months after her divorce from Louis.[4]

When Louis got word of what Henry had done, he was beyond livid. He felt not only betrayed but also humiliated because Henry would now govern more territory in France than he would. Louis responded by mustering troops and recruiting Stephen's son Eustace to help him lead an invasion into Anjou. Henry was in Barfleur at the time preparing to sail to England when he got news of the French king's invasion. He immediately led his troops back towards Anjou, causing the French troops to quickly disperse.

Meanwhile in England, King Stephen was working to secure his son Eustace as the rightful heir to the throne. He insisted on having his son preemptively crowned as a sort of 'king in waiting' but the archbishop of Canterbury refused to do so without express written permission from the pope. Stephen sent the archbishop of York, Henry Murdac, to Rome to plead his case to the pope. When Murdac returned to England in early 1152, the response from the pope was not what Stephen expected. The pope refused to acknowledge Eustace as the rightful heir to the throne of England. The previous pope, Innocent II, had been the one to approve of Stephen's accession to the throne, but Innocent died in 1143. The new pope, Eugenius III, would not endorse Pope Innocent's prior decree.[5]

Stephen then called all his barons together at the Easter court of 1152 and made them swear an oath to uphold his son's rights to the throne. He also demanded that the archbishop of Canterbury, his own brother Theobald, crown Eustace as future king but he stoutly refused. Theobald would not risk excommunication from the church by disobeying the pope and besides, he didn't trust Stephen.[6] Theobald was so sure Stephen would force him to officiate over Eustace's quasi-coronation that he fled into exile. The new pope levelled a further blow by refusing to renew Bishop Henry's papal legate. Stephen had officially lost the support of both the pope and his own clergymen.

Stephen received the worst news of all just one month later when his beloved wife, Queen Matilda, died on 3 May 1152 after a short illness. She was more than just a wife, she was his partner in all manner of things. When he was in captivity, it was Queen Matilda who secured his release and chased his enemies out of London. She had been a model medieval queen in both her diplomatic and political skills. Stephen was somewhere between the ages of 55-60 years old when his wife died. He had spent the last fifteen years fighting and he was worn down, both physically and mentally. His greatest challenge was still to come. Would he be ready for it?

13

Henry's Final Invasion

After multiple delays, Empress Matilda's son Henry began his third and final attempt to depose Stephen and take the throne for himself in January 1153. This time he sailed with a much larger army than his previous attempts and had his English supporters on standby ready to join his impending invasion force consisting of 140 knights and 3,000 foot soldiers. They landed on England soil on 5 January 1153, which was well out of the campaigning season. The weather was dreadful with bone-chilling cold temperatures combined with non-stop rain and snow, making it extremely difficult to move an army around much less feed it. The reason for Henry's unusual timing was to break Stephen's siege of Wallingford Castle, the stronghold of Brian fitzCount. Stephen thought that by taking control of Empress Matilda's secure bases in England, it would demoralise their supporters. However, the people holed up in Wallingford Castle sent to Henry for help and he made the bold move of sailing an invasion fleet into England in the dead of winter.[1]

After Henry landed in England, he travelled first to his mother's stronghold of Devizes Castle to set up his base of operations. It was decided that he should first take his troops north and attempt to capture the royally garrisoned castle at Malmesbury. Henry laid siege to the castle and Stephen responded swiftly by mustering troops to nearby Cirencester but the confrontation never materialised. Some chroniclers say that the swollen River Avon prevented Stephen's army from crossing it safely and so he had no other choice than to retreat. Other chroniclers say that Stephen's magnates were so tired of the war with Duke Henry that they simply refused to fight. It was probably a combination of both these reasons that no pitched battle took place and instead Stephen offered a temporary truce, allowing him to withdraw his troops peacefully.

Despite the poor weather, Henry continued on with his quest for the crown, capturing castles and gaining more supporters from England's most powerful men. Shortly after the siege of Malmesbury, Henry received a boon to his cause when English noble Robert of Leicester left Stephen and came to Henry's side, bringing with him thirty castles in the Midlands of England which hugely increased Henry's powerbase. In July 1153, Henry's army went on the march towards Wallingford in order to break the siege set by Stephen who had brought up an 'inexpressibly large army from every part of his kingdom'.[2] Along the way to Wallingford, Henry's army succeeded in capturing both Nottingham and Stamford. Stephen was losing more traction by the day and things got even worse when his son and heir Eustace died suddenly and unexpectedly on 17 August 1153.

At this point Stephen's crown was hanging by a thread and he knew it. He was around 60 years old, he had lost most of his supporters in England, and his heir was dead. He had been fighting Empress Matilda and her son Henry for the entirety of his reign, nearly eighteen years. No matter what he did, he could not stop Henry's momentum, and he was growing weary of trying. It was at this point that the two sides began to negotiate a permanent truce to bring about an end to the civil war.

Throughout the months of September and October 1153, Archbishop Theobald of Canterbury and Bishop Henry of Winchester mediated between the two parties in a series of slow, pain-staking negotiations. Finally, after two months of arbitration they agreed on the terms of the truce which would become known as the Treaty of Winchester which put an official end to the Anarchy. Per the agreement, Stephen was allowed to rule England until his death but then Henry would become king of England, essentially disinheriting Stephen's only living son, William. In a show of solidarity, Stephen and Henry left Winchester together and set off on a slow progress to London where Henry was received 'with splendid processions, as was fitting for so great a man'.[3] Stephen could now for the first time in his reign enjoy peace in his kingdom.

Unfortunately, Stephen did not have much time left to enjoy the peace. On 25 October 1154, less than one year after the Treaty of Winchester was signed, King Stephen died after being 'violently assailed by a pain in his guts, accompanied by a discharge of blood'.[4] In all likelihood, his health had been in serious decline for quite some time, due to so many years of campaigning, not to mention the fact that he had been wounded twice in battle and held captive by Empress Matilda for nine months.

Duke Henry was with his mother Matilda in Normandy when the unexpected news of Stephen's death reached them. Henry immediately prepared to sail to England to claim his throne, leaving the administration of his French territories to his very capable mother. After a brief delay for weather, Henry crossed the Channel on 7 December 1154. He was crowned King Henry II of England by Archbishop Theobald on 19 December 1154 at Westminster Abbey. Usually the death of a king caused great instability in a kingdom. But for the first time since the death of William the Conqueror in 1087, there was a peaceful succession in England.[6]

14

Was King Stephen a Usurper?

Stephen's reign as king of England from 1135 to 1154 was dominated by the English civil war known as The Anarchy. Although he began his tenure as a popular, well-liked ruler, the abundance of years spent battling Empress Matilda and Henry weakened his hold on the throne. His inability to put down his rivals shook the confidence of both his English nobles and commoners. Unlike William the Conqueror, Stephen did not contribute to improvements in the governance of the kingdom, nor did he leave any lasting legacy of note. He was more inclined towards peace than fighting, which was not a strong characteristic for a medieval king. His inability to maintain law and order caused his people to turn against him and look for another alternative.[1]

King Stephen I of England has long been considered a usurper for stealing the crown from his cousin Matilda. There was no precedent at that time for a female ruler and Stephen was very nearly the closest male blood relative to Henry I. Stephen also claimed that Henry chose him to succeed on his deathbed. So, was Stephen really a usurper?

Let's remind ourselves of the formal definition of the word usurp which is 'to seize and hold (a position, office, power, etc.) by force or without legal right'.[2] In twelfth-century England, there were no strict rules when it came to succession. It was very much a fluid thing at that time, usually with the eldest legitimate male heir inheriting from his father. But obviously, there were situations when there was no legitimate male heir to inherit. In those cases, it was basically up to the ruler to make his choice, although there were no laws forcing the people to follow the king's choice.[3]

King Henry I selected his legitimate daughter, Matilda, as his heir because he lacked a legitimate male heir. This must have been a stunning announcement at the time since England had never witnessed a female ruler. However shocking it might have been, there was no law against it.[4] Not only did Henry announce Matilda as his heir, he went to great lengths to have his barons swear oaths of fealty to her, including her own cousin Stephen.

When Henry I died, Stephen saw the chance to overpower what he saw as a stereotypical weak woman so he could steal the crown for himself. Stephen had no legal right to the throne. He had never been named by Henry as an heir despite his claim that King Henry named him as his successor as he lay dying. In fact, Stephen wasn't even closest in blood line to Henry I. If male succession had been strictly followed, Robert Curthose would have been king after William the Conqueror, and Robert's son William Clito would have been next in line after that. Due to King William's conflict with his son Robert, he chose to bypass Robert and pass the throne to his second son William, who in turn passed it to his brother Henry I. Being that Stephen had no legal right to the throne and stole it away from Matilda, Stephen is very deserving of the title of a usurper king.

Part III

King Henry IV (1399–1413)

15

Edward III and the Succession Problem

enry IV was born on 15 April 1367 at Bolingbroke Castle in Lincolnshire, England. Known in his youth as Henry Bolingbroke, he was the fourth-born son of the mightiest English land magnate at that time, John of Gaunt, Duke of Lancaster and son of King Edward III. John had a total of fourteen children with two wives and a mistress who later became his wife. Only eight of John's children lived to adulthood, with Henry Bolingbroke being the oldest legitimate son.[1] Not only was Henry raised with the expectation of inheriting his father's vast lands and wealth one day, he was also a high ranking member of the royal family which put him close in the line of succession to the English throne, automatically making him one of the most powerful men in England.

Henry Bolingbroke was the grandson of King Edward III, a 'victorious and honourable king who had won respect abroad and popularity at home'.[2] When Edward III was just a teenager, his mother and her lover deposed his father, King Edward II, and Edward III became the new king of England. Edward II was a terrible king who allowed his favourites to rule in his stead. He was very controversial because of his flamboyant style and it is very likely he was gay. In fact, throughout his reign he had two very close councillors that were purported to be his lovers: Piers Gaveston and Hugh Despenser.[3] Edward II's long-suffering wife, Queen Isabella, tolerated her husband's outrageous behaviour for years but finally reached her breaking point in 1325 and allied herself with Roger Mortimer, the earl of March, to bring about a rebellion against her husband. At some point early in their alliance, Isabella and Roger became lovers. Together the queen and the earl made a powerful duo and quickly exerted their will on Edward II's court.

In 1326, Isabella and Roger mounted a successful takeover of England in which they captured King Edward II and the king's current favourite, Hugh Despenser. Hugh was given a traditional traitor's execution for that time. First, he was dragged behind a horse and then he was hanged. Before he passed out from asphyxiation, he was taken off the gallows so he could be disemboweled and castrated. Then he was quartered, and his body parts were sent around England to show the people how traitors would be dealt with under Isabella's and Mortimer's rule.[4] King Edward II was dealt with more gently. He was imprisoned and forced to abdicate his throne to his eldest son, Edward III, who was only 14 years old at the time.

Although Edward III was now the ordained king of England, he would not yet be allowed to rule on his own since he was a minor. Until he reached the age of 18, he was supposed to be ruled by a council of noblemen, however, the real power resided with his mother and her lover. They made all the decisions for him and pulled all the levers in the machinations of government. They were only using Edward III as a puppet king.

For all their talk about Edward II's misrule, Isabella and Roger turned out to be no better. They plundered the royal coffers for their own enjoyment and took counsel from no one. They failed to protect their subjects from continuous Scottish attacks. They had neither the courage nor the money to fund a military campaign. Most damning of all were the restrictions they put on young Edward III. They limited his financial allowance, they prevented him from making decisions in government matters, and they blocked his new young wife from being coronated as queen of England.[5]

Young Edward endured three years of Isabella's and Roger's tyranny before he was old enough and courageous enough to make a bid for control of his own kingdom. He knew they would not step down willingly. He would have to mount a coup to overthrow them. Edward gathered a small circle of his most loyal supporters and broke into Isabella and Roger's apartments at Nottingham where both were taken as prisoners. Roger was tried before parliament on 26 November 1330, found guilty, and hanged three days later. Isabella was held as a prison of honour at several castles, finally settling in at Castle Rising in Norfolk where she lived for nearly thirty years.[6] Young Edward III had proven himself successful in wielding his authority in England and banishing those with evil intentions, even if it was his own mother. Empowered and in control of England, now he would turn his attention to France.

All future kings of England would trace their heritage back to Edward III because he not only had English royal blood but also French royal blood (his mother Isabella was the sister of King Charles IV of France). When Charles IV died childless in 1328, young King Edward asserted his right to the French crown as Charles' nearest male relative. The French rejected his claim citing Salic Law which stated that inheritance could not be passed through a female line. The throne went instead to Philip of Valois, Charles' cousin through a completely male line.[7] Edward was greatly aggrieved and felt that he was cheated out of his rightful inheritance. He vowed to make France pay and he set his sights on winning the throne of France by conquest.

By October 1337, Edward was styling himself as the king of England and France, and in 1340 he formally claimed his right to the throne of France.[8]

The Hundred Years' War was the result of Edward III's bid to win the throne of France. The early years of the war did not go well for him but as he grew in both age and experience, he began to make considerable advancements against the French.[9] The first major victory for the English was the Battle of Crécy in October 1346, followed by the Battle of Poitiers in September 1356. But then Edward's fortune started to turn again. The English ran out of money and men to fight the unrelenting French army, therefore, Edward was forced into a number of peace treaties. Edward suffered further degradations when a new French king was crowned in 1364: Charles V. King Charles was merciless in beating back Edward's aggressions and forced him to give up his claim to the French throne via the Treaty of Bruges in 1375.[10] The treaty reversed all the hard-fought work Edward and his soldiers had undertaken over the past thirty years.

Edward would never quite recover from the humiliation of losing his bid for France. He began to shrink into the background and allow his councillors to rule in his name, just as his father had done. Not only was Edward III crushed by his failures in France, he had also lost his third and favourite son, Lionel of Antwerp, in 1368, and his wife, Queen Philippa, in 1369.[11] He still had plenty of sons left though, among them his first-born son Edward of Woodstock, nicknamed the Black Prince, either for his brutality or for the black armor he wore on the battlefield.[12]

Edward of Woodstock was born in 1330, the fourth year of his father's reign, the year in which Edward III gained control of government over his own mother and her lover, Roger Mortimer. Edward of Woodstock was made heir to the throne of England when he was invested as prince of Wales in 1343 at the age of 13. Only three years, later young Edward proved himself as a gifted military leader during England's decisive victory over the French at the Battle of Crécy and then at Poitiers in 1356. He helped his father fight the battles of the Hundred Years' War for over twenty years and was poised to one day make a magnificent, chivalrous, and knightly king. In fact, all of King Edward III's hopes for the future relied on the Black Prince, but even the best laid plans sometimes go awry.

In the fall of 1368, the Black Prince fell ill and from that point forward he was seriously debilitated. We don't know the specific ailment, but we do know that it followed him for the rest of his life and the condition seems have been both physical and mental. He would endure extreme bouts of lethargy that confined him to his bed for months at a time. He also experienced physical maladies, including discharges of blood, presumably from his genitals or anus because he was unable to ride a horse and had to be carried around in a litter. Contemporary chroniclers speculate that he may have been suffering from rectal or prostate cancer.[13] He expired from his long illness on 8 June 1376.

The devastated King Edward III now had to select a new heir. Fortunately for him, he had many other legitimate living sons to draw from. Unfortunately, not all were good candidates to be the next king of England. His youngest sons, Edmund of Langley and Thomas of Woodstock, were too young and had shown little appetite for government. The most logical heir for King Edward would be his eldest living son, John of Gaunt. He was the only son who had demonstrated the ambition and the intelligence to rule the kingdom.[14]

Although John of Gaunt was a spare heir, he had been raised to be a chivalrous prince and mighty warrior whose role in the family would be to aid his brother Edward, the Black Prince, in ruling England. John witnessed his first military campaign during the 1355 expedition to France the tender age of 15 and took part in at least another eleven major military expeditions, often alongside his father and his brother in France during the Hundred Years' War.[15] In 1359, John of Gaunt made a highly profitable marriage to Blanche, the only child of the duke of Lancaster, Henry Grosmont, which made her an heiress. After Grosmont's death in 1361, John of Gaunt inherited, on behalf of his wife, the entire duchy of Lancaster which was the largest singly held territory in England. This made him immensely wealthy, second only to the king of England. When you were wealthy and powerful in medieval England, you were often accused of being overly ambitious. Rich, mighty nobles made the people suspicious that they might have designs on the crown for themselves. John of Gaunt was no different. Although he proved his loyalty to Richard II time and time again, there were continual whispers that Gaunt was going to try to usurp the throne from his nephew.[16]

After the death of the Black Prince and with his own health failing, 64-year-old King Edward III finally wrote his will in late 1376. His will was called the 'Act of Entail' and in it he established the succession of the throne following 'tail male' rules which excluded heirs through his daughters. Rather than naming his eldest living son (John of Gaunt) to be the next king, King Edward did something slightly unusual, although not unprecedented.[17] He named his grandson, Richard of Bordeaux, eldest living son of the Black Prince, to be next in the order of succession using a device called 'Right of Substitution'. Essentially since the Black Prince died prematurely, his son Richard was accepted as a substitute. After Richard, he named the next in line for succession to be John of Gaunt and the male heirs of his body, followed by King Edward's other living sons, Edmund, Duke of York, and Thomas, Duke of Gloucester.

Interestingly, the 'Act of Entail' was kept secret from the public. The only people who knew about it were those named in the entail and the king's closest confidants who bore witness.[18] Certainly, as the main beneficiaries, Richard, Gaunt, and Henry would have been made aware of their status in line for the throne. Unfortunately, the document must never have been introduced to parliament to put into law or else we would have seen in recorded in the Parliament Rolls.

There are a few possible reasons for the secrecy. First, many rulers were hesitant to publicly name an heir because that gave discontented subjects someone to rally around and possibly attempt a coup. Secondly, it is possible King Edward hid the Act of Entail because he was afraid of a backlash since John of Gaunt was so unpopular in London. John was haughty, overmighty, and openly flaunted his relationship with longtime mistress Catherine Swynford who bore him three illegitimate children. Thirdly, Edward may have kept it secret because it defied the English tradition of primogeniture, which states that the next eldest child inherits, regardless of gender. If King Edward III would have followed primogeniture, the next in line to the throne would have been the first earl of March, Roger Mortimer, who was the son of Edward's second eldest living child, Isabella.[19] Instead, Edward III chose to exclude females from the royal succession, in favour of his living sons and grandsons.

16

Rival Cousins

Henry of Bolingbroke would have known about King Edward III's Act of Entail and that he was third in line for the throne after his cousin Richard and his father John of Gaunt. Since Richard was only three months older than him, Henry could hardly have hoped to outlive Richard to wear the crown himself one day. Richard would surely marry and have children who would inherit the throne. If Edward III would have named John of Gaunt as his heir instead of Richard, Henry most certainly could have expected to inherit the throne one day from his father. Even so, being third in line to the throne wasn't so bad for Henry. He lived a very comfortable life as a royal prince and spent his youth preparing to be a successful ruler, whether by kingship or as an elite nobleman to his cousin Richard.

Born in 1366 at Bolingbroke Castle in Lincolnshire, Henry was raised around the royal court alongside Richard.[1] As royal princes, they would have both been taught the rules of chivalry, the art of the joust, and how to behave at court. Unlike Richard, Henry fully embraced his martial education and became one of the most respected knights in all of Europe. Not only did he travel abroad on crusades, he also befriended many foreign rulers and made magnificent trips to be entertained at their courts.[2] It was with those foreign rulers that he learned the valuable lesson of working together with nobles and to forge alliances with them rather than trying to control them, which would be one of Richard's downfalls. Unlike Henry, Richard had none of the skills required for a strong medieval warrior king. He had no aptitude towards physical feats, such as jousting, and found no joy in combat training or weaponry.[3]

Richard was only 9 years old in 1376 when his father, the Black Prince, died. Then the very next year, old King Edward died. Suddenly young Richard was thrust into the spotlight and would have to deal with the pressure of being a child king under the enormous shadow of his grandfather. Edward's reign had started with great promise but ended in huge disappointments, especially over the losses in the Hundred Years' War. The people of England hailed Richard II as the saviour of the kingdom, the answer to all England's woes.[4] It gave him a big head and perpetual case of paranoia. He was quite distrustful of those around him who held power and grew suspicious that someone in the group would eventually try to challenge his authority as the king of England.

Although Henry and Richard grew up together as young boys, they were not good friends, in fact, quite the opposite. Richard absolutely hated Henry. Richard was none of the things that Henry was. Richard was not strong and athletic, he did not joust, and he was not an experienced military leader. He was basically the antithesis of his once mighty grandfather Edward III. Richard was terribly jealous of Henry and felt threatened that Henry or his father might one day try to wrestle the crown from his head.[5]

Richard II was crowned king of England on 16 July 1377 at Westminster Abbey. His cousin, Henry of Bolingbroke, participated in the coronation ceremony as did Henry's father and Richard's uncle, John of Gaunt. They had every intention of supporting Richard as king and assisting him in good governance, but Richard didn't exactly make it easy. In the early years of his reign, government was essentially run by Gaunt and the other prominent nobles and churchmen. But in January 1380, Richard II declared his minority to be over as he thought himself old enough to rule. That's when all the trouble started.

To be fair, England had been in tumult for many years as a result of King Edward III's decline in health and ambition. The commoners were tired of being pinched for more and more money every year to fund fruitless expeditions to France but Richard and his councillors didn't really care that they were making life extremely difficult on their subjects. They mercilessly passed additional poll taxes to pay for the war repeatedly in the first few years of Richard's reign. Not only were their expeditions to France a failure, the French had gained an upper hand and went on the offensive. England now faced the serious threat of invasion on their own land. It was one thing to fight a war in another country, it was quite another for the war to come to you.

The breaking point between the commoners and the king came in early 1381 when the king's commissioners travelled to the shires to collect the newest round of taxes instituted by the Northampton Parliament. When the commoners resisted, Richard sent his biggest thugs to intimidate them into submission.[6] The people were appalled at the rough treatment by their king and it only fueled their desire to mount a resistance. So widespread was the discontent that many counties rose up together and challenged the king in what would become known as the Peasants' Revolt.

The first to revolt against the king's authority came from Essex in late May 1381. As news spread that the villagers had taken up arms and murdered the royal sheriff, other towns began to rise up as well. Within days, the rebels, led by Wat Tyler and John Ball, organised themselves into one cohesive group and designed a strategy to keep their momentum going. They went from town to town throughout England stirring up the discontented and recruiting more commoners for their mighty mob which would soon march on London. From the very beginning the rebels pledged their allegiance to King Richard II and swore that their aim was to set government right by expelling corrupt leaders and reforming the treatment of all England's peasants.[7]

For the next ten days, the rebels built up their armies and started dispensing justice in small little towns across southeastern England. They found the corrupt royal appointees who had been complicit in Richard's excessive taxation policy and in many cases murdered them.[8] Once they had spilled enough blood in the shires, it was now time to take their complaints to the king in London. Richard had been well informed of the peasants' activities in those first two weeks of June and he was prepared to negotiate.

On 11 June 1481, Richard sent his royal messengers to Canterbury, inviting the rebels to meet with him in person the following day at Blackheath, just east of London. The peasants eagerly agreed and immediately set off west towards Blackheath but they didn't travel peacefully. All along the way the mob hunted down whom they considered to be traitorous and burned down building after building inciting terror all along their path. Meanwhile, Richard spent the day moving the royal court from Windsor Castle to the Tower of London, the safest fortress in the city. Included in Richard's group was his cousin Henry Bolingbroke and hundreds of royal guards and courtiers.

The following day the peasants gathered at Blackheath in the tens of thousands. Clearly their numbers intimidated the king's party who had travelled down the Thames to the meeting place. Richard decided not to go ashore just yet. Instead, he sent a messenger to get the rebels petition so he could learn their demands. Richard and his party were shocked at what they read. The rebels outright demanded the execution of a long list of Richard's closest advisors, including John of Gaunt, Simon Sudbury, Archbishop of Canterbury, and Treasurer Hales.[9] Clearly Richard was not going to allow that to happen, so he sent a message back saying they should discuss the matter further next week.

The rebels felt betrayed and humiliated by the royal snub. On 13 June they began a march of vengeance, their target being the capital city of London. If Richard would not administer justice, the rebels would take matters into their own hands. King Richard did nothing to protect the city against the invading mob. Instead, he locked himself up in the Tower with his closest adherents. Richard left the citizens of London to fend for themselves when the rebel mob was literally at their gates. Londoners feared the mobs' destruction but they did not have the numbers to hold them back from London Bridge, so they opened the gates to the city.[10]

The rebels ran through the city hunting down their political targets and setting free all the prisoners in the city jails. Since John of Gaunt was at the top of their hit list, they headed towards his luxurious Savoy Palace, the grandest residence in all of England next to the king's. Luckily John was north on the Scottish borders and not home at Savoy when the rebels invaded his property. They piled up all his belongings, including his clothing, furniture, and tapestry, and set it all on fire. They threw all of his coins, plate, and jewels into the Thames and then set the palace itself on fire. So complete was the destruction that the entire building collapsed.[11] There was literally nothing left.

Richard and his councillors looked out from the Tower to see a city on fire and the rebel army heading their way. When the rebels arrived, they encircled the Tower, effectively imprisoning Richard and his companions. Richard sent a messenger down who announced that the king was prepared to pardon them all if they would promptly leave London. It was a ludicrous offer, one with no advantage for the rebels. They laughed it off. Richard tried again, this time proposing that they meet the following day at Mile End, not far from the safety of the Tower. This time, Richard did show up.

On 14 June 1381, Richard and a large group of adherents arrived at Mile End to an enormous group of rebels, again numbering in the tens of thousands. Richard asked them what they wanted and this time they put forth a more reasonable set of demands like a reform of the justice system, maximums for rent, minimums for pay, and freedom from serfdom. They did not call for the heads of Richard's closest advisors like they had done at Blackheath. Richard was prepared to accept almost any terms they put forth so it was lucky for him that he didn't have to agree to the deaths of his closest advisors. But for some unexplained reason, after agreeing to the rebels' demands Richard then proclaimed that they were also free to capture those they considered traitorous and should bring them before the king for lawful judgement.[12] He essentially gave them free licence to roam his kingdom and dole out their own law and order.

Their first targets were the noblemen hiding in the Tower. By giving the peasants free reign to round up those they deemed traitorous, Richard had inadvertently unleashed the rebel mob on those he was trying to protect most. The rebels easily overtook what little guards were left at the Tower and the destruction began. Several of Richard's councillors were killed, including Simon Sudbury, the archbishop of Canterbury. They dragged Simon to Tower Hill and had him beheaded, then they staked his head on a spike and nailed his archbishop's hat to his skull. Fifteen-year-old Henry Bolingbroke only survived the attack because of the intervention of one of the guards, John Ferrour, who dissuaded the mob from taking the young boy's life. No doubt the terror of the event left a lasting impression on Henry, in more than one way.[13]

Even though the king and the rebels had come to an agreement on 14 June 1381, the unrest in London had not settled down one bit. The rebels were still inhabiting the city and wreaking havoc on their targets. They performed their own trials and levied executions without the approval of Richard. On 15 June, the rebels burst into Westminster Abbey and dragged out prison warden Richard Imworth, then took him to Cheapside for a public beheading. This was the straw that broke Richard's back. He accepted that his Mile End agreement was already failing and sent yet another royal messenger to the rebel army demanding that they meet him again for more negotiations, this time at Smithfield.

For Richard's third meeting with the rebels, he did not send a messenger but appeared himself face-to-face with their leader Wat Tyler and asked for his demands. Tyler demanded not only an end to serfdom but also an end to lordship as a whole. Richard told him he could have anything he wanted as long as he left the city immediately. As Tyler considered the king's offer, a scuffle broke out in which Tyler pulled out a dagger and the mayor of London responded by sticking his own dagger in Tyler's neck.[14] Chaos and confusion broke out among the rebels. The royal army surrounded the rebels and presented to the king Wat Tyler's head on a spike. With their leader now gone and executed as a traitor, the rebels lost their will to fight. They begged the king's forgiveness and meekly marched out of London to return to their homelands. King Richard II had narrowly survived the first serious threat to his reign. Although it was the first, it certainly wouldn't be the last. Richard had succeeded in subduing the commoners but next he would face an even bigger threat from his own noblemen.

17

The Lords Appellant

Despite the frightening events at the Tower and the abandonment of Henry by Richard, the real estrangement between the cousins didn't occur until 1382. Up until then, Henry was a loyal member of Richard's court and a highly visible presence at all the royal celebrations, including festivities and jousts. His father, John of Gaunt, continued to be a trusted member of Richard's court and was heavily involved in governmental matters. Both Henry and John looked the other way when Richard granted away lands to his favourites who in many cases were men of lower birth. There was a growing contingent of noblemen who were growing resentful of Richard's new up-and-comers. Henry and John tried their best to keep the peace, but the situation soon became untenable.

In 1382, there was a dispute between landowners in Buckinghamshire where Henry of Bolingbroke held land. The dispute was so great that King Richard was brought into the matter. Instead of ruling in Henry's favour, King Richard ruled in favour of the Despensers, old allies of King Edward III. As a result, Henry was completely ostracised from court.[1]

Gaunt too was having major issues with Richard. At a February 1385 council meeting there was a heated debate about what to do next in France. John of Gaunt recommended another French invasion and wanted King Richard himself to lead the army. But Richard had none of it and angrily rebuked John, blaming him for all of their military failures in France. Gaunt stormed out of parliament as did Richard's two other royal uncles, Gloucester and York. Next, quite shockingly, King Richard put out a hit on Gaunt.[2] He didn't order his arrest or trial, he ordered his outright assassination. Gaunt was tipped off which allowed him to escape before the deed had been done. Months later, at the encouragement of Richard's mother, the two men were formally reconciled, but they would never again trust each other.

It wasn't just Henry and John who had trouble with the king. The nobles too were suffering from rough royal treatment. As Richard reached adulthood, he became more tyrannical and violent. He continued to award great offices of power to his favourites while snubbing those noblemen who were traditionally placed in those roles. In July 1383 he raised his lowly friend Michael de la Pole, son of a wool merchant, to be the chancellor of England, the highest office in the kingdom. In another example of Richard's bad behaviour, he had a disagreement with the archbishop of Canterbury. Rather than working it out diplomatically, Richard immediately drew his sword and had to be stopped from murdering the churchman.[3] Less than one year later, Richard argued with the earl of Arundel and punched him in the face hard enough to knock him down.[4] The nobles were terribly unhappy with Richard's brutal style of kingship, lack of military experience, misguided attempts to negotiate with France, reckless financial spending, attempts to degrade the power of parliament, and general misrule resulting from his circle of favourites. They had finally had enough.

In what became known as the 'Good Parliament' of October 1386, Richard's tyranny was held in check. The king's chancellor, de la Pole, announced that the government would need £150,000 immediately for the defence of the realm against France. The nobles and commons strongly protested and instead suggested that the expenses of the royal household should be examined. The nobles were well aware that Richard spent money on himself indiscriminately, all the while extorting huge sums of money from his citizens to pay for the war against France which had proven so far to be a huge failure. When members of parliament pushed back on his newly proposed poll tax to fund next year's efforts in France, Richard angrily stormed out of Westminster Abbey, abruptly ending the entire parliamentary session.

The nobles then put up a united front against the king, threatening to depose him if we would not cooperate, just as his great-grandfather Edward II had had done to him.[5] Deposition would be a complete disaster for Richard on many levels, especially since at this point he was married but childless. If he were to be deposed, his untrustworthy uncle Gaunt would become the next king of England, followed by his hated cousin Henry. With little other choice, Richard returned to parliament. He himself escaped deposition, however, his chancellor did not. Additionally, a council of fourteen lords were appointed to rule England and reform government for the term of one year.[6] This group became known as the lords Appellant and they would be a thorn in Richard's side for much longer than their initial one-year appointment.

To say King Richard was humiliated would be a massive understatement. Given Richard's vengeful nature, the lords Appellant knew Richard would find a way obstruct their reforms. Indeed, he spent much of 1387 travelling the kingdom so he could avoid them. Although the lords had control of his entire administration, Richard found one thing legally he still had the power to do: appoint an heir. Richard declared that he as king, not the lords Appellant, had the right to choose his own heir and that he would not follow the line of succession put forth by Edward III. He threw out his grandfather's Act of Entail and instead declared that his heir would be 12-year-old Earl of March, Roger Mortimer, great-grandson of King Edward III.

Roger Mortimer was the son of Phillipa, the daughter and only child of King Edward's second-born son Lionel of Antwerp. Even though Lionel was deceased, Richard used the right of substitution in selecting Roger, just as Edward III had done in selecting Richard as the Black Prince's substitute. However, it was highly unusual to name an heir through a female line, especially when there were other capable male heirs closer in line to the throne. Richard selected the Mortimers so that John of Gaunt, Henry of Bolingbroke, and the entire Lancastrian line would be excluded from the succession. Richard's declaration was met with great resistance from the lords of his realm who were already disgruntled from enduring years of his tyrannical treatment.

Finally, November 1387 rolled around and another parliament was summoned which was a relief to Richard because he thought he had outlasted his enemies and the lords Appellant would be disbanded. Quite the opposite happened though. Instead, the lords Appellant put forth charges of treason against five of the king's closest councillors including Robert de Vere, Michael de la Pole, and the archbishop of York.[7] Richard agreed to hold the five men in his custody until the charges could be heard by parliament in early 1388. He did nothing of the sort. Instead, he tipped the men off, allowing most to flee the kingdom for their own safety. Only de Vere decided to stay in England to stand his ground against the charges.

When they learned Richard had allowed the accused to escape, the lords Appellant held a special meeting on 12 December 1387 at Huntingdon to decide how to deal with the king. It is at this time that Henry first joined the lords Appellant.[8] Up until that point, he had refrained from joining the dissident group and their activities. Henry knew of Richard's vengeful tendencies and that he would probably be destroyed if he openly allied with the Lords against their king. However, it was nearly impossible not to invoke Richard's wrath, whether it was deserved or not, so against his father's advice, Henry threw in his lot with the reforming lords.

The Lords Appellant now had two options before them. They had already mustered a large army numbering in the thousands and were debating whether to march to London to confront the king militarily, or march west to intercept de Vere's army which was on the way to London to reinforce the royal army. The Lords settled on going after de Vere first. The five lords split up their forces so they could encircle de Vere and cut off his line of retreat. When de Vere discovered the trap, he attempted to make his way into London but was blocked by Henry's forces at Radcot Bridge on the

Thames. After a brief skirmish, de Vere's army was quickly overwhelmed and fled the field. Seeing his last hope of victory dissolve before his eyes, King Richard left Windsor and placed himself in a more secure location, the Tower of London, to await his fate.

Emboldened by the victory of de Vere at Radcot Bridge, the victorious rebel Lords marched into London with their armies, ready to make a more forceful rejection of Richard's rule. On 27 December 1387, they met with Richard at the Tower of London and laid down their demands. They would give him one more chance to avoid impeachment if he agreed to have his favourites arrested and tried. They also made him agree to honour Edward III's Act of Entail which placed John of Gaunt back in line to the throne after Richard. To all of this Richard agreed because he had no other choice.

In the spring of 1388 what was to become known as the 'Merciless Parliament' convened, named so due to the ruthless way in which the victims were treated. The session lasted several months as all of the king's favourites were rounded up and put on trial. All in all, eight men were executed, including de la Pole and de Vere. Seven other men had their titles and lands revoked, plus they were exiled from England.[9] It seemed as if the lords finally had the upper hand over Richard, but the king was not content to let others supplant his royal authority.

For the next several years, Richard tried to retaliate against the lords Appellant. He continually threatened the lords and nobles with arrest, confiscation of lands, titles, goods, and even exile if they didn't bend to his every whim. The situation had become so untenable Henry decided to leave England. From 1388 to 1393, he set off on several overseas trips where he showed off his knightly skills and built long-lasting relationships with foreign leaders. His demeanor and his gallantry at the jousts earned him great respect and a reputation as one of the best knights in Europe. He eagerly accepted an invitation from renowned French knight Boucicaut, Sir Jean le Maingre, to compete in the famous St Inglevert jousts in March 1389.[10] It was a great honour to be invited to the jousts and Henry's father, John of Gaunt, announced the news all around England, which must have irked Richard and inflamed his jealousy. Boucicaut was so impressed with Henry that he invited him to join him on crusade in Tunisia but Richard refused to grant Henry permission to take the trip.

Undeterred, Henry set about a plan to fight a holy war in Lithuania. He left England in August 1390 with a huge entourage and joined up with a contingent of German knights. Together, they found initial success by sacking the town of Vilnius; however, the castle at Vilnius held out for weeks. Henry's food supplies and gunpowder ran out and a great number of men in his army died from the cold, inhospitable conditions. Henry retreated with his army and waited out the cold winter at Königsberg before travelling back to England in May 1391 where he received a glorious welcome back reception.[11]

By the spring of 1392, Henry's mind had returned to his foreign glories and he began planning another trip to Lithuania. He set sail in July but was disappointed to learn upon landing that the two sides had made peace and there was nothing for him to do there. He certainly couldn't return to England without achieving something to show for his expensive trip so he came up with an ingenious idea: a pilgrimage to Jerusalem. Very few Englishmen had ever been to Jerusalem. To have done so would have immediately made you sort of famous. The one-way trip from England (and from Lithuania) was well over 4,000 kilometres and to get there one had to make their way through warring nations and extremely dangerous travelling conditions. Even with Henry's considerable resources, the trip took him nearly a year to complete.[12]

Upon his return to London in June 1393, he probably expected a huge welcome but instead he was greeted with serious unrest within his cousin Richard's court. The root of the current discontent stemmed from the peace treaty which had just been made between England and France, which was negotiated by John of Gaunt and John's brother Thomas, Duke of Gloucester. In order to secure the peace, they agreed to give away Richard's claim as the real sovereign of France, which obviously proved to be highly unpopular back in England. Henry was linked to the disastrous treaty just by family association. Richard was likely behind the treaty since he was an advocate of peace over war, but he was content to let Gaunt and the Lancastrians take the fall for it.

Although John of Gaunt and Henry Bolingbroke stayed loyal to their kinsman Richard over many tumultuous years, the king did not return the same respect or appreciation. In 1394, Richard again changed the order of succession to suppress the power of his uncle and cousin. As soon as John of Gaunt set sail on an expedition to France in September 1394, Richard changed the line of succession.[13] John of Gaunt and Henry posed too much of a threat to his throne, plus he could never forgive Henry for his part in the lords Appellant. For those reasons, Richard decided that the person who would be the least threatening to his reign would be Edward III's fourth son, Edmund of Langley, Duke of York, who was an arthritic invalid. From this point forward, Richard's demeanor towards his Lancastrian relatives was very chilly. No more warm familial welcomes, no new titles or awards; he virtually ignored them.

18

Henry's Invasion

The year 1397 was a turning point in Richard's reign. He felt confident enough in the tactics he had used to get the lords out of the picture and he decided it was time to take it to the next level. Richard's rule was reaching the pinnacle of tyranny at this point and he cared not what anybody else thought. He believed he was the divine ruler and as so he would do as he pleased.

In July 1397, Richard went on a vengeful mission to arrest and punish the senior members of the lords Appellant for usurping his royal authority from 1386 to 1388.[1] The earl of Arundel was publicly beheaded. Thomas Arundel and Thomas Mortimer were banished from the kingdom. Thomas of Woodstock, Duke of Gloucester, died in custody while awaiting his trial. Then in September 1397, Richard called parliament to meet and it was during this session that the king declared he would grant pardons to all who had offended his majesty, for the sake of peace in England — all except for fifty men he listed out specifically. Then Richard revoked all laws and charters made since 1386, the year the lords Appellant were first appointed to guide Richard's rule. In doing so he revoked the pardons which had been granted to the lords in previous years, including Henry Bolingbroke. Henry was now in serious danger and it wasn't out of the question that he would end up exiled or even worse if he offended Richard in any way. Indeed, Richard didn't have to wait long to find an event in which he could utilise to ruin his cousin Henry.

In December 1397, a seemingly innocent exchange between Henry and Thomas Mowbray, Duke of Norfolk, precipitated such an event.[2] The two dukes' courts were on the move and their trains passed each other on a road outside of London. They happened to be the two remaining dukes of the lords Appellant who had not been punished by Richard. As the two men chatted, Mowbray shared his belief that there was a plot afoot to take them both down. Henry told the story to his father, John of Gaunt, who in turn confronted Richard but was stunned to learn that Mowbray had been plotting a second assassination attempt on John's life.

By late January 1398, John of Gaunt and Henry travelled to Shrewsbury to speak to King Richard about the Mowbray situation. Richard told Henry that he could not accuse Mowbray of an assassination attempt without putting it in writing and presenting the charges formally to parliament, so Henry did just that. At the next parliamentary meeting, Henry repeated what Mowbray had told him back on the road outside London: there was a plot afoot to kill Henry and Mowbray by the king himself.[3] Mowbray denied the charges. Richard was shaken to hear the charges Henry laid out and he abruptly called parliament to a close.

After Henry and Mowbray were unable to reconcile, Richard declared that the matter must be solved by a duel.[4] This was a bit unusual, there aren't many cases in the medieval chronicles suggesting it was normal for two such high dukes to battle out their differences in combat. It, in fact, turned in to quite a spectacle as the men would settle their differences by jousting. The event was held at Coventry on 16 September 1398 and attracted thousands of people from all over England as well as France. As the two men spurred on their horses during their first pass on the lists, a yell to 'Halt!' stopped them before their lances met. It was King Richard who ordered the fight to end before it had even begun. The king retreated for a couple of hours and then sent one of his heralds to read a newly drafted royal declaration. The king ordered both Henry and Mowbray exiled from England: Henry for ten years and Mowbray for life.[5] By 13 October, Henry was on a ship headed for France where he was to be hosted by King Charles VI.

Only two months into Henry's exile, John of Gaunt fell seriously ill and lingered on his deathbed for nearly six weeks before dying on 3 February 1399.[6] Richard did not allow Henry to return to England to attend his father's funeral. In fact, with his uncle John out of the picture, Richard was ready to deliver the deathblow to his cousin Henry. Unprovoked, Richard announced on 18 March 1399 that all previous pardons issued to Henry were revoked and that the entire Lancastrian inheritance would revert to the king. He also extended Henry's banishment from ten years to life.[7]

This was an absolutely devastating outcome for Henry, it was the worst-case scenario. Everything had been taken away from him in the blink of an eye. With his father's death, he was now the preeminent member of the Lancastrian family, yet he had no power, no lands, and no home. Henry had two choices: he could embrace the life of a royal exile, travelling around foreign royal courts, or he could make a bold move to reclaim his English lands and remove Richard from power. If Henry's father John of Gaunt would have been alive at the time of his exile, Henry could have lived a quiet life outside England while John would have undoubtedly worked towards renewing royal favour for his son. But with Gaunt no longer in the picture, Henry was free to make his own choice. His father had always held him back from confrontation but this time Henry Bolingbroke would take destiny into his own hands.

It was a matter of personal honour as a renowned chivalrous knight that one should defend himself when he was wronged. This was a common medieval attitude where honour meant everything. Henry was also set on defending Edward III's Act of Entail and thought he would be setting things right. Richard had certainly wronged a number of powerful people in his twenty-two-year reign. Henry decided to recruit those noblemen who had suffered at Richard's hand to join him in a rebellion. Henry also had on his side the people of England. Although he had never been given much power in government, his jousting and crusading exploits had earned him huge respect and admiration from the people. This was in complete opposition to Richard who was not well loved by anyone, except maybe his favourites.

While Henry brewed over his choices, Richard was about to make a fatal mistake. He pompously believed that Henry was out of the picture and would not seek retaliation, so turned all of his attention to another foe: Ireland. Immediately after levying the crushing punishment on Henry, Richard began planning an invasion of Ireland. England was technically the overlord of Ireland, but the unruly Irish people pushed back against English rule. For some reason, Richard chose this as the opportune time to lead an army north to Ireland, leaving most of England largely unprotected.[8] Word of Richard's movements reached Henry in France by mid-June 1399. If Henry was going to make an invasion attempt, now was the perfect time to do so while the king was away, but he would have to move fast.

Henry immediately sent out secret letters to his most trusted allies in England asking them to muster men in support of his invasion.[9] He had no way of knowing whether they would show up once he arrived in England and unfurled his banners calling men to arms. There simply wasn't enough time for the recipients to respond because Henry had to leave France immediately. The first recruit to Henry's revolution was Thomas Arundel, the exiled archbishop of Canterbury. Next came Louis, the brother of the current king of France.

Within two weeks of learning that Richard was in Ireland, Henry set sail with a small force of loyal retainers. Henry spent some time sailing up and down the coast, spreading the word of his invasion and picking up supplies. He finally landed in the town of Ravenspur on 4 July 1399.[10] Then his retinue rode about sixty kilometres west to Pontefract Castle in the Lancastrian heartlands where he could feel some measure of safety. Immediately after his arrival, his friends and colleagues came to join him at Pontefract, bringing with them thousands of men to fight for Henry's cause.[11] Henry was a famous knight, well-known throughout the realm and esteemed as just, pious, and brave. Men willingly flocked to his side to help take back the kingdom from the tyrannical Richard.

After circulating letters to local towns making his case against Richard II and inviting them to join him, Henry moved his army a few kilometres to Doncaster where he joined up with several other discontented English land magnates and their armies. It was there at Doncaster on 13 July 1399 that Henry swore to his followers the purpose of his mission: to take back his Lancastrian inheritance and set up a council to oversee Richard's government.[12] At this point in his journey, Henry did not plan on deposing Richard, or if he did, he did a good job keeping his intention secret.

For the next two weeks, Henry's army travelled around England, gaining more men to his cause every day. They started south towards London but then changed course and went southwest instead for an especially important meeting. The king's newly named heir Edmund, Duke of York, had been left back in England as regent while Richard was away in Ireland. Edmund knew full well of Henry's activities in England but the old man delayed a response, preferring to instead hold four days of discussions with King Richard's councillors in which they decided not to raise an army against Henry but to instead broker a deal. Henry arrived at Berkeley Castle on 27 July 1399 and held a meeting with his uncle Edmund. Henry pleaded his case and remarkably, Edmund who was supposed to be protecting the realm in Richard's absence, agreed to let Henry go forth with his plans to depose Richard.[13] He would not assist Henry but he would not stop him either.

When Richard received news of Henry's activities, he immediately set sail for England and landed in Milford Haven, Wales on 24 July 1399. Their ships had been scattered and the royal army was seriously depleted. Richard marched his men to his stronghold of Carmarthen Castle where he had planned to set up his base of operations. As soon as Richard arrived at the castle, he received news of Edmund of York's betrayal and decided to reverse course. Realising that his army could not put up a fight against Henry, Richard sent the earl of Salisbury north ahead of him to raise an army. On 31 July 1399, Richard snuck away from his army and fled north with just a dozen retainers. He arrived at Conway Castle on 6 August 1399 expecting to find reinforcements but was disappointed to find only around 100 men.[14]

With few options before him, Richard decided on diplomacy. He sent the dukes and earls of Exeter, Surrey, and Gloucester to Chester for negotiations with Henry. Immediately upon their arrival, Henry had them arrested. Then Henry sent the earl of Northumberland to Conway to come to terms with King Richard. Northumberland was steadfast that Richard must agree to three rules: that Henry's 'inheritance be restored to him; that a parliament be summoned over which he would preside as steward; and that five of the king's councillors – the dukes of Exeter and Surrey, the earl of Salisbury, the bishop of Carlisle and Richard Maudeleyn – be put on trial for treason'.[15]

Richard took several days to consider Henry's offer and finally decided to agree to his terms. After Northumberland departed Conway to give Henry the good news, Richard's true intentions were revealed. He told his friends at Conway that Henry 'will be put to bitter death for this outrage that he has done to us. Doubt not, there will be no parliament held at Westminster on this matter' implying that Richard would find illegal means to rid himself of Henry.[16] Northumberland promptly arrested Richard and held him prisoner at Flint Castle. Henry arrived at Flint immediately afterwards to confront his longest rival and cousin. Henry said that the commons had long been unhappy during Richard's reign and that he, as the duke of Lancaster and next in line to the throne, would help him rule. Richard had little other choice than to agree to Henry's demands.[17]

Henry and his men then took custody of Richard and started the long march towards London, over 350 kilometres away. Several times during the trip, Richard tried to escape, and so when they arrived in London on 30 August 1399, Richard was put in the Tower of London, the strongest fortress in the city.[18] As Henry was paraded through the city as a hero, Richard heard the jeers and insults of his people as he shamefully made his walk to the Tower.

Now Henry and his councillors had to carefully decide what to do next. The king was safe in captivity and clearly would not be allowed to rule any longer. According to Edward III's Act of Entail, Henry Bolingbroke was next in line to the throne. But if kings had the right to name their own successors, then Henry was not Richard's heir. Richard had most recently named his aging uncle Edmund as his heir. Henry's legal strategy was to return to the laws of Edward I's reign (1272–1307) which said succession was to be through the king's male heirs and could not pass through the female line. If Henry could get this ancient law reinstated in England, that would have made him Richard's legal heir. Without it, the 8-year-old Edmund Mortimer would have been Richard's heir since Mortimer's mother was the daughter of Edward III's second son, Lionel of Antwerp.

All legalities would have to be settled by parliament which was scheduled to meet at Westminster on 29 September 1399. Prior to parliament, Henry and his councillors held meetings with Richard in the Tower asking that he peacefully resign. Richard was livid and at first refused but then acquiesced as he saw no other choice.[19] When parliament began, a lawyer read Richard's resignation out loud and said that Richard wanted Henry to be his successor. Thomas Arundel, the former archbishop of Canterbury, stepped up and asked the crowd if they would take Henry as their king to which they responded with shouts of 'yeahs!'[20] Henry was led to the empty throne and he knelt, making the sign of the cross on his head and chest, symbolically becoming the new ruler of England. His official coronation was held two weeks later on 13 October 1399 at Westminster Abbey.

Former King Richard was kept a prisoner at the Lancastrian stronghold of Pontefract Castle until his death in February 1400. The exact cause of his death is not known but the story given by most chroniclers is that he was starved to death by his keepers. Henry worried his enemies would rally to Richard and attempt to take back the throne. In fact, a plot to kidnap Henry and his sons by one of Richard's adherents was thwarted in December 1399. Henry knew there would be no peace in England while Richard was alive, so it is quite feasible Henry had Richard starved or abused in some way to bring about his death.

19

Was Henry IV a Usurper?

Henry IV is considered one of the most famous usurpers off all time. He has been accused and convicted in the court of public opinion for deposing his cousin, King Richard II, and seizing the throne for himself. In fact, that was the crux of Shakespeare's Henry IV plays, but is that how it really happened? Was Henry Bolingbroke right to overthrow Richard II in order to restore justice to the kingdom of England? Did he take advantage of the poor circumstances of Richard's reign to claim the throne for himself? Did Henry seize the throne from Richard illegally or was he the rightful heir to the crown?

Since we know Henry IV did not take the throne from Richard II by force, the only remaining question is whether he took it legally. The legality of Henry's rise to king was somewhat dependent on the past which brings up even more questions. Were any laws broken when Edward III named his grandson Richard as his heir instead of his eldest living son John of Gaunt? Likewise, did Richard break any laws when he bypassed Edward's entail and named Roger Mortimer and Edmund of Langley as his heirs? Did Henry break any laws when he accepted the crown for himself and deposed his cousin Richard? Should kings have to uphold entails from their predecessors or was it legal for them to change it to their own personal liking?

In England during the Middle Ages, there was no law that strictly defined the order of succession. Other European kingdoms, such as France, observed Salic Law which prohibited women from being crowned as well as their sons. Germanic kingdoms followed semi-Salic rule which allowed a woman to inherit but only if all the men in the royal bloodline were dead. England had no set rules or laws regarding succession.

European neighbours had a great influence on England's laws and customs, which were typically mish-mash. Since England had not put the order of succession into a legal act up until this point, it was basically up to the current ruler to choose the next heir to the throne. Is it any wonder England had so many disputes over who should rightfully rule England during the Middle Ages? With no legal rules governing the order of succession it became open to interpretation and that's when the royal heirs and nobility used it to their advantage. It made it much more possible to manoeuver their own royal relatives into positions where they might someday have a shot at the throne themselves.

Henry IV has long been regarded as one of the most famous usurpers in history, but was he really? It is my judgement that Henry IV was not a usurper. To be a usurper, one must either seize authority illegally or by force. Although Henry did amass a sizable army, it did not resort to violence to solve the conflict. The army was merely a show of force so that Richard would take them seriously and understand the gravity of the situation. Furthermore, Richard's own regent and heir, Edmund of Langley, did nothing to stop Henry. In fact, it was his acquiescence that made Richard's overthrow possible.

Lastly, Henry was careful to use lawyers to find legal ways to depose King Richard II and thus overturn his previous statute naming Edmund of Langley as his heir. With Richard deposed and all of his previous acts of parliament voided, the order of succession had to revert back to the previous king. That would make King Edward III's act of entail valid again and Henry of Bolingbroke next in line to the throne.

Part IV

King Edward IV (1461–1470 & 1471–1483)

20

The Inept King Henry VI

The reign of Henry VI was one of the most disastrous of all the medieval kings of England. He came to the throne when he was only 9 months old after the sudden death of his warrior father, King Henry V. Henry VI was raised and educated to be a powerful monarch, but he never really took to it. Being a child king, he never had the benefit of learning from his father's example of good kingship. Instead, he formed his ideals of kingship from chivalrous medieval books and religious texts. As a result, he became extremely pious and preferred peace over conflict.[1] These would be admirable qualities for a modern-day ruler, but no good if you were expected to rule a large, unruly medieval kingdom such as England.

In November 1437, just days shy of his sixteenth-birthday, King Henry VI dismissed his regent council and declared that his minority was over, meaning he was ready to rule independently on his own. It was a disaster from the very beginning. Henry had no ability to discern between good advice or bad advice from his councillors. As a result, he was very easily swayed to change his position depending on the last person to catch his ear. Plus, he wasn't really that interested in affairs of state, so he mostly let the people around him make decisions for him. His strong preference for peace with France would be a monumental error that would contribute to his downfall, not to mention the loss of the Hundred Years' War with France.[2]

While Henry struggled to establish his reign in England, his cousin Richard, Duke of York, was on his second tour of duty as lieutenant-general of France. Although Richard was very close in the line of succession, his position at court was quite precarious. He was a prince of royal blood, however, he was continually denied his rightful place at court. King Henry VI had abdicated authority to his personal favourites and they were dead set on pushing the powerful duke of York completely out of the picture in order to maintain control over King Henry and his government. Richard spent his entire adult life trying to wrestle away power from the king's greedy councillors in order to protect his lands and titles for himself and his heirs, including his son Edward, Earl of March, the future King Edward IV. Richard's actions in the 1450's laid the groundwork for his son Edward to one day overthrow Henry VI and ascend the throne of England for the House of York.

Edward IV's father Richard had been involved in court politics from a fairly young age. When he was only 6 years old he joined his cousin King Henry VI's household[3]. At the tender age of 13, he was knighted.[4] When Richard was 19 years old, he was appointed as the temporary constable of England while the duke of Bedford, Henry VI's uncle, was out of the country. On 1 May 1436, when he was 25 years old, Richard, received his first major royal appointment: lieutenant-general of France, in charge of directing military campaigns in the long-running Hundred Years' War.[5] This was an extremely prestigious position and Richard led several early victories, including the capture of several small French towns, but before long, things in France became untenable for Richard. He was not given the proper manpower, money, or resources to fight a successful war in France. The wages he had been promised by Henry VI for both himself and his soldiers were far into arrears, forcing Richard to fund the war effort entirely out of his own pocket.[6] This was the beginning of the tension between Richard and Henry that would eventually erupt into a full-blown civil war between the houses Houses of York and Lancaster known today as 'The Wars of the Roses'.

Despite the issues he experienced during his first tour of duty as lieutenant-general of France, Richard returned for a second tour in July 1440. This time he took his young family with him, including his wife, Cecily Neville, and their 2-year-old daughter Anne, and set up their primary residence at Rouen in Normandy. Edward Plantagenet, the future King Edward IV, was born in Rouen on 28 April 1442. After Edward, Richard and Cecily went on to produce six more sons (only three lived into adulthood) and three daughters (two survived).

Shortly after Edward's birth, King Henry recalled Richard to England and granted the lieutenancy of France to his new favourite, John Beaufort, who had also just been given the dukedom of Somerset. Richard was greatly perturbed at being recalled from France, especially since he had established his family there and had invested so much of his own money and resources. In fact, the king still owed him over £20,000 for funding the French offensive out of his own pocket.[7]

The duke of Somerset's brief time as lieutenant-general of France was a total disaster. First, he invaded the French duchy of Brittany by mistake even though it was an English ally. Henry VI was forced to pay reparations to mend the rift Somerset had caused with Duke Francis of Brittany. After further misfortunes, Somerset fled back to England alone and abandoned his army in France. Somerset's failure was so profound that even King Henry refused to receive him at court. Somerset died in May 1444, most likely by suicide for the shame that his actions in France had caused for himself and his family.[8] Against all odds, his only legitimate daughter, Margaret Beaufort, would go on to play a major part in English politics and would reverse his family's fortunes in a monumental way through her only child, Henry Tudor.

Due to Somerset's colossal failure, Henry VI had no other choice but to negotiate a hugely unpopular truce with France in 1444. Henry sent one of his most trusted advisors, William de la Pole, Earl of Suffolk, to manage negotiations and directed him to make peace at any cost. The result of Suffolk's negotiations was the Treaty of Tours which was concluded on 28 May 1444. Henry was so desperate for peace that he astoundingly agreed to renounce the whole of England's claim to the French throne. Even more outrageous was Henry's agreement to cede two major territories back to France: Maine and Anjou. Lastly, the peace treaty was sealed with a marriage contract between King Henry and a French princess: Margaret of Anjou. The choice of Margaret was highly questionable, and the English people were outraged since Margaret brought with her no titles, lands, or dowry.[9] Typically, foreign marriages of royalty came with hefty dowries, but Margaret's father was broke.

The biggest opponent of Henry's treaty with France was his uncle Humphrey, Duke of Gloucester. Humphrey was Henry VI's closest living male relative and therefore the heir to the throne since Henry had not yet sired any children. Humphrey had fought alongside Henry's father, Henry V, in the Hundred Years' War and had served as co-protector of England while Henry VI was a child. Duke Humphrey was livid at Henry for going against his advice and making the disastrous treaty. He was disgusted at Henry for handing over the English-held French territories that Henry V had died fighting for. Duke Humphrey was particularly outraged that young King Henry released his father's prisoner, the duke of Orléans, who had been held captive since the Battle of Agincourt in 1415. In fact, Humphrey felt so strongly that he came out of retirement and led public protests against his nephew's policy.[10] The king's councillors were eager to silence Humphrey. In April 1447 he was arrested and charged with treason for plotting to overthrow the king, which was an obvious lie. Gloucester would not have to face the charges because he mysteriously died just a few days after being taken into custody. The official story is that he had a heart attack or stroke due to the shock of his arrest, but many suspected it was murder.[11]

After the death of Humphrey, the closest male relative to Henry VI was Richard, Duke of York, which made him next in line to the throne. Only months after Humphrey's death, King Henry started to succumb to pressure from his councillors to eliminate all rivals to his throne and they considered Richard to be the most serious threat of them all. Richard was one of the wealthiest men in England and his influence was so vast that he could raise a large army on short notice, which made him very dangerous. To remove him from having a direct hand in England's governance, Richard was appointed to the lieutenancy of Ireland for a period of ten years. This was a big step down from being the lieutenant of France and was twice the usual appointment length. In fact, many saw it as a political exile.[12]

Richard arrived in Ireland on 6 July 1449 and made his way to Dublin where he would set up his home base of operations. Within three months York had many of the local lords swearing fealty to him. This was an astonishingly quick success since Ireland had been all but ungoverned and ungovernable for hundreds of years. In France, the situation was the exact opposite. King Henry's favourites Suffolk and the new Somerset, Edmund Beaufort, had completely bungled their military campaigns and lost even more of the English-held territories. Henry's refusal to punish his favourites incited a great uproar in London and the people decided to take justice into their own hands. As England was now too dangerous for him, Suffolk fled the country and sailed for Burgundy on 2 May 1450. Shortly into his voyage, his ship was intercepted by a small English fleet and was brought aboard their ship, *Nicholas of the Tower*. The crew staged a mock trial and found Suffolk guilty of treason. They beheaded him with a rusty sword and shoved his corpse overboard, leaving it to wash up unceremoniously on the shores of Dover.[13]

Further disorder struck the kingdom of England shortly after Suffolk's death when news came of the crushing defeat at the Battle of Formigny. The English army of 3,000 men was nearly decimated by the French and the great stronghold of Normandy was lost.[14] It was greatly unsettling for the people of England, not just for the loss of life but also for fear that the French army might now bring the fight to English shores. Immediately after Henry received news about the devastating loss at Formigny, he ordered the people of Kent to muster men and gather weapons in case of a French invasion.

As the Kentishmen nervously watched the shores for any sign of French ships, a rumour began circulating that King Henry held the people of Kent responsible for Suffolk's recent death at sea. As punishment, many Kentishmen would be brought to trial and hanged, while the king also planned to turn the whole of Kent into a royal forest.[15] This rumour incited hysteria among the Kentish people. They blamed Henry and his corrupt councillors for putting them and the whole of England in this precarious situation and, feeling their backs were against the wall, they chose to defend themselves.

In the summer of 1450, a huge discontented Kentish mob numbering in the tens of thousands marched upon London to challenge the king and his corrupt councillors.[16] The mob was led by a mysterious character named Jack Cade. His real identity was rumoured to be an Irishman named John Mortimer who was related to the House of York. In a lengthy manifesto, Cade asserted that the king was surrounded by false councillors who drove the kingdom into poverty and left the country lawless. The rebels complained that 'the lords of his royal blood have been put from his daily presence, and other mean persons of lower nature exalted and made chief of his privy council'.[17]

King Henry spent June 1450 in London attempting to put down Cade's rebellion, but he failed miserably. By late June he conceded to the rebels by granting them permission to arrest and try those they deemed as treasonous, and Henry fled London for the safety of Kenilworth Castle. They set up a traitor's court at Guildhall where they tried and executed about twenty men.[18]

With no help coming from the king, the citizens of London decided to take matters into their own hands and mount their own defence. On the evening of 5 July 1450, a small army of armed citizens marched to London Bridge and confronted the Kentishmen in a bloody battle that lasted until the next morning. At least forty London citizens were killed but they did succeed in pushing Jack Cade's men out of the city. The next day, Queen Margaret, who had stayed behind in London, offered pardons and terms to which the rebels accepted, except for Jack Cade. The queen put a price of 1,000 marks on his head and he was captured just days later. He died during the trip back to London but nevertheless his head was lopped off and placed on a pole above London Bridge.[19]

King Henry and Queen Margaret returned to London in late July 1450 believing the unrest to be over, but they couldn't have been more mistaken. Henry learned no lessons from the Kentish uprising. He dismissed all the rebels' concerns, especially the ones about replacing those evil councillors about him. In fact, Henry did quite the opposite when shortly thereafter he awarded the office of constable of England to the duke of Somerset, Edmund Beaufort. Emboldened by Cade's rebellion and Somerset's rise, York was now ready to force the issue and demand his rightful place next to King Henry VI helping him govern the realm.

21

The Wars of the Roses

In September 1450, the duke of York made an unexpected trip home from Ireland. The reason for York's trip to England is not entirely clear but most likely he had heard of Cade's Rebellion and decided he needed to return to England to help Henry get control of his kingdom. He had also no doubt heard about the death of Suffolk and wanted to take his place as Henry's chief advisor.[1] However, York's arrival in England wasn't reassurance to Henry, it instead caused panic among his councillors. They distrusted York and feared the impetus for his trip was to wrestle the throne from Henry, especially after the Cade manifesto made references to Duke Richard being left out of the governance of England.

Upon hearing of Richard's sailing, King Henry and his councillors took a defensive stance, putting the port towns along northwestern England on high alert and ordering them to delay York's disembarkation as long as possible. When York landed in September 1450, he was turned away from Beaumaris in Wales by the king's officers, greatly confusing Richard because he believed himself to be in good favour with the king. Richard's suspicions were aroused by Henry's hostile actions so he headed towards the safety of his homelands where he would gather a force of his most loyal men to accompany him to London.

On the way to London, Richard sent a letter to Henry pledging his loyalty to the king and complaining of his treatment at Beaumaris. He also took the opportunity to accuse 'certain persons' of plotting to bring him down. When the king responded, he put York in his place, politely telling him to butt out: 'When the work requires it, or it is necessary, I will call upon your assistance.'[2] But Richard, was nowhere near backing down. In fact, Henry's response only served to inflame his passion on the matter. When Richard arrived in London on 27 September 1450, he went directly to Westminster Abbey to speak with Henry but was forbidden to enter the king's presence. York would not be deterred. He forced his way into the king's chambers and pleaded his case, insisting that he was loyal to the king and that his only reason for returning to England was to help restore good governance to the realm. York's speech evidently worked because by the end of 1450, the king allowed him to move against his councillors by submitting a formal petition of complaint to parliament naming the councillors he believed were corrupting the king, namely Somerset. The result was Somerset's impeachment and banishment from the kingdom, however, Henry did not enforce the punishment and Somerset remained in England.

Throughout 1451, York and Somerset continually antagonised each other, trading barbs that grew more hostile and aggressive with each passing month. It was in this year that the two men became open enemies. The duke of Somerset was determined to take revenge on York for causing his impeachment and began spreading rumours about York's ulterior motives, causing Richard to write yet another letter to Henry pledging his allegiance. Later that month, Somerset's men attacked York's chamberlain, Sir William Oldhall, within the walls of St Martin's church in London, which was considered particularly sinful. Richard at this point had had enough and began distributing letters to Shrewsbury and neighbouring towns lamenting the loss of France, the lack of justice in the kingdom, and laying blame for all of England's woes squarely on Somerset's shoulders. In his letters, Richard asked his fellow Englishmen to join him at Ludlow to array and then march to London to force a confrontation with the king.

By mid-February 1452 York had raised several thousand men who led in a march to London.[3] Negotiations between the two parties occurred in the first few days of March and York had only one demand: arrest Somerset and remove him from the king's presence permanently. Not unlike before, Henry agreed to York's demand in the moment, but then failed to enforce the agreed punishment for Somerset. After the negotiations had been concluded, York disbanded his army and travelled to Blackheath on the southeast outskirts of London to meet with the king personally, relieved that they had come to an amicable conclusion. But when York entered Henry's tent, he was shocked to see Somerset there by the king's side as if nothing had happened. Supposedly when the queen received word of what the negotiators had agreed to, she immediately cancelled the order to arrest Somerset and restored him to power.[4] A shocked York was then taken into royal custody and forced to march back to London at the head of King Henry's army. He was publicly humiliated by being required to take a very public pledge of fealty at St Paul's Cathedral promising that he would be loyal to Henry and would not raise an army without the king's approval. As soon as Henry released him, York retreated to his castle at Ludlow to lick his wounds and think about his next steps.

With York temporarily out of the way, King Henry turned his attention to the security of the throne for the Lancastrians. Since he and the queen were still childless, he began preparing his half-brothers Edmund and Jasper Tudor to be his heirs but then miraculously, in the spring of 1453, Queen Margaret of Anjou found out she was finally pregnant after eight years of marriage. A royal heir would change everything. Not only did the pregnancy bring the king and queen great joy, it was also a tidy way to get the Yorkists out of the line of royal succession.

The hope was short-lived, though, as devastating news came from France. On 17 July 17 1453, the English royal army was utterly destroyed by France at the battle of Castillon, giving the French control of the entirety of Gascony.[5] This was the last of the English-held territories in France and the loss was a huge blow to everyone in England, both nobles and commoners alike. Thousands upon thousands of Englishmen had given their lives or lost family members in the fight over France and it turned out to be all for nothing. France was lost and the Hundred Years' War was over.

King Henry had been staying at his hunting lodge in Clarendon when he news of the disaster in France reached him. Upon hearing of the loss, the king suffered a complete mental collapse. He basically became catatonic; he could not move his body, nor could he communicate in any way. He was in a sort of daze or stupor that lasted an entire eighteen months. The exact diagnosis of his condition is unknown but it is quite possible that an already depressed Henry was shocked into a major depressive episode upon hearing of the final loss in France and he essentially checked out, both mentally and physically.[6]

Henry was still mentally incapacitated when Queen Margaret gave birth to their first child, a son named Edward, born on 13 October 1453. Sadly, when the queen presented the baby to Henry, the king had no reaction whatsoever. This was a problem because kings were required to recognise children as their own in order to be considered an official heir.[7] The lack of King Henry's acknowledgment of Edward as his son mean that York was still the de facto heir to the throne.

As Margaret and Henry's fortunes seemed to be falling, York's were indeed rising. He was accepted back into politics and came to London in November 1453 for a meeting of the Great Council. Wisely, he did not come with a large retinue, but he did come with an agenda: to oust Somerset and take what he felt was his rightful place as the king's closest advisor. To achieve this goal he recruited one of his closest allies, the duke of Norfolk, to give an impassioned speech to the royal council in which he accused Somerset of overstepping his authority in royal matters and also put the blame for the crushing loss of France squarely on Somerset's shoulders. Norfolk was a dynamic speaker and his efforts were successful. Two days later Somerset was arrested and imprisoned in the Tower of London where he would reside for the next sixteen months.[8] The pendulum of power was clearly swinging in York's direction after this seemingly easy victory over his nemesis.

With Somerset locked away and King Henry unable to rule, only Queen Margaret remained to protect the interests of the House of Lancaster. With York gaining more momentum by the day, Margaret decided to make a bold power grab before it was too late. In early February 1454, she introduced a bill of five articles to parliament in which she petitioned to be the regent of England, giving her complete control of the government. Her bill was met by stunned silence as the audacity of the move sunk in that a woman, no less a French woman, wanted complete control of the kingdom as if she were a king. Without alienating her too much, parliament politely declined her request.

For many months Queen Margaret and the king's close attendants managed to keep the true nature of the king's illness a secret but they knew it wouldn't be possible to hide forever. As soon as the truth came out, they anticipated a strong challenge on behalf of York and his allies, and that's exactly what they got. On 23 March 1454, a group of York's allies including three earls, three lords, three bishops, and two viscounts visited King Henry at Windsor Castle. They required his input in the appointment of a new chancellor and archbishop of Canterbury after John Kemp's death but they were appalled to see King Henry in such a sorry state, unable to understand what they were saying and definitely unable to respond.[9] They went back to parliament and reported that Henry was unable to perform his duties. With the king so obviously incapacitated, parliament had no choice but to appoint a protector to govern England. The obvious choice was York, and there were no other suggestions put forth. He was formally invested as Protector and Defender of the Realm on 27 March 1454. York was now the most powerful man in England.

Interestingly, when parliament appointed York to the role of protectorate, they did not say his term would end when Henry recovered. Instead, they said York would be protectorate until Prince Edward came of age. Parliament clearly had little hope of the king's recovery. This was a perfect spot for York as he would essentially have control of the kingdom for the next fifteen years until Prince Edward was old enough to rule on his own.

Nine months into York's protectorate, the pendulum of fortune suddenly swung back in favour of the Lancastrians. On Christmas Day 1454, King Henry inexplicably woke up from his stupor with no memory of the past eighteen months. A grateful Queen Margaret presented their son whom this time was formally recognised by his father. Upon meeting his son

King Henry 'held up his hands and thanked God'.[10] Margaret wasted no time filling him in on everything that had happened over the past eighteen months and the two set about undoing the work of York. They immediately released their closest ally Somerset from the Tower of London and formally pardoned him, much to the chagrin of the Yorkists. On 9 February 1455, York's post of protectorate, was officially dissolved and shortly thereafter his allies whom he had appointed to the most powerful positions in England were also released from their posts and Henry's men were restored.

Adding insult to injury, the king revoked the title of captain of Calais from York and granted it to Somerset. This show of favour towards Somerset and against York greatly offended Richard who had shown himself to be a much more capable leader than Somerset had ever been, both in France and in England. But York was not a man to quietly retreat like a dog with his tail between his legs. Instead York and his ally Salisbury retreated to their castles, began calling men to arms, and planned out their next moves.

A few months after York's protectorate ended, he and his allies were invited to attend a meeting of the Great Council on 25 May 1455 at Leicester which was in the heart of Lancastrian territory. York remembered not so long ago when Henry's brother Humphrey, Duke of Gloucester, was disgracefully arrested and imprisoned upon his arrival at parliament. York feared this too could also be his fate and that the king was trying to entrap him. So instead, the duke and his allies, the earls of Salisbury and Warwick, decided their best move would be to intercept Henry before he made it to Leicester. Richard Neville, the earl of Warwick, was the son of Salisbury and the nephew of Richard of York. Due to a very advantageous marriage, he inherited vast wealth and lands from his wife's side of the family, making him the preeminent noble in the north. His involvement with the duke of York and Edward would later earn him the nickname of 'the Kingmaker'.

The king's scouts brought word to Somerset that York was on the move with a large army but what they got wrong was York's direction. Somerset believed York's army was heading to Leicester to force a confrontation at the upcoming council meeting, but York was really heading towards London to intercept King Henry before he made it to Leicester. Somerset sent out an array of arms and gathered as many nobles as he could to reinforce the royal army which he led out of London, along with King Henry, on 21 May 1455. They barely made it out of the city before receiving distressing news: York's army was a mere fifteen kilometres away, much closer than they had ever imagined.[11] Somerset marched the royal army ten kilometres further towards the town of St Albans and found York's army already encamped there. King Henry whole-heartedly believed that York would negotiate a resolution and that this confrontation would not lead to violence. In fact, he believed it so much that he and his men did not put on their armor before arraying themselves within the town streets of St. Albans. Negotiations between the two sides went back and forth but made no progress. The king flatly refused to get rid of Somerset and so York ordered his army into formation.

At around 1.00am on 22 May 1455, the first battle of the Wars of the Roses commenced with a Yorkist assault against the king's forces within the town of St Albans. Due to the locale, it was more of a street skirmish than a traditional medieval pitched battle which usually took place in a wide-open field. The king's army was reported to be between 2,500 to 3,000 men strong while York's army was said to be much larger, approximately 5,000 men.[12] At first, Somerset's barricades worked to keep the Yorkists out of the town, but it didn't take long for Warwick and his men to break through and overwhelm the unprepared royal army. Many of Somerset's men fled the bloodshed rather than stand with him and be slaughtered.

The First Battle of St Albans was the shortest battle of the Wars of the Roses, lasting altogether less than one hour.[13] Many of the king's closest nobles were killed that day, including Somerset who was specifically targeted for death by York and his commanders. King Henry's life was spared and after the battle ended, York and his allies approached him peacefully. Together they kneeled before him, pledged allegiance, and swore that they meant him no harm. They promised that their only goal was to rid the king of the evil councillors who surrounded him. King Henry willingly gave himself over to the Yorkists and he was taken into custody. Henry was now essentially a puppet king and the Yorkists would use his name and rule the kingdom through him. Just four days after the battle of St Albans, King Henry was made to open parliament, which only a king could do, and then he was packed off to Hertford Castle to join the queen and take a back seat in the governance of his realm.

After gaining control of Henry VI's government, York swiftly placed his allies in positions of power. His own position became even stronger just a few months later when King Henry again fell into another paralysing bout of depression.[14] On 15 November 1455 York was once again named 'Protector and Defender of the Land'. York's second term as protectorate would be much shorter than the first, lasting only three months. In February 1456, the Lancastrian party managed to rouse King Henry just enough to come to parliament and declare York released from the role of protectorate. Then that summer, Queen Margaret moved the king's entire court from Yorkist-popular London to Coventry in the Midlands, a traditional Lancastrian stronghold. Although King Henry is not known to have been ill during this time, he had grown increasingly passive about politics and allowed Queen Margaret to take the helm of his government. [15]

Queen Margaret spent the next two years rebuilding the Lancastrian powerbase in the Midlands. By the winter of 1457, she felt sufficiently prepared to make a full-court press to win back control of the kingdom. She started the Lancastrian revival by moving the royal court back to London and calling a council meeting on behalf of her husband. By mid-February 1458, London was brimming with tension as the council members began to arrive for the meeting, all of them with large retinues of men in the hundreds. It seemed as if an armed confrontation was unavoidable, but it was surprisingly peaceful and conciliatory. After a few weeks of negotiations, York and Warwick agreed to the king's terms of compensation for St Albans in which they would pay a large sum of money to the families of slain noblemen as well as paying for masses to be sung at St Albans in remembrance of the lost lives.[16] Lastly, and most importantly, they agreed to thousands of pounds in bonds which were meant to ensure good behaviour.

The king, queen, and lords shortly thereafter celebrated the successful negotiation and newfound unity in a very public way. On 25 March 1458, what would become known as 'Love Day', the reconciled lords of both the Houses of Lancaster and York intermingled with the king and queen in a great procession to St Paul's Cathedral where together they would give thanks to God for the newfound peace. Even the duke of York and Queen Margaret walked side-by-side with hands held. It was a great show for the citizens of London, one in which the leaders tried to demonstrate that all was well in government and everything was in perfect order. To the citizens watching the show, it looked a little too good to be true, and they were right.

Despite both sides agreeing to this ten-year peace deal, they were only able to tolerate each other for ten months before the fighting broke out once again. The impetus for the confrontation that broke the Love Day reconciliation was the rise of Richard Neville, Earl of Warwick. Since being appointed Captain of Calais in the Autumn of 1456, Warwick had done much to turn around the state of affairs in Calais. He paid the back wages owed by King Henry to the angry garrisons, reinforced its defences, and expanded its naval fleet. So great was his power that he practically ruled the English channel and on many occasions fought off foreign fleets and participated in pirate raids in which he took possession of foreign goods.[17]

Queen Margaret became concerned about the level of authority Warwick wielded and sought to put him in his place. She commissioned an investigation of Warwick's alleged misdeeds in Calais and summoned him to appear before the council in November 1458 to explain himself.[18] Warwick arrived in London with a large force of armed men, causing quite a disruption, including at least one brawl and one attempt on Warwick's life. Queen Margaret revoked his role as captain of Calais and ordered his arrest, but Warwick managed to escape England before Margaret could get her hands on him. Love Day now seemed to be a distant memory as the two sides headed back down the path towards inevitable confrontation.

In late June 1459, Queen Margaret called a meeting of the Great Council in Coventry with the express intent of doling out punishment to York and his allies for opposing the king's authority. York, Salisbury, and Warwick were not invited to the meeting. Fearing an armed retaliation from the Lancastrians, the Yorkists retreated north to Ludlow Castle and began raising troops. Whispers and rumours spread through the country that both the Yorkist and Lancastrian leaders were preparing for battle by mustering men and stockpiling weapons.

In September 1459, the Yorkists set their plans in motion. Warwick sailed from Calais to England with a force of 600 men and marched his army towards Ludlow Castle, the planned rendezvous point with his allies York, and Salisbury. Salisbury also left his castle and marched towards Ludlow with a huge armed force of about 5,000 men.[19] The Yorkist allies sent oaths of allegiance to King Henry, insisting that their only aim was the good governance of his realm but Queen Margaret wasn't buying it. She was aware that the three nobles had mustered men and were headed to Ludlow so she set out to stop them before they could join into one huge army. Salisbury's location was the closest in proximity to the king's army, which was at Kenilworth, so she ordered the royal army to block Salisbury's progress. Salisbury was able to evade them at first, but on the morning of 23 September 1459, his advance guard ran into another royal army, this one led by aging military leader Lord Audley. Audley's Lancastrian army of nearly 10,000 men barred the route of Salisbury's Yorkist army in a farming area known as Blore Heath.[20] Helplessly outnumbered, Salisbury ordered his army into a pretend retreat and when the royal soldiers started pursuing them through the woods, the Yorkists turned and cut them down as they were crossing a waterway. This turned the tide of victory in the Yorkists favour and they fought through the night until they stood victorious over the Lancastrian army in the Battle of Blore Heath. Salisbury led his victorious troops to Ludlow where they would join up with the armies of York and Warwick.

A little over two weeks later, on 12 October 1459, the combined Yorkist army faced off with the royal army fronted by King Henry himself at Ludford

Bridge. The sight of the king in person seemed to give some of the Yorkists cold feet. To fight against a king in battle was certainly treasonous plus they were severely outnumbered by the royal army, perhaps as much as two to one.[21] The Yorkist leaders sent several messages to Henry proclaiming their loyalty and begging him not to fight but their pleas went unanswered. The tension was too much for one Yorkist leader named Andrew Trollope. In the middle of the night under cover of darkness, he and his troops defected from the Yorkist side and joined the king's army. At this point the Yorkist leaders realised defeat was unavoidable. To preserve their lives, they fled not only the battlefield but England entirely. The duke of York, went to Ireland with his 16-year-old son Edmund, Earl of Rutland. Warwick, Salisbury and York's 17-year-old son Edward, Earl of March, fled to Calais.

Parliament was summoned to meet immediately to deal with the volatile situation and to dole out punishments on Yorkist rebels. On 20 November 1459, an Act of Attainder was levied against York and his allies in which they were stripped of all titles and proclaimed traitors. Furthermore, their heirs were forbidden from inheriting those lands and titles in the future. This was a devastating punishment, one that was meant to completely ruin them. In fact, this session came to be known as the 'Parliament of Devils' due to the ruthlessness of the sentences they passed without any sort of trial. It was meant to destroy the Yorkists once and for all, but Margaret and Henry's councillors seriously misjudged the resolve of the leaders of the House of York.

22

The Rose of Rouen

Despite their defeat at Ludford Bridge and being stripped of their lands and titles at the Parliament of Devils, not all was lost for the Yorkists. They still had strong support from the Commons and the people of London, and they were starting to gain international support for their cause.[1] In Dublin, the Irish parliament passed a law making it a treasonable offense to attempt to kill lieutenant of Ireland, giving Richard some measure of protection from King Henry's faction. In Calais, Warwick's navy had rallied around him, despite the fact that he wasn't the captain of Calais any longer. That title had been given to the younger duke of Somerset, Henry Beaufort, but the citizens had refused to acknowledge him. On 15 January 1460, Warwick further harassed the Somerset and the Lancastrians by destroying a fleet of ships being specially built to aid Somerset against Warwick in Calais.

Slowly but surely, support was building again for the Yorkists and their cause. In the spring of 1460, the people of Kent, who were the instigators of Cade's Rebellion ten years earlier, sent a letter to Warwick pledging their support and their men to fight in his army. That was the little support the Yorkists needed. With momentum seemingly on their side, Warwick and York held a secret war council in March 1460 where they laid plans for an invasion of England. Those plans were put into action just three months later when Warwick, Salisbury, and York's 16-year-old son Edward sailed from Calais and landed their invasion fleet at Sandwich on 26 June 1460 with about 2,000 soldiers.[2] Their march to London was carefully planned so that it passed through the county of Kent where they expected to pick up several thousands of men to join their army.

The king and queen's army was in Coventry and only a small royal force was left behind in London, commanded by Lord Scales. The king ordered Londoners to resist the Yorkists but they defied King Henry and allowed Warwick's army to enter the city on 2 July 1460.[3] The fact that Londoners allowed Warwick to enter unopposed suggests that they were ready for an able leader to take control of the kingdom, for they knew that King Henry was unable to govern them. Warwick himself was reported to say 'our king

is a dolt and a fool who is ruled instead of ruling'.[4] Warwick was also a sort
of a celebrity at that time, having been renowned for his exploits in Calais
but mostly for leading the Yorkists to victory at the First Battle of St Albans.
London citizens clearly liked and respected Warwick better than Richard of
York, whom they had turned away from London in 1452 when he tried to
take the city by force.

It didn't take long for the news of Warwick's London takeover to reach
the king and queen who had remained at Coventry in the Lancastrian
Midlands, counting on Londoners to repel Warwick's rebel army. It was
only when the Yorkist army departed London headed for Coventry that the
king finally acted. Around July 6, King Henry departed Coventry at the
head of the royal army and headed southeast towards London to confront
the approaching Yorkist army. The Yorkists and the Lancastrians were on an
unavoidable collision course.

On 10 July 1460, the two armies faced off against each other at the
decisive Battle of Northampton after days of failed negotiations. The
Yorkist army, led by Edward of March, Warwick, and Lord Fauconberg,
initiated the battle and quickly overwhelmed the royal army with their
superior numbers.[5] Paving the way for the Yorkist victory was the desertion
of Edmund Grey, one of the leading Lancastrian commanders. He ordered
all his men to lay down their weapons and allow Warwick to penetrate the
royal army's defensive line unmolested. The king's soldiers tried to flee the
slaughter but once again they found themselves trapped on the battlefield
by a river. With no other escape route, many royal soldiers drowned while
trying to flee across the river. King Henry's most ardent supporters, including
the dukes of Buckingham, Shrewsbury, and Beaumont were hunted down
and slaughtered on the battlefield. Mercifully, the battle only lasted a half
an hour.[6]

The Battle of Northampton was a huge victory for the Yorkists, even more
so since they were able to take back possession of King Henry VI. The king
was found in the royal tent and willingly gave himself over to the Yorkists.
Warwick, Edward, and Fauconberg immediately pledged fealty to the king
and transported him back to London. He was once again their puppet king.

With King Henry in the hands of the Yorkists, Queen Margaret felt
increasingly threatened, not only for herself but for the safety of her son,
Prince Edward. She had not gone to Northampton with the king and his
army but instead stayed back in Coventry with Edward. When she received
news of the Lancastrian defeat and the capture of her husband, she fled
with her son to Jasper Tudor's Harlech Castle in Wales but then was
moved to Denbigh Castle which was thought to be safer than Harlech. She

remained in Wales for the next five months trying to rally more supporters to her cause.[7]

Meanwhile, back in London Warwick was still leading the Yorkist takeover. His next step was to have King Henry summon a meeting of parliament for 7 October 1460. There were two main items on the agenda: reward Yorkist supporters and reverse the Act of Attainder from the Parliament of Devils that took away all of the Yorkist nobles' lands and titles. It wasn't until after the summons for parliament went out that the duke of York finally sailed from Ireland to join his allies in England, a whole two months after the Yorkists' colossal victory over the Lancastrians at Northampton. After arriving in England, York took his time slowly making his way across England, showing himself to the people in a rather kingly way as if he were on a royal progress.[8]

When York, finally arrived in London on 10 October 1460, it was apparent to everyone that he had a new motive. York had a different demeanor this time and carried himself majestically, even decked himself out in a special blue and white uniform embroidered with Plantagenet symbols. He made a great show as he and his 500-man Yorkist army made their official entry into London with trumpeters announcing his arrival along with a great display of royal banners.[9] He then proceeded to Westminster where parliament was in session and made his intent known. After barging into the Star Chamber, York walked straight up to the king's throne and placed his hand upon it. This was a symbolic gesture that he was officially staking his claim to the throne of England. Members of parliament were shocked and horrified. York was in turn equally shocked when no one rose to support his claim, instead there was only a stunned silence.[10] He withdrew from the chamber but then six days later he formally asserted his right to the throne based on his supreme lineage over Henry VI to which he provided a genealogical roll. He claimed that Henry IV had unlawfully seized the crown from Richard II, thus cutting out the Mortimer line from royal succession.[11]

In a closed session, leading nobles wrestled over how to respond to York's claim without angering him but also how to honour the rights of the sitting monarch, King Henry VI. After two weeks of debates, a compromise called the Act of Accord was reached on 24 October 1460. In the agreement, King Henry VI was declared the rightful king of England until his death or voluntary resignation. Richard, Duke of York, followed by the heirs of his body were declared next in line to the throne, essentially disinheriting the king's son, Prince Edward.[12] The Parliament Rolls record King Henry's reaction when he was told of their verdict: 'to avoid the shedding of Christian blood, by good and serious deliberation and the advice of all his lords spiritual and temporal, agreed to the settlement'.[13]

Why would Henry agree to remove his son from succession? Some say it's because he didn't believe Edward was really his son. Rumours about Edward's parentage had been circulating for years and perhaps Henry believed them. It was well known that the king and queen required coaching in the bedroom and Henry was notoriously pious, abhorring the sight of naked skin.[14] Perhaps he knew for sure that Edward was not his son because he and his wife were in a sexless marriage. The most likely explanation of Henry's acquiescence could be that he really had no other choice. One London chronicler wrote that 'the king for fear of death granted York the crown because he was kept at Westminster by force and strength'.[15]

One person who was surprisingly unpleased with the Act of Accord was Warwick. He was distressed at York's bold attempt to take the throne upon his recent arrival in London. He may have also been shaken by the lack of support in parliament for the Yorkist cause. He was also offended that York swooped in to steal the glory after Warwick had orchestrated the invasion that led to the victory at Northampton and had been holding the city of London waiting for York's late arrival.

Obviously, Queen Margaret was supremely unhappy about the Act of Accord since it cut her son out of the line of royal succession. Unlike her husband, she was not ready to give in to the Yorkists, it simply made her more determined to fight for her son's cause. In December 1460, she took the reins of the Lancastrian party by sailing to Scotland with the purpose of soliciting financial and military support from Mary of Guelders, the dowager queen of Scotland. Soon with Scotland's help, as well as Lancastrian supporters in northern England, Queen Margaret had raised an army of nearly 15,000 men and they began a campaign of raids on the England-Scotland border.[16]

With Lancastrian uprisings springing up across the kingdom, the duke of York had no choice but to split up his forces. He sent his son Edward to Wales to put down Jasper Tudor's uprising. Warwick would stay in London to protect the capital. York took his second eldest son, Edmund, north with him along with 6,000 soldiers to confront the Lancastrians.[17] On the way north York learned that the queen's army was much larger than he had anticipated so he decided to stop at his own Sandal Castle, just south of the town of Wakefield, on 21 December 1460 to await reinforcements from his son Edward. At some point thereafter, the two sides called a temporary truce to last over the Christmas holiday.[18]

As the traditional story goes, on 30 December 1460 a small Yorkist foraging party was sent from the castle to look for any food they could harvest or supplies they could gather. Although it was still the Christmas season and the truce still active, the Lancastrian army appeared before the foragers and a fight erupted. The duke of York left the castle to join in the melee, but it quickly turned into a full-scale battle for which he was not prepared.[19] The Lancastrian army encircled and outnumbered York's men. York was pulled off his horse and unceremoniously hacked to death. His son Edmund was captured by Lord Clifford, whose own father had been killed by Yorkists at the Battle of St Albans. Lord Clifford cut Edmund down after declaring 'By God's blood thy father slew mine and so will I do thee and all thy kin.'[20] Salisbury was captured and publicly beheaded. The heads of York, Salisbury, and Edmund were placed on spikes at Micklegate Bar so all those entering York on the main road from London would see what the king did with traitors. A paper crown was placed on York's head to mock his lost battle to be crowned king of England. The Battle of Wakefield was a severe blow to the Yorkist cause and it opened the door for the queen's army to march south into London.

It was mid-January 1461 when Edward of March received the disastrous news that his father and younger brother Edmund had been killed by the Lancastrians at the Battle of Wakefield. Now Edward would step up to become the de facto leader of the Yorkist rebellion as he was next in line to the throne according to the Act of Accord. In Edward there became a Yorkist revival of sorts because this new young candidate, unlike his ambitious and haughty father Richard, fit the ideals of a medieval ruler. He was the complete opposite of the pathetic King Henry VI. Edward was tall, handsome, young (only 19 years old), and had a reputation as a fierce warrior and capable military leader. He had inherited his father's leadership skills and he also had a few vital qualities that York was lacking: he was charming, charismatic, and chivalrous.[21] He was exactly what the people of England wanted in a king. He was a breath of fresh air after the disastrous reign of Henry VI. The people may have been hesitant to back his father's claim to the throne, but would they be more eager to support this new prince of York?

After the disaster at Wakefield and the death of his father and brother, Edward mustered his army of mostly Welshmen and prepared to leave Gloucester for London to help Warwick defend the city against Queen Margaret's army who was barreling their way south. Shortly after departing Gloucester, Edward received news that a Lancastrian army led by Jasper and Owen Tudor was nearby and making their way towards London to join up with the queen's main royal army. Edward decided that the best course of action would be to intercept the Tudors' army before they could reach the royal army and bring an even bigger threat to the Yorkists. Edward reversed course and led his army north to a town called Mortimer's Cross to confront the Tudor forces.

On the way to Mortimer's Cross, Edward's forces witnessed a rare meteorological phenomenon where it appeared as if there were three suns in the sky (a sundog or parhelion). At first Edward's men were afraid it was a bad omen, but Edward twisted it to his own benefit and calmed his men's fears by telling them it was a sign from God that Edward should be king of England.[22] This special sign from God rallied the Yorkist troops as they lined up at Mortimer's Cross to block the Tudors' path to London.

The Lancastrian and Yorkists armies drew up into battle position on 2 February 1461. Walter Devereaux, Edward, and Sir William Herbert each commanded the left, right, and centre flanks of the Yorkist army. The Lancastrian army was led by Jasper Tudor, Owen Tudor, and Sir James Butler, Earl of Wiltshire. The Lancastrians were first to attack, assaulting Devereux's flank with such a force that it began to collapse and the Yorkist soldiers began fleeing the battlefield. Seeing Devereux's flank in such deep distress, Edward swung his centre flank in Devereux's direction to help push back the Lancastrian army. Edward's forces were successful and the Lancastrian army was forced into full retreat.

The Yorkists chased the fleeing Lancastrians until they caught the officers, one such officer being Owen Tudor, father to Jasper Tudor and stepfather to King Henry VI. Owen was taken to the marketplace at Hereford and publicly beheaded. Before placing his head in the block, he reportedly said 'That head shall lie in the stock that was wont to lie on Queen Catherine's lap.'[23] Afterwards, it was said that a mad lady washed the blood off his face, combed his hair, and placed 100 candles around his head.

The Battle of Mortimer's Cross was a complete disaster for the Lancastrians but especially for Jasper Tudor. Not only was his father killed but as many as 4,000 of his Welsh soldiers were massacred.[24] He was now being hunted by the Yorkists and he had no choice but to go into exile. Now the last hope for the Lancastrians would be Queen Margaret. With momentum on their side, the Yorkists wasted no time in forcing another confrontation, this time with the queen.

On 12 February 1461, just ten days after the Yorkist victory at the Battle of Mortimer's Cross, Richard Neville, Earl of Warwick left London with a huge army numbering some 9,000 men. They were marching north to face Queen Margaret's army which was presently marching south from York. Margaret's force was larger, estimated to be around 12,000, but they were mostly contained undisciplined northern soldiers, Welshmen, and Scottish mercenaries.[25] It was reported that her army wreaked havoc everywhere they went. They were said to have pillaged, raped, and destroyed any town unlucky enough to be in their path. Realistically, an army that large required a huge amount of resources to sustain itself so it's no wonder they had to go out through the villages and countryside to find food and other resources. It was also said that Queen Margaret had no money to pay her soldiers, so they took their compensation in other ways.[26] The truth is probably a little bit of both but nonetheless it gave Queen Margaret's army a very bad reputation which would end up damaging their cause.

As Margaret's army barreled south towards London, Warwick's army slowly marched north on their inevitable confrontation with the Lancastrian army. On 13 February 1461, Warwick's troops arrived at St Albans, the site of the Yorkist victory at the very first battle of the Wars of the Roses six years prior. Believing the queen's army was further away than it actually was, Warwick decided to set up camp there for the night. Little did he know that the queen's army had just sacked the Yorkist outpost at Dunstable fifteen kilometres away and were now on their way to St Albans.[27] Margaret had managed to get her army there so quickly because she marched them all through the night. The move paid off and they took the Yorkists by complete surprise when they lined up for battle once again at the town of St Albans.

This time it would be a complete reversal of fortunes compared to the first Battle of St Albans where the Yorkists easily beat an unprepared royal army. During the Second Battle of St Albans, the royal army overtook the unprepared Yorkists in the market square, pushing them back, breaking their lines of defence, and forcing them into a full retreat. It could not have been a greater victory for Queen Margaret, especially because she was able to take back possession of King Henry who had been 'under the protection' of the Yorkists for the past seven months. This was a devastating loss for the Yorkists and especially for their commander Warwick since this was his first loss in battle. Overall, the Yorkist army lost around 4,000 men and the Lancastrians lost about 2,000 men.[28] Warwick and Edward retreated west to Cotswolds in southern England to regroup and refresh their troops.

After Queen Margaret's victory, her army lingered at St Albans as they made plans to march south and enter London. There was just one problem: it seems Londoners were not eager to welcome the queen and her reputedly destructive army without reassurances of good behaviour. The city council sent an envoy of three noble women to negotiate with Queen Margaret: Cecily Neville, Richard of York's widow, Jacquetta Woodville, Edward's future mother-in-law, and Lady Scales, widow of loyal Lancastrian and commander of the Tower Thomas Scales. By sending women to treat with Queen Margaret, it demonstrates how much everyone knew that she was the one in charge of the Lancastrians now, not her husband, King Henry. Margaret was a tough negotiator and would only agree to part of their demands so in response the city refused them entry. Desperate for provisions and too weakened to face Edward's oncoming army, the queen departed St Albans and marched her army north to the safety of the Lancastrian heartland so she could prepare her army to take London by force.

In the meantime, Warwick's and Edward's combined Yorkist army swiftly made their way to London to attempt entry even though they had been on the losing side of the latest battle. When they arrived in the city on 26 February 1461, they were very pleasantly surprised when Londoners opened the city gates for Edward and cheered his arrival. It was quite a bold move for citizens to openly turn their backs on the anointed king and invite in his main rival to take his place. Technically what they did was treason, but they probably didn't believe King Henry was capable of enforcing law and order at this point. In their eyes, Henry was an incompetent ruler and it was time for the next man in line to take his place on the throne.

Although the Yorkists had control of London, they did not have control of King Henry, therefore they could not rule through him as Richard and Warwick had done. Instead, they needed to come up with a legal reason why Edward should be the rightful ruler. To that end, Edward accused King Henry of breaking the Act of Accord by defecting from the Yorkists and rejoining with the Lancastrians after the Second Battle of St Albans. According to Edward, the consequence of breaking the Act of Accord was forfeiture of the crown. To reinforce Edward's case, Warwick staged two public exhibitions where he asked Londoners if Henry deserved to rule or if they would have Edward. Reportedly they all shouted nay for Henry and yea for Edward.[29]

On 4 March 1461, in Westminster Palace, Edward was formally declared King of England in a rushed, quasi-coronation. There was no time for the usual celebrations and festivities that surrounded a typical royal coronation because they had just received news that Queen Margaret was preparing another attack. Edward turned his attention to readying his own army for battle once again. Part of his preparations included the issuance of his first two royal proclamations. In the first proclamation he asked the people to accept him as their king and to refrain from assisting the dethroned King Henry VI. Secondly, he offered a pardon to any Lancastrian who surrendered in the next ten days, except for the leaders which he listed specifically, including the exiled Jasper Tudor.

23

The First Reign of Edward IV

Now that Edward had been officially enthroned as Edward IV, King of England, his first priority was to secure his rule by putting down the army of the deposed King Henry VI. If Edward didn't put an end to the Lancastrian power, he would never be able to find any safety in his reign. Luckily, he would not have to do it alone as he had many capable Yorkist allies with huge numbers of men and resources at their disposal. Together in London they planned their strategy. They would each leave London separately and retreat to their power bases to recruit more men for their army and gather the needed weapons and resources for their next battle.

The duke of Norfolk was the first of Edward's allies to leave London. On 5 March 1461, he left the city for East Anglia where he would gather his full army. Two days later, Warwick left London for his home base in the Midlands where he would raise his banner calling men to arms. On 11 March Lord Fauconberg departed London with a large force and finally on 13 March Edward left London with the main body of the Yorkist army, now technically the king's army.

The disparate Yorkists armies met up and joined forces at Pontefract Castle on 27 March 1461, except for Norfolk who was running late. Their intelligence informed them that the Lancastrian army was only twenty kilometres away on the opposite side of the River Aire near the village of Towton. Warwick led a small force to try to infiltrate the enemy, making a river crossing at Ferrybridge where the Lancastrians were standing guard. At first, Warwick was successful in pushing back the Lancastrians and he even gained a little ground. But as his army slept that night, a large force of Lancastrians, including Warwick's own great-uncle Sir John Neville, launched an ambush. Warwick's army was completely taken by surprise and they quickly fled to avoid the slaughter. Edward rushed to the scene with the royal army and was able to push the Lancastrians back. That evening Edward was able to get his men through the river crossing. They encamped near Towton only a couple of kilometres away from the Lancastrian army and prepared to do battle the following day.

On the morning of 29 March 1461, the two armies donned their armor and lined up into position for the Battle of Towton, the bloodiest battle of the Wars of the Roses.[1] The duke of Somerset led the Lancastrian army of 60,000 men including most of England's surviving nobles and around sixty knights. The Yorkists had 48,000 men and much fewer men of rank on their side.[2] The Yorkist lines were commanded by King Edward, Warwick, and Lord Fauconberg. The Lancastrian army's lines were led by Sir Andrew Trollope, the earl of Northumberland, Lord Dacre, and the dukes of Exeter and Somerset. This was by far the largest battle of the Wars of the Roses so far in terms of the sheer number of soldiers in each side's army. Towton was no minor skirmish; it initiated a full-scale civil war and each side had fully prepared themselves for what they believed would be a decisive battle to end the conflict once and for all.

The weather that morning was terribly cold and windy. To add to the misery, it began snowing just as they were lining up for battle. Lord Fauconberg, the leader of Edward's front line, noticed that the wind had shifted and was now blowing into the faces of the Lancastrian army, making it very difficult for them to see. Fauconberg had the idea to unleash their archers immediately so that the Lancastrians would quite literally be blind-sided. As the Yorkist arrows rained down, the Lancastrian archers fired back but the harsh wind stopped their arrows just short of the Yorkist army. Seeing that his forces were being overwhelmed by arrows, Somerset ordered his line forward for hand-to-hand combat. The fighting was fierce and soon the entirety of both armies were involved in the melee. So many dead bodies lay on the field that fighting had to be paused a few times to clear out the corpses.[3]

After many hours of hand-to-hand fighting, the Lancastrians slowly gained an edge over the Yorkists. Then the Lancastrians unleashed what they intended to be their death-blow: they had hidden a secret force of men at Castle Hill Wood and now that group descended on the already weakened Yorkists. Edward's army was pushed all the way back to their camp and on the verge of collapse when the belated Norfolk finally arrived with a large force of fresh soldiers.[4] Norfolk was an absolute god send and it was his arrival that saved the battle for the Yorkists. Within an hour, the Yorkists forced the Lancastrians into a full retreat. So many Lancastrians were killed fleeing across the river, it was said the bodies formed a bridge.[5]

Henry, Margaret, Prince Edward, Somerset, Exeter, Lord Roos, and Sir John Fortescue fled to the safety of Scotland. Many of their nobles weren't so lucky. Among the Lancastrian nobles who lost their lives that day included the earl of Northumberland, the duke of Buckingham, Sir Andrew Trollope, and Lord Dacre. More than forty-two of their knights were executed. In all, more than 28,000 men died in the Battle of Towton the single largest loss of life ever to occur on English soil.[6]

After the victory at Towton, Edward rode north to York and ordered the removal of the heads of his father, brother, and uncle from Micklegate Bar, and gave them all a proper burial. With his family laid to rest Edward then rode to London and made his official entry into the city on 26 June 1461. Now that the Lancastrians had been chased out of England, Edward could have the big, grand coronation that he skipped three months earlier. Following the long-held royal tradition, Edward inducted thirty-two new Knights of the Bath, including his two brothers George and Richard.[7] Additionally, he raised his brothers up to the preeminent positions of English nobility by granting the dukedom of Clarence to George and the dukedom of Gloucester to Richard. The two brothers' stars were rapidly rising thanks to their older brother's powerful new position. George was especially prideful because he was now next in line to the throne until such time as Edward married and had children.

The next three years gave way to many Lancastrian-inspired revolts from both Scotland and Wales. Queen Margaret and her army of English, Scottish, and French soldiers spent most of these years encamped in Scotland where they received financial and military support from King James II and his queen Mary of Guelders.[8] From Scotland, Queen Margaret could menace Edward with continual border raids into English territory.

The first border raid occurred in May 1461 when Margaret of Anjou's army crossed over from Scotland and attacked the English town of Carlisle. When the citizens refused to cede their town, Margaret laid siege to the castle. Warwick soon received news of Margaret's siege on Carlisle and sent Lord Montagu to chase the Lancastrian army back across the Scottish border, which he did with little trouble.

One month later, Margaret's army made another border crossing into England. This time her plan was to recruit as many supporters to her cause as possible before attempting another attack on an English town. She believed she would find many English volunteers to join her army but she was unpleasantly surprised that so few men were willing to join old king Henry. The city of York had pledged their allegiance to the new king, Edward IV, and they weren't about to anger him. After the plan to expand her army in England failed, she then received alarming news that Warwick was headed her way with his large army in tow. Seeing no other choice, Margaret fled with her army back to Scotland again.

With his allies doing a good job keeping Margaret at bay in Scotland, Edward IV turned his attention to troublesome Wales, a thorn in his side and another hotspot for Lancastrian rebels. On 8 July 1461, he commissioned William Herbert and Sir Walter Devereaux to raise troops and make preparations to subdue the rebels in Wales. Two weeks later he raised William Herbert to the peerage, probably meant to replace Jasper Tudor as his most powerful representative in Wales. With business in Wales delegated to his trusty men, Edward went on royal progress, lodging at Ludlow Castle from August to November 1461.[9]

Herbert and his men attacked Pembroke Castle in southern Wales and it easily fell to them on 30 September 1461. By taking the castle, Herbert had become the de facto earl of Pembroke, ousting Jasper Tudor who had escaped and was now on the run. Herbert also took over Jasper's wardships, including that of 4-year-old Henry Tudor, Earl of Richmond, the only son of the wealthy Lancastrian heiress Margaret Beaufort. Henry Tudor inherited the earldom of Richmond from his father Edmund Tudor, half-brother of King Henry VI, and he stood to gain his mother's huge inheritance one day, making him one of the most valuable wards in all of England. Having the wardship of Henry was a huge boon for Herbert and he would use it to his best advantage. Although he did have to pay £1,000 for the privilege of Henry Tudor's wardship, he did plan to eventually marry Henry to his daughter Maud, which would elevate Herbert's family even more.[10]

After the fall of Pembroke Castle, Herbert led his army into northern Wales in pursuit of Jasper Tudor who was thought to be hiding in the mountains of Snowdon with Henry Holland, Duke of Exeter, and a small army. Herbert's army caught up to Jasper and their two armies faced off on 16 October 1461 at Twt Hill in Caernarvon. It was a decisive win for Herbert and his Yorkist army. Luckily though, Jasper managed to escape once again and together with the duke of Exeter he sailed to Scotland to join up with Margaret and Henry in what little was left of the Lancastrian court. Jasper had now lost his nephew, his lands, and his titles with the Yorkist takeover but that only strengthened his resolve to restore his half-brother King Henry, and thus himself and his nephew Henry Tudor.

Meanwhile in Scotland, the Lancastrian leadership desperately searched for aid from foreign sovereigns who might be friendly to their cause. In August 1461 they sent an envoy to meet with King Charles VII of France whom they were confident would provide aid but during the envoy's journey to France, King Charles died suddenly from an infection. Charles was succeeded by Louis XI who was quite hostile towards the Lancastrians. He persuaded Mary of Guelders to pull back on the manpower and financial support she had been giving to Margaret and her Lancastrian followers. But Margaret found support elsewhere and even plotted a gigantic multi-national invasion of England with the help of Denmark, Burgundy, Aragon, Castile, Portugal, and Navarre. Together they would have had over 100,000 soldiers in their armies but the plot was foiled in February 1462 when communications from Margaret to one of her co-conspirators was intercepted by Edward's men.[11]

With several failed attempts now under their belts, Scotland finally withdrew their support from the Lancastrians and signed a peace treaty with the Yorkists. With little other choice, Margaret, her son Edward, Jasper Tudor, and a small entourage of loyal Lancastrians left Scotland in June 1462 and sailed to France to plead for Louis' help. King Henry VI stayed back in Scotland. This was Margaret's first return to her homeland since becoming queen of England seventeen years earlier. She was heartily welcomed and did indeed find support from her relatives but at a huge cost. King Louis agreed to assist her with an invasion of England but in return she would have to cede Calais.[12] Calais was a hugely important port town in France that the English had managed to hold beginning in 1347 all through the Hundred Years' War. Louis was eager to possess Calais and was willing to aid the Lancastrian rebels in order to get it. This agreement was sealed in the Treaty of Tours on 28 June 1462.

Margaret and her Lancastrian entourage spent much of the summer of 1462 in France preparing their fleet of forty ships and 2,000 French soldiers.[13] On 25 October 1462, Margaret invaded Northumberland, taking control of Bamburgh Castle, followed by Dunstanburgh, and then Alnwick Castle. Their progress was halted however, by the arrival of King Edward's forces who numbered around 7,000 and were commanded by Warwick.[14] Edward himself was sidelined with a case of the measles so he trusted his cousin to lead the royal army against the Lancastrian rebels. Warwick split up his forces into three separate armies and each laid siege to the castles under Margaret's control. The Lancastrian garrisons were not prepared for a prolonged siege and quickly ran out of supplies. Bamburgh and Dunstanburgh surrendered to the Yorkists on Christmas Eve 1462. Alnwick Castle finally surrendered to the Yorkists on 5 January 1463. One of Margaret's biggest supporters, Henry Beaufort, Duke of Somerset, defected from the Lancastrians and pledged fealty to King Edward IV. Edward flaunted his newfound Lancastrian defector around court and brought him into his close circle of trusted allies.

Despite losing their English castles and one of their leaders, Margaret and her Lancastrian supporters would not be deterred. After fleeing Bamburgh for Scotland, Margaret regrouped and launched another round of English border raids in the spring of 1463. This time her raids were successful in capturing Bamburgh Castle, Dunstanburgh Castle, and Alnwick Castle in northeastern England. Bolstered by these small wins, Margaret plotted an even bigger move.

In June 1463, Margaret and King James of Scotland led a full-scale invasion force into England and laid siege to Norham Castle. King Edward dispatched Warwick and Montagu to deal with what he assumed was another small-scale raid but this time it was different. In fact, when Warwick arrived, he was so taken aback at the huge Lancastrian force that he immediately sent word to Edward to send reinforcements to him. Edward himself led his men north to join Warwick but was delayed in Northampton. Warwick and Montagu proceeded without him, managing to sneak up to Norham undetected. The Lancastrian army, surprised and panicked, quickly fled back to Scotland, as did Margaret and Prince Edward who made it to Berwick Castle after a perilous journey, but suddenly found they were unwelcome visitors. Margaret had promised to cede several English border counties to Scotland in exchange for their support but without regaining the rule of England, she had no way to fulfill her promises.[15] Again, with seemingly no other choice, Margaret and Prince Edward sailed to France to ask for Louis' help once again. She left King Henry behind in England. They would never see each other alive again.

The penniless Margaret took her small Lancastrian retinue first to Burgundy to ask for Duke Philip's help but he only gave her a small amount of money and then sent her on her way. Dejected, Margaret led her entourage to her father's lands of Anjou where she would beg for his mercy. Meanwhile, King Edward worked with foreign Lancastrian supporters to end their aid to Margaret once and for all. On 8 October 1463, Edward signed a peace treaty with King Louis XI of France in which Louis agreed to give no further aid to the Lancastrians. On 3 December 1463, Edward signed a similar agreement with Scotland. Margaret's former allies had now abandoned her. The Lancastrian cause looked as bleak as ever.

The original version of the popular 1620 painting of William the Conqueror.

Panel from the Bayeux Tapestry depicting Bishop Odo of Bayeux, Duke William, and Count Robert of Mortain (11th century).

Ethelred the Unready, circa 968–1016.
Illuminated manuscript, The Chronicle of
Abindon, c.1220. MS Cott. Claude B.VI folio
87, verso, The British Library.

Statue of King Alfred
the Great in Wantage,
Oxfordshire, erected in
1877.

Scene 57 from the Bayeux Tapestry depicting the death of King Harold at the Battle of Hastings (11th century).

An illustration of King Stephen from the illuminated manuscript of Matthew Paris, a monk in the 13th century.

Portrait of Empress Mathilda, from "History of England" by St. Albans monks (15th century).

Drawing from a 14th century manuscript depicting King Henry I and the sinking of the White Ship.

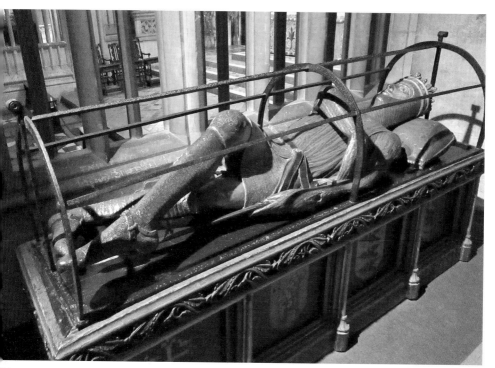

Photo of the tomb of Robert, Duke of Normandy, which rests in Gloucester Cathedral (2020).

Enamel effigy of Geoffrey Plantagenet, Count of Anjou, from his tomb, 1151. Formerly at Le Mans Cathedral, now in the Museum of Archeology and History in Le Mans.

Oil painting of King Henry IV by an unknown artist, circa 1597–1618.

John of Gaunt, Duke of Lancaster, circa 1593 by Lucas Cornelisz de Kock.

Portrait of Richrd II by an unknown artist, circa 1390.

The bronze effigy of Edward III in Westminster Abbey, 1377.

The tomb of Edward of Woodstock, the Black Prince, in Canterbury Cathedral, 1376.

A depiction of the imprisonment of Charles, Duke of Orléans, in the Tower of London from a 15th-century manuscript. The White Tower is visible, St Thomas' Tower (also known as Traitor's Gate) is in front of it, and in the foreground is the River Thames.

Richard II meeting with the rebels during
the Peasants' Revolt. From a 1470s copy of
Jean Froissart's Chronicles.

Posthumous portrait of King Edward IV circa
1520, from original circa 1470–1475.

Portrait of Queen Elizabeth Woodville by an unknown artist, circa 1471.

Portrait of Richard, Duke of York, by an unknown artist, circa 1450.

Portrait of King Henry VI by an unknown artist, circa 1540.

Queen Margaret of Anjou from the illuminated manuscript of Talbot Master, circa 1445.

Illustration of the Battle of Barnet from the Ghent manuscript, late 15th century.

An illustration of Richard Neville, Earl of Warwick, from the Rous Roll, 15th century.

Portrait of George Plantagenet,
Duke of Clarence, by Lucas
Cornelisz de Kock, 16th century.

An illuminated miniature depicting
the beheading of Edmund Beaufort,
4th Duke of Somerset, while
King Edward IV watches, late
15th century.

Portrait of King Richard III by unknown artist, circa 1520.

Middleham Castle, home of Richard III and Anne Neville. Photo 2007.

Image of Henry Stafford, 2nd Duke of Buckingham, by unknown artist, 18th century.

Painting of the Princes in the Tower by John Everett Millais, 1878, Royal Holloway Collection.

Henry Tudor, Earl of RIchmond, in his youth, painted by an unknown French artist, circa 1470–1480.

Bust of King Henry VII by Pietro Torrigiani. This bust was based on a plaster cast taken from the dead King's face, circa 1512.

Portrait of Queen Elizabeth of York by an unknown artist, circa 1500.

Portrait of the Royal Tudors by an unknown artist, circa 1503–9. At left, Henry VII, with Prince Arthur behind him, then Prince Henry (later Henry VIII), and Prince Edmund, who did not survive early childhood. To the right is Elizabeth of York, with Princess Margaret, then Princess Elizabeth who didn't survive childhood, Princess Mary, and Princess Katherine, who died shortly after her birth. Circa 1505 and circa 1509.

Pembroke Castle, home of Henry Tudor and Jasper Tudor. Photo 2007.

Oil painting of Margaret Beaufort by an unknown artist, 16th century.

Portrait of Arthur, Prince of Wales, circa 1500.

Oil painting of Catherine of Aragon, wife of Arthur and Henry VIII, at 40 years of age. Author unknown, early 18th century.

Portrait of young Henry VIII by Meynnart Wewyck, circa 1509.

A stained glass window featuring Jasper Tudor at Cardiff Castle, date unknown.

24

Warwick's Rebellion

Just as it looked like the end was near for Henry and Margaret, fortune's wheel turned their way in 1464. First, their former ally Henry Beaufort, Duke of Somerset, defected from Edward's side and rejoined the Lancastrian cause, reuniting with Margaret's court at Bamburgh Castle in Northumberland. Secondly, Lancastrian loyalists began flocking to Bamburgh to join the royal army which gave them leverage to reopen negotiations for assistance with Burgundy and France. Third, common support for King Edward had begun to sour and civil unrest broke out in many counties across England over excessive taxation and the new martial state in which they lived.[1] There was also a huge frustration among the people of England over Edward's tendency to cry out for financial assistance whenever there was a threat but then rarely follow through with campaigning after getting the money. For example, in June 1463 Edward requested £37,000 from parliament to fight against Scotland but he took no action after receiving the money.[2] In February 1464, he postponed parliament until May and during March 1464 he was 'making rather leisurely preparations to go north in person'.[3]

With the Lancastrian cause gaining momentum in the north, Edward finally decided it was time for him to take some sort of decisive action to put down the resistance. On 27 March 1464, Edward made a public proclamation that he would lead an army north to confront the Lancastrian rebels and put them down once and for all.[4] As he was building up troops in preparation to leave London, his ally John Neville, Lord Montagu, who was already on his way north, had an unexpected skirmish with the queen's army. He was travelling north to Scotland where he would pick up Scottish envoys and escort them across the English border and into York to negotiate an Anglo-Scottish peace treaty. On his way, Montagu's army was ambushed by a small Lancastrian force but managed to escape and make it to Newcastle where he could get reinforcements for his trip.

From Newcastle, Lord Montagu continued north towards Scotland, this time with a much larger army, and was again set upon by the Lancastrians, this time at Hedgeley Moor in Northumberland. The newly defected

Duke of Somerset, Henry Beaufort, led the Lancastrian army that blocked Montagu's path north, forcing him into a confrontation. Few details survive from the battle but we do know the Lancastrians had about 5,000 men in their army, easily outnumbering Montagu's Yorkist forces.[5] Very early into the battle Ralph Percy, one of the leaders of Northumberland and a loyal Lancastrian, was cut down on the battlefield. This was a monumental loss, so much so that a number of Lancastrian soldiers began fleeing the battlefield. Now that he was outnumbered, Somerset withdrew his troops to Alnwick Castle to regroup, and the Yorkists claimed another victory over the Lancastrian rebels.

The Lancastrians may have been defeated temporarily but they did not intend to back down. They decided that they needed something to keep their momentum going, some small win against the Yorkists before King Edward arrived with the bulk of the royal army, which they expected at any time. Upon receiving news in early May that Edward's army was heading north, the Lancastrians marched south, hoping to attract more supporters to their cause. They were also looking for an opportunity to catch Montagu off-guard as he travelled home from Scotland so they could redeem themselves by cutting down his army. The Lancastrians arrived at Hexham in Northumberland on 14 May 1464 and made camp. Unbeknownst to them, Lord Montagu was very nearby with his army. The next morning Montagu's army launched a surprise attack on the clueless Lancastrians which caused them to break rank and flee. The ones who remained were quickly overtaken. Somerset was executed by the Yorkists as were Lords Roos and Hungerford. By 19 July, more than two dozen other Lancastrian leaders were executed.[6]

The Yorkists nearly caught King Henry at Bywell Castle but he managed to escape just before they arrived. Henry was able to live on the run for over a year, continually moving between friendly allies who took turns hiding him. The Yorkists finally caught him on 13 July 1465 near Ribblesdale, Lancashire. He was bound up and taken to London where Warwick promptly arrested him in the name of King Edward and imprisoned him in the Tower of London. Warwick ordered that he be treated with proper respect due to his position and gave Henry a clothing allowance plus a number of servants to attend to his daily needs.[7] Henry would spend the next five years in Yorkists' captivity.

After Hexham, the Yorkists then successfully won back the castles of Alnwick and Dunstanburgh when the inhabitants swiftly surrendered. Bamburgh Castle initially held out against a Yorkist takeover but after cannon fire started crumbling walls, they gave up and handed over possession of the castle to the Yorkists. Margaret and Prince Edward fled England and sought exile in France. They would remain in France for several years at the graciousness of her father, Rene, king of Naples, who supported her and her court of around fifty loyal Lancastrians.[8] It seemed as if the Lancastrian resistance was over but Margaret was not yet ready to give up. Although she had lost her husband the king, her son Prince Edward was nearing his teenage years and would soon be ready to take the helm of the Lancastrian cause.

With the Lancastrians definitively chased out of England and their leading magnates either executed or imprisoned, the Yorkist position in the summer of 1464 was the strongest it had ever been. King Edward IV was a force to be reckoned with and international channels opened up to him. He was well-positioned to restore honour and dignity to the monarchy of England. One of the best ways to do this in medieval Europe was by landing an advantageous foreign marriage. Edward had already turned down a marriage proposal from the king of Castile to his daughter Isabella, who would go on to become the queen of Castille and the mother of Catherine of Aragon. More recently, Warwick had negotiated a prestigious French marriage with Bona of Savoy, the sister-in-law of King Louis XII of France.[9] Warwick favoured the French match because it had the added bonus of securing peace between the two nations who had just recently come out of the epic Hundred Years' War.

Despite Warwick's labours, the impetuous young Edward made a decision that would ultimately lead to a fracture in their relationship which caused Warwick to rebel against the man he had helped place on the throne. On 30 April 1464 as Edward travelled through Stony Stratford he stopped at Grafton Regis, a manor house belonging to the Woodville family.[10] There he happened upon a beautiful young woman named Elizabeth Woodville and instantly fell in love. Elizabeth was not only an unsuitable match because she was just a minor noble, but she was also five years his senior, had been previously married, was the mother of two sons, and her family was loyal to King Henry, even fighting against Edward in the most recent battles. Despite the terrible match, Edward's passion got the best of him and he threw caution to the wind. He returned to Grafton Regis on the morning of 1 May 1464 and married Elizabeth Woodville in a secret ceremony with few witnesses.

Edward made a monumental mistake with the marriage and it would ultimately be his undoing. Edward knew full well that his marriage to Elizabeth would be controversial, so he determined to keep it secret for as long as possible. It was not until a Great Council meeting at Reading Abbey on 28 September 1464 that he was forced to reveal his secret. When his councillors pressed him for a decision on the French marriage with Bona of Savoy, Edward finally admitted that he was already married.[11] Everyone was completely shocked but especially jolted was Warwick. To him, keeping this marriage a secret for over four months while he laboured on Edward's behalf for a French marriage was humiliating.

Edward's secret marriage to Elizabeth Woodville was just the latest in a string of disappointments for Warwick. He had put a lot of time and energy into building a relationship with France, despite Edward's preference for building an alliance with France's rival Burgundy. Warwick also had a difficult time standing by and watching the new queen's family welcomed so heartily to court, overshadowing his own prestigious Neville family. Elizabeth Woodville's family was huge: five brothers and seven sisters. King Edward would arrange for each Woodville sibling an advantageous marriage to the most eligible noblemen and women in all of England.[12] He freely gave them lands and titles confiscated from the Lancastrians, honours that Warwick felt should have been granted to him. After all, without Warwick, Edward would not have been able to win the crown of England for the House of York. Warwick was becoming inpatient with Edward and worried about his growing independence. Whereas Edward used to rely on Warwick's guidance and opinions, he now sought the council of his Woodville relatives. The Herberts of Wales had also taken a strong position in Edward's court which further pushed Warwick out of Edward's inner circle.

Warwick was also aggrieved at Edward's hesitance to approve marriages for his two daughters who were at a marriageable age. The problem was the lack of eligible bachelors since the Woodville sisters had all been married off to Edward's noblemen. In Warwick's mind, there were only two eligible bachelors good enough for his daughters: Edward's two brothers and heirs to his throne, George and Richard. If Warwick couldn't be king himself, he would try to put his daughters in a position where they might be queen one day.

Marriages of this magnitude could not be done without the king's blessing but when Warwick asked Edward for permission, he was denied. So in the fall of 1467, Warwick went behind Edward's back and requested papal dispensation for the marriage of his daughter Isabel to Edward's brother George.[13] Edward found out about Warwick's manouevre and was able to send his own letters to the pope decrying the marriage which resulted in the pope refusing the dispensation. In January 1468, King Edward summoned Warwick to explain himself, but Warwick refused to come to him. The two men spent the entirety of 1468 in a power struggle, neither refusing to bend to the others' will. Warwick was exacerbated at Edward's choice to ally with Burgundy and Brittany to fight a joint war against France, but Edward really didn't care what Warwick thought. He was being counseled by the Woodvilles now.

By February 1469, Warwick was actively plotting to overthrow Edward and replace him with his son-in-law, George, Duke of Clarence.[14] Warwick began trouble by stoking little rebellions all around England. He even started a rumour that Edward was illegitimate and therefore his brother George was the rightful king of England. Warwick had plenty of support, especially in the north, and was directly involved in the April 1469 rising led by Robin of Redesdale. The uprising was very similar to Cade's Rebellion under Henry VI's reign. Robin of Redesdale issued a manifesto, probably penned by Warwick himself, which called on Edward to rid himself of his evil advisors, mainly the Woodvilles and the earl of Pembroke, William Herbert. The earl of Northumberland put down the first instance of the northern rebellion. In June 1469, another major rebellion exploded in the north forcing Edward to gather his army and set off north from London to deal with them personally. At this point Edward didn't believe Warwick was behind the rebellions, despite the rumours going around, but all of that was about to change when Warwick finally showed his true colors.

While Edward was on the road with his army, Warwick slipped away to Calais with his daughter Isabel and Edward's brother George. In open defiance of King Edward, Isabel and George were married on 11 July 1469 by the archbishop of York, George Neville, who conveniently was Warwick's brother. The day following the wedding, Warwick issued a manifesto in favour of the rebels and against Edward's deceitful and covetous councillors, an obvious jab at the Woodvilles.[15] He invited all who would join his cause to muster at Canterbury 16 July for a march north to join Robin of Redesdale's rebel army.

When Robin got word that Warwick was coming north to join them, he led his army south to join Warwick, but he didn't anticipate the presence of rival armies in his immediate vicinity. William Herbert, Earl of Pembroke, led his army to Nottingham to join up with Edward's forces and even though Herbert's army was twice the size of Robin's, the emboldened rebel couldn't resist the temptation to fight. On the morning of 26 July 1469, the two opposing sides lined up into battle position. Robin and the rebel army attacked Pembroke's army of Welshmen twice, but no ground was made by either side. Pembroke's army got a boost in morale when the earl of Devon appeared with his army to join them in battle and for a time they had the upper hand over Robin's army. But then Robin's fortunes improved once again when Warwick arrived on the scene with his army. We do not know the size of Warwick's army but it must have been intimidating because Pembroke's army immediately broke ranks and fled the battlefield. The casualties for both sides were significant. Over 2,000 men from Pembroke and Devon lay dead on the battlefield.[16] Pembroke and his brother were taken prisoner and later executed on Warwick's orders. Robin of Redesdale was killed during the battle.

Edward had been travelling with his army to meet up with Pembroke and Devon when he received news of the devastating Yorkist loss at the Battle of Edgecote. Disheartened, his army broke rank and abandoned him. With only a few men still with Edward, Warwick knew that now was the perfect time to strike. But there was no fighting or bloodshed. Warwick's brother, the archbishop of York, intercepted King Edward and requested that he go with him to Coventry to be taken under the earl of Warwick's protection. With little other choice, Edward allowed himself to be taken into Warwick's custody.[17]

Although Edward was technically Warwick's prisoner, he wasn't locked up in a dungeon or mistreated in any way. He was well kept and maintained, first at Warwick Castle and then further north at Middleham Castle. With news spreading about the king's captivity, law and order started to break down all over the kingdom. Not only were crimes becoming more prevalent across many towns and villages, so too were mini-rebellions. Cropping up at all ends of the kingdom, people were protesting Warwick's capture of Edward and the disintegration of the king's authority across the land. There were even Lancastrian-inspired uprisings taking place on the border of Scotland. Warwick's resources were spread too thin to respond to all the uprisings and he realised he had no choice but to release Edward or be overthrown himself.[18]

Edward was allowed to leave Middleham Castle in August 1469, only one month after his capture. He quickly regained control of his kingdom and things went back to normal except for his relationship with Warwick. Edward could not rid himself completely of Warwick because he played an important role in government and provided much needed support in the north. Warwick was the richest land magnate in all the realm having inherited the earldom of Salisbury from his father and the earldom of Warwick through his wife Anne Beauchamp. He had vast swaths of land and would have thousands of men at his disposal if he were to issue a call to arms. Therefore, Edward decided to tread lightly around his cousin. The king asserted his independence from Warwick, yet he was careful not to say anything that could inflame Warwick's ire. In December 1469,

Edward staged a public reconciliation at Westminster with Warwick and Clarence which included a feast of peace and forgiveness. Although Edward believed them to be reconciled, Warwick and George were secretly working against him.[19]

In March 1470, a new set of uprisings cropped up in the north. As Edward's army left London and headed north, Warwick and Clarence mustered their armies as well. They wrote to Edward pledging support but secretly they were planning to ambush him.[20] Warwick's ally, Lord Welles, marched his army to Leicester to rendezvous with Warwick but Edward's army met them at Stamford and cut them off before they could reach Leicester. Although Edward had been suspicious of Warwick and Clarence's activities, he had no idea they were planning to join Welles' rebel army until he saw Welles' soldiers wearing the livery of Warwick and Clarence. Edward led his army in an attack and before long, the rebel army broke ranks and fled the battlefield. Many stripped off their uniforms as they ran, as if to erase their affiliation with Warwick and Clarence, hence the name 'Lose Coat' in this aptly named Battle of Losecote Field.[21] In one of the coats, letters from Welles to Warwick were found, confirming the king's suspicion that they were indeed plotting against him. Lord Welles was beheaded on the battlefield.

After the battle, Edward summoned Warwick and Clarence to come to him at Stamford but to only bring a small retinue of men. Warwick wrote back agreeing to Edward's demands but instead of following the king's orders, he sent orders for his northern supporters to muster their armies and join up with him in Rotherham. The king had received word of Warwick's movements and issued a proclamation giving Warwick and Clarence five days to turn themselves in or else they would suffer a traitor's death which usually involved hanging, drawing, quartering, and beheading. Still Warwick refused to obey Edward.

25

The Second Reign of Edward IV

W arwick had no plans to surrender to the man who sat upon the throne of England because of his help. Warwick ignored Edward's summons and continued marching his army to Rotherham but when he arrived, he was very disappointed to see so few supporters there to join him. So he tried a different mustering point, moving his troops to Lancashire where he erroneously thought he had could count on support. Upon his arrival he found that none of the nobles there would help him either. Helplessly outnumbered by the king's army, Warwick and Clarence fled to Dartmouth where they took a ship to France to hide in exile. They tried to land in Calais but the king had sent advanced word to the town to repel the two men. As Warwick sailed along the French coast looking for a safe place to land, his daughter Isabel, wife of Clarence, went into labour and her child was stillborn.[1]

Desperate, Warwick sent a message to his old friend King Louis XI and was granted political asylum in France. Louis was a staunch Lancastrian supporter and soon persuaded Warwick that he had a better chance of ruling England through old King Henry than through a strong, warrior king like Edward. Convincing Margaret of Anjou to join forces with Warwick was another thing as it took all of King Louis' powers of persuasion to convince her to join in their plan. Louis, Warwick, and Margaret met at Angers on 22 July 1470 to seal their joint alliance against Edward. A few days later, Margaret's son, Prince Edward, was betrothed to Warwick's youngest daughter Anne. This move ensured Warwick that his daughter would be queen one day and he would be the grandfather of kings.

With Warwick in command of the Lancastrian invasion, he once again called on his northern supporters to launch uprisings to make King Edward leave London with his army and head north to deal with the rebellions. While Edward was distracted in the north, Warwick took his opportunity to issue a new proclamation calling on his fellow countrymen to help him rescue Henry VI from the Tower. Warwick and his new allies set sail from Calais on 8 September 1470 with a large fleet of sixty French ships. They landed at Exeter and then marched nearly 250 kilometres to Coventry, gaining members along the way until their ranks swelled to a reported 30,000 soldiers.[2]

When Edward received news of Warwick's invasion, he immediately left York and headed south to intercept Warwick's Lancastrian army. He stopped for the night at Doncaster and there he received the disastrous news that Lord Montagu had defected and joined the Lancastrians. Furthermore, Montagu's army was quickly approaching Doncaster with orders to capture the king. In a panic, Edward and a small retinue fled the town and travelled to King's Lynn where he procured three ships to take him and his party to Burgundy, arriving on 11 October 1470. Edward had long cultivated an alliance with Burgundy and could count on them for protection, especially since his own sister Duchess Margaret was married to Charles, the duke of Burgundy.

Meanwhile Warwick's forces had overtaken London and gained possession of the Tower. King Henry was promptly rescued and moved back to his royal apartments at Westminster Palace. On 13 October 1470 Warwick staged a second coronation for King Henry VI at St Paul's Cathedral in London. After the ceremony, Henry was taken back to his royal apartments while Warwick took over running the country.[3] At the 26 November parliament, Warwick had Edward declared a usurper and revoked all the lands of titles of Edward's allies. Warwick also had the line of succession legally established: after Henry VI, the throne would pass to George, Duke of Clarence, and the heirs of his body, followed by Edward's other brother Richard, Duke of Gloucester.

While Warwick established his authority in London, Edward was in Burgundy planning his comeback. With the Burgundian assistance of ships, money, and 1,500 soldiers, Edward sailed home to England, landing 12 March 1471 at Ravenspur on the Norfolk coast. There he was met by his loyal brother Richard and the queen's father, Richard Woodville, Earl Rivers. As they headed north to York, their numbers swelled as nobles and common men flocked to join Edward with the understanding that he was there to reclaim his duchy of York, not the throne of England.[4]

On 14 March 1471 messengers arrived in London reporting Edward's invasion of England. Warwick gathered all the men he could and rode hard to Coventry where he planned to rendezvous with George's troops. Unbeknownst to Warwick, George had reconciled with Edward and flipped back to his brother's side. Fortune was seemingly on Edward's side but then news came that Margaret and her army had just landed in England. Suddenly, it was a race to London to get control of the city before Margaret could arrive and sack it. Although Warwick was the de facto leader, London opened its gates to his enemy. Edward was hastily re-crowned king before it was time to muster men once again to deal with the impending arrival of Warwick's army.

Edward left London on 13 April with an army of 9,000 men and marched them up the Great North Road to the town of Barnet where they camped for the night.[5] Edward's scouts reported that Warwick's men were on the opposite side of the ridge so Edward launched a rare night attack in the thick fog which caused much confusion.[6] Warwick's men mistook each other for the enemy and unknowingly slayed each other, causing cries of treason to reverberate through his army until many abandoned the field. Warwick perceived the situation to be hopeless and fled but was captured and executed by Edward's men. The Battle of Barnet was a decisive victory for Edward as he finally overpowered his one-time ally Warwick who had helped put him on the throne ten years prior.

Edward had little time to celebrate his victory over Warwick at the Battle of Barnet. Two days after the battle, Edward got news that Margaret and her army had landed in England. She was supposed to have joined Warwick's offensive against Edward but bad weather had delayed her sailing from France and now she was suddenly without Warwick's assistance. She turned her army towards Wales where she could count on protection from Jasper Tudor but now Edward's army was in hot pursuit of her. After marching her army relentlessly for days, Margaret had to stop and rest at Tewkesbury on the evening of 3 May, where Edward caught up to her and the two sides prepared for battle.

In the early morning hours of 4 May 1471, the king's brother Richard, Duke of Gloucester, opened the Battle of Tewkesbury against Margaret's army. King Edward had the advantage in numbers and position which served to quickly overwhelm Margaret's army. As her soldiers fled from the battlefield, Edward's men chased them down and put them to death, including Margaret's own son, Prince Edward. Margaret hid in sanctuary at a local abbey for three days before she surrendered herself to the final victor in this battle, King Edward IV.

On 21 May 1471, Edward made a triumphant entry into London with his brothers and loyal nobles, as well as the former Queen Margaret whom he paraded in a carriage. That very night Henry VI died in the Tower. The official story from Edward's government was that Henry died of natural causes. That's a little too coincidental to be believable that Henry died the very day Edward regained control of the kingdom. Nevertheless, Edward was immediately re-crowned king of England and ruled his country with no further threats to his reign until his unexpected death in 1483. He did, however, have to deal with lots of trouble from his greedy brother George as well as the few remaining Lancastrians who were now hiding in Brittany, France.

26

Was Edward IV a Usurper?

Much of this chapter focused on Edward's father Richard, Duke of York and with good reason. If not for Richard's efforts, Edward would have never been in a position to be king. So, to answer the question of whether Edward was a usurper, we also have to pass judgement on his father's actions.

Richard was the leading land magnate in England during the reign of Henry VI which made him a very rich and powerful man. He had royal blood on his paternal and maternal sides of the family: both his mother and father could trace their descent to King Edward III. His father was the son of Edmund of Langley, King Edward III's fourth surviving son, making Richard the great-grandson of Edward III. Richard's mother, Anne Mortimer, was the great-granddaughter of Lionel of Antwerp, Edward III's second surviving son.[1] By contrast, King Henry VI could only claim English royal blood through his father, not his French mother, Catherine de Valois. Technically, Richard of York had more English royal blood in his veins than Henry VI, which gave him a very valid claim to the throne. Richard knew it, Henry knew it, and the people of England knew it too.

Richard tried repeatedly to gain his rightful spot in Henry's government as next in line to the throne. During Henry's bouts of madness, Richard served as the protector of England twice. Despite the inroads he made during his protectorates, Henry's councillors always found a way to push him out of Henry's court. When Richard died at the Battle of Wakefield on 30 December 1461, his eldest son Edward picked up where he left off and continued the Wars of the Roses against King Henry VI.

In March 1461, the citizens of London, exhausted by years of conflict, welcomed Edward with open arms and accepted him as their new king. It's not hard to see why. He was the polar opposite of King Henry VI. Not only was Edward young, handsome, and charismatic, but more importantly he had demonstrated his skill and prowess on the battlefield. After too many years of tumult, the people of England believed Edward had the aptitude and the ambition to protect them and lead their kingdom. Although he had some years of peace during his two reigns, he was continually faced with rebellions, both from his enemies and his own family members. As the years went on, these troubles took a toll on Edward. He became complacent about running his government and turned to pleasures of the flesh. Multiple chroniclers wrote about his insatiable lust for women and his multiple mistresses.[2] He became gluttonous in his later years and gained a great deal of weight. He was even said to take emetics so that he could continue gorging himself with food. There is no doubt his licentious and lustful lifestyle contributed to his death at an early age.[3]

Edward's first reign as king of England began in 1461 after the Battles of Mortimer's Cross, the Second St Albans, and Towton where his army succeeded in killing a large number of Lancastrian knights fighting for Henry VI. In 1470, Edward went into exile in Burgundy after Warwick's invasion, then Edward won back the throne by defeating Warwick's army at the Battle of Barnet, followed by the destruction of Queen Margaret's army at the Battle of Tewkesbury. He returned to London and served as king of England until his death in 1483. Was Edward IV the rightful king of Edward or was he a usurper?

As we saw in Part III, Henry of Bolingbroke deposed his cousin King Richard II, yet we judged Henry innocent of the title usurper because he gained the throne by legal means and without any physical violence. Edward, on the other hand, as well as his father, Richard of York, did invoke physical violence against the sitting king of England on multiple occasions which was especially treasonous since Richard and then Edward were next in line to the throne and should have been assisting the king to keep the peace.

Both Richard and Edward were ambitious and over-reaching, but especially Richard who dreamed of being king and was willing to do anything to achieve his goal. You don't often hear of Edward IV being referred to as a usurper but the evidence proves otherwise. Despite the desire of English citizens to rid themselves of the inept King Henry VI, there were no legal movements to depose King Henry VI and Edward very clearly used violence, not once, but multiple times against the sitting king of England. With these facts well known, Edward clearly deserves to be considered a usurper of the crown.

Part V

Richard III (1483–1485)

27

Loyalty Binds Me

Richard III is quite possibly the most controversial king ever to rule England. Many people think of him as an evil monster of a man, mostly due to his unfair portrayal in Shakespeare's historical plays. On the other end of the spectrum we have the Ricardians, a group of Richard III superfans who started a movement to glorify Richard III who they say is a much maligned, misunderstood king. With such drastically different viewpoints, who was the real Richard III? Was he a disfigured, plotting, scheming murderer, or was he a loyal, chivalrous, underappreciated ruler?

The future King Richard III was born Richard Plantagenet on 2 October 1452 at Fotheringhay Castle in Northamptonshire. He was the eleventh of twelve children born to Richard of York, the infamous duke who nearly succeeded in wrestling the crown away from King Henry VI. Richard III's mother, Cecily Neville, was also of high noble blood. She was the daughter of an earl, the aunt of Warwick the Kingmaker, and the sister of the earl of Salisbury, who was among the men killed alongside her husband Richard and son Edmund at the Battle of Wakefield on 30 December 1460.

Richard's eldest son Edward, Earl of March, became the de facto leader of the House of York after the death of Richard at Wakefield. With his family thrown into turmoil, 8-year-old Richard was too young to offer any real help, he could only stand by helplessly and pray that God would keep his brother Edward safe and grant him victory over the Lancastrians. Undoubtedly this early childhood experience would have a great effect on his future role as Edward's most loyal councillor. As a young boy Richard resolved to become a mighty warrior so he could serve his eldest brother in his pursuit of the throne of England.

It wasn't long after Richard of York's death that Edward got the chance to show his skills on the battlefield. On 29 March 1461, Edward scored a resounding victory against the Lancastrians at the Battle of Towton. Edward's destruction of the Lancastrian army was so complete that it caused Queen Margaret and King Henry VI to flee England for the next four years. When 19-year-old Edward made his victorious procession through the city of London as their new king, his younger brothers Richard and George were by his side.[1] They were created Knights of the Bath and given dukedoms shortly after Edward's coronation. George, the second eldest brother, became the duke of Clarence and Richard became the duke of Gloucester.

Edward treated his brothers very well and made sure they received the best education possible so they could be of service to him when they became adults. Edward arranged for Richard to enter the household of the great duke of Warwick, otherwise known as The Kingmaker. Richard spent several years at Warwick's Middleham Castle where he trained to be a chivalrous knight, adept at weaponry, hunting, hawking, as well as the more refined skills of a royal prince, such as playing the harp, singing, and dancing.[2]

By the spring of 1465, 13-year-old Richard was considered old enough to leave Warwick's wardship and enter his brother's court in London.[3] Richard unknowingly entered a very tense environment as a result of his brother Edward's surprise marriage to Elizabeth Woodville in the year prior. The royal court was being overrun by the ambitious Woodville faction while Richard's mentor Warwick was slowly but surely falling out of royal favour. Warwick deeply resented Edward IV for pushing him out of his inner circle of councillors and replacing them with his new Woodville relatives. Young Richard was unfairly put in the middle and felt pressure to choose sides.[4]

Richard's loyalty was severely tested in 1469 when Warwick came out in open rebellion against King Edward. As if that wasn't bad enough, Richard soon learned that his brother George was in on Warwick's scheme. George was in fact the figurehead of the insurrection and their plan was to depose Edward in order to place George on the throne. Richard had to choose between two brothers and his mentor, which must have been incredibly difficult for him, but in the end he chose his brother Edward.

While Edward marched his royal army from London to northern England in the summer of 1469 to deal with uprisings that Warwick had instigated, Warwick sailed to Calais with his eldest daughter Isabel and the king's brother, George. Against Edward's order, Warwick had Isabel and George married on 11 July 1469. If Warwick could place George on the throne, then his daughter Isabel would be queen of England and he himself would hypothetically be the grandfather of the next king of England. The day after the forbidden marriage took place, Warwick issued a public manifesto against Edward's evil councillors (i.e. the Woodvilles) and invited those who wished to join his cause to muster at Canterbury on 16 July 1469.[5]

Edward and Richard were at Nottingham Castle mustering their own troops as Warwick and his rebel army quickly tore across England. Warwick's forces easily overcame Edward's trusted ally, the earl of Pembroke, as he was on his way to meet up with king. When Edward learned of Pembroke's fate, he tried to hide but Warwick's men found him and took him prisoner. Warwick could not kill an anointed king without serious repercussions, but he could rule through him as he had done with King Henry VI. However, Warwick's coup did not go according to plan. When news of the king's capture made its way around England, law and order effectively broke down and the country was consumed with little uprisings everywhere. Warwick did not have the resources or the manpower to handle all the insurrections. He had no choice but to release King Edward from captivity, allowing him to resume control of the kingdom.[6]

As a result of his loyalty throughout their recent family crisis, King Edward showered Richard with rewards and titles, including Constable of England (the leading law enforcement officer in the entire country) and Chief Justice of South Wales, and the earldom of March.[7] Surprisingly, Edward did not punish Warwick, rather, he staged a formal reconciliation between the three York men. During the Christmas 1469 celebrations, Edward hosted both Warwick and George at his court in London. Edward believed it to be a true reconciliation but just months later, Warwick and George would betray him again.

By March 1470, Warwick and George were stoking considerable uprisings in the north. Their goal was to lure the king away from London so they could ambush him. This time Warwick meant to put a permanent end to Edward since his previous plan of holding him as prisoner and ruling through him had not worked out. However, Warwick's plan backfired when King Edward easily overtook Lord Welles' rebel army at the Battle of Losecote Field on 12 March 1470. The battle got its name 'Losecote' not from the location of the battle but for the way the Yorkist soldiers dropped their coats emblazoned with Warwick's livery as they fled the battlefield.[8] In one of these jackets, Edward's men discovered letters confirming the involvement of Warwick and George in the recent northern uprisings. In response, Edward summoned Warwick and George to appear before him to explain themselves. They feared they would be arrested if they put themselves in the king's presence so they decided to flee England for France. In a terrible stroke of luck, Warwick's daughter Isabel went into labour during their voyage across the English channel. When they arrived at Calais, they were denied entrance and had to drift off the coast with no help from a midwife for Isabel. Her first child, a son, was stillborn.[9]

Turned away from his former stronghold of Calais, Warwick managed to find safe refuge with King Louis XI of France. Warwick nurtured the king's support in his bid to overthrow King Edward IV and was willing to do anything to gain control of England. In a shocking turn of events,

Warwick agreed to forge an alliance with his old enemy, Queen Margaret of Anjou. Now instead of placing Edward's brother George on the throne, Warwick's new strategy was to free King Henry VI from the Tower, reinstate him as king of England, and rule through him. At first, Queen Margaret was very distrustful of Warwick's proposal, but she knew it was the best option available to her. The two former adversaries came together at Angers Cathedral on 22 July 1470 to finalise their alliance. They sealed the deal with the marriage of their children, Prince Edward and Anne Neville.

All throughout the summer of 1470, King Edward IV was actively preparing for an invasion from the newly combined duo of Warwick and Margaret. Although George had flipped to Warwick's side, Richard stayed loyal to Edward and was with him in the Midlands during all the war preparations.[10] When Warwick began a fresh round of northern uprisings, Richard rode with his brother Edward and the royal army to put down the minor revolts. While Edward was in northern England, Warwick took the opportunity to sail his invasion fleet, landing at Plymouth in southwest England on 13 September 1470. His plan was to march his enormous army to London to free King Henry VI from the Tower and take over the city.

When King Edward got work of Warwick's landing, he immediately gathered his men and headed south from York with all the speed they could muster. After seventy kilometres travelled, the king halted his army at Doncaster.[11] This is where he planned to rendezvous with Marquess Montagu's army so they could ride to London together. At Doncaster, Edward received the shocking news that Montagu had defected to Warwick's side and was presently approaching Doncaster with orders to capture Edward.

With no time to think, Edward and his adherents jumped on their horses and fled Doncaster before Montagu arrived. They dashed 160 kilometres southeast until they reached the coast, eventually ending up at King's Lynn in Norfolk. It was there they boarded a ship and set sail for Burgundy on 2 October 1470. Burgundy would be a safe place for Edward to hide because his sister Margaret was the reigning duchess there. She would be able to supply him with ships and soldiers to fight Warwick and gain control of England. With Edward in Burgundy were his most loyal noblemen, including his brother Richard, plus Lord Hastings and Lord Rivers.[12]

With King Edward in political exile, London was Warwick's for the taking. After landing in England on 13 September 1471, Warwick and George headed northeast to face down King Edward. Along the way they gathered supporters and their army was said to be as large as 30,000 men.[13] Warwick was at Coventry when he received the delightful news that King Edward had fled the kingdom. Warwick then rode to London as fast as he could and promptly freed Henry VI from the Tower on 6 October 1470. One week later, Henry was re-coronated as King of England with Warwick by his side. Now Warwick was the effective ruler of the realm.

It wasn't long before Warwick's power would truly be tested. In Burgundy, Edward wasted no time preparing his own English invasion to take back his throne from Warwick. He had also used his in time in Burgundy to mend rifts with his brother George, who through the use of secret messengers, conveyed to his brother Edward that he planned to desert Warwick and flip back to Edward's side.[14]

On 11 March 1471, Edward set sail from Burgundy with a small army of 1,500 men.[15] The following morning, he tried to come ashore on English soil but found that many of the port towns were blocking his entry at the commandment of Warwick. Even in York, his own duchy, the capital city turned him away at first. The citizens only allowed him entry after he promised him to seek the restoration of his dukedom, not the throne. As he moved south towards London, men flocked to his banners and his army soon grew, but it was not as large as the army Warwick was leading north to stop him. When Edward learned of Warwick's location at Coventry, he tried to force the earl into battle, but Warwick retreated inside the castle walls and refused to fight.

With the earl unwilling to give battle, Edward swung his army around and marched with all speed to London where he was heartily welcomed by the citizens on 11 April 1471.[16] That evening Edward heard good news that his plan to draw Warwick out of his castle had finally worked. Edward's scouts reported Warwick's army was located at St Albans, a mere thirty kilometres from London. The very next morning, King Edward marched his large army out of London and headed towards the inevitable confrontation with Warwick. When he arrived at Barnet that evening, he discovered that Warwick's army was on the other side of the town less than two kilometres ahead. Under the cover of darkness, Edward ordered his men into battle position and around 4.00 am that morning. Edward commenced the battle in those early morning hours, taking Warwick and his troops completely unaware.[17]

What won the Battle of Barnet for Edward on 14 April 1471 may have been the weather. A misty rain and thick fog had descended on the battlefield, causing confusion among Warwick's army. Some of Warwick's men mistook their fellow soldiers for Edward's men and began slaying each other. The battlefield rang with cries of treason and the disoriented Lancastrian soldiers fled for their lives.[18] Soon Warwick himself was running away from the battlefield but he was quickly hunted down by Edward's men and stabbed in the throat.[19] Edward's mentor-turned-nemesis was dead, leaving only Queen Margaret and the last of the Lancastrian stragglers standing in Edward's way.

Queen Margaret and Jasper Tudor had planned to join up with Warwick's army prior to the Battle of Barnet, however, the weather had delayed their sailing. Upon arriving on English soil on 14 April at Weymouth in southwest England, Margaret received the devastating news of the loss at Barnet and the death of Warwick. Undeterred, the queen moved her army on, intent to face down Edward and win back the throne for her husband and young son, Prince Edward. Her supporters had raised men in southwest England and Margaret led them north at breakneck speed to reach Jasper Tudor in Wales before King Edward IV could hunt her down.

Edward received news of Margaret's landing on 16 April 1471, giving her a two-day head start. Within a week he raised an army large enough to confront Margaret's impressive Lancastrian army. Edward and his soldiers left London on 24 April and by 3 May they arrived at Tewkesbury, covering an impressive 190 kilometres in only ten days.[20] Margaret had also been thrashing her army, forcing them to march for two days straight without rest or refreshment.[21] She had nearly made it to the safety of Wales but was having difficulty finding a safe place to cross the swollen Severn River. That's when Edward's army arrived and pinned Margaret's army up against the uncrossable river. Her exhausted soldiers had no choice but to stand and fight for their lives.

On the morning of 4 May 1471, Margaret of Anjou's army lined up in battle array against the army of King Edward IV. By Edward's side were his brothers Richard and George, as well as his closest friend, Lord Hastings, all of whom were his military commanders. King Edward struck the first blow and after a fierce bout of hand-to-hand fighting, Margaret's army began to fall back. They were losing ground against the king's superior fighters and before long they completely fell apart. Margaret's men began fleeing the field, their only escape route was by river. As it was too high to cross safely, many of her men chose to drown while trying to make their escape rather than being cut down by the Yorkists.[22]

Queen Margaret's son, Prince Edward, was not immune to the devastation. King Edward's men found the young prince on the battlefield and immediately slayed him.[23] Some of Margaret's men hid in sanctuary at a local abbey but King Edward had them dragged out, tried, and beheaded in the marketplace of Tewkesbury. Queen Margaret herself was found hiding in a different abbey a few days later and was taken as King Edward's prisoner. The Battles of Barnet and Tewkesbury effectively destroyed the House of Lancaster. It would be twelve years before a little-known exile named Henry Tudor would revive the Lancastrian cause and challenge the House of York.

28

The Unravelling of George, Duke of Clarence

To commemorate the Yorkists' epic victory over the Lancastrians at Tewkesbury, London held a huge celebration to welcome King Edward and his men back into the city. The king made his triumphant entry on 21 May 1471 with his brothers Richard and George leading the procession through the city. In their train, King Edward's enemy and now prisoner, Margaret of Anjou, was put on full display as a sort of trophy to cap off Edward's victory. That same evening, King Edward and his brothers took a bold step they deemed necessary in order to secure Edward's new reign. They knew that keeping King Henry VI alive in the Tower would only encourage more Lancastrian rebellions, so they decided to do something about it. On the very night of Edward's re-entry into London, old King Henry died in the Tower. The official report from Edward's government was that the feeble old king died of natural causes, but that is highly suspect.[1] The York brothers had the motive and the means to snuff out the last Lancastrian king, and they knew they had to distinguish all rivals to the throne or Edward's reign would never be secure.

King Edward's rule was infinitely steadier after the death of King Henry VI and soon everything else fell into place. His reinstatement as king of England caused Calais to surrender to his authority, and even Wales was now under relative control.[2] Edward's new man in Wales, Sir William Herbert, became the new earl of Pembroke after forcefully taking Pembroke Castle from Henry VI's half-brother, Jasper Tudor. Jasper feared Edward would put them to death like he had Henry VI, so Jasper fled with his 12-year old nephew, Henry Tudor, and sought exile in Brittany, France.

After sixteen years of fighting between the Houses of York and Lancaster, it finally seemed as if the war was over and all the leading Lancastrians flushed out of the kingdom. England had itself a glorious, young, warrior king who was handsome, charming, and chivalrous. His throne was secure as there were no remaining Lancastrians with a strong enough royal bloodline to challenge Edward's rule. The difficulty now for Edward would come from within his own house. It seems there were certain family members who were not content with the rewards they received for helping Edward win back his crown. The result was infighting between the three York brothers and the Woodvilles which would ultimately lead to the downfall of Edward IV, the death of his two young sons, and the crowning of King Richard III.

A bitter quarrel developed between Edward's two brothers not long after they were back in London. The main cause of the strife was the distribution of lands and titles from their turncoat cousin Warwick.[3] Since George was married to Warwick's eldest daughter Isabel, he expected to get the bulk of Warwick's estates. Richard threw a major wrench into George's plan when in June 1471 he asked King Edward permission to marry Warwick's other daughter, Anne Neville, and split George's inheritance. Although he certainly had a lot to gain in the marriage, there are indications that Richard and Anne genuinely loved each other. They had grown up together at Middleham Castle and had been childhood sweethearts, so the marriage wasn't entirely for Richard's financial benefit.[4]

George threw an enormous tantrum when he learned of Richard's marriage proposal. Edward ordered George to back down and accept Richard's upcoming marriage, but George did just the opposite. He took physical custody of Anne and hid her away at a friend's house so Richard couldn't marry her.[5] When Richard returned from fighting the Scots in the North, he had to search for her desperately before he found out that his brother George hid her. Once he did find her, he smuggled her away and kept her safely in sanctuary until they could be married in the spring of 1472. The newlyweds set up their primary household at Middleham Castle, their childhood home. The following year, Anne gave birth to the couple's first and only child, a son named Edward in honour of his uncle, the king.

George deeply resented both brothers for infringing upon the Neville estates and he decided to take action. By the spring of 1473, he was plotting a new rebellion with the staunch Lancastrian earl of Oxford, and King Louis XI of France.[6] Throughout the summer George waited for the right moment to take revenge on his brother Richard. In September 1473, Richard led his army south at the king's request, leaving northern England vulnerable. George took the opportunity to stir up another rebellion with the northerners. George's ally, the earl of Oxford, raised his banner calling men to muster but King Edward's men quickly encircled and captured him. Although George had never got so far as to raise his own army, King Edward found evidence that he was involved in Oxford's attempt at a rebellion. As usual, Edward was extremely lenient with George and did not punish him at all for this recent bout of misdoings.[7] Once again, King Edward found himself in the role of peacemaker, trying to reconcile his two brothers. Soon Edward's 'great enterprise' would bring the three of them together in harmony, at least for a brief time.

In 1475, all of King Edward's attention would be focused on preparing to invade France. He had promised to pick up the reins from Henry V and press England's claim to the French throne, or at the very least win back some of the French territories that were lost during the reign of Henry VI. Such a huge expedition required a lot of financial support and parliament readily made several large grants of money to Edward. The king also coerced the wealthiest nobles and citizens loan him money which he termed 'benevolences'.[8] Next, Edward needed a huge army for his expedition and for that his brothers and noblemen raised as many as 12,000 men.[9] Although impressive, it wasn't nearly enough to make an impression in France so Edward allied with Burgundy to launch a joint invasion.

On 4 July 1475, Edward's huge fleet sailed across the English Channel and landed in Calais, one of the few places in France that the English still commanded. It was there that the duke of Burgundy was to rendezvous with Edward and join their forces into one gigantic army. Charles was late, not arriving until 14 July, and even then he did not bring an army but only a small retinue of his personal bodyguards. Charles explained to Edward that his army was engaged hundreds of kilometres away at Lorraine and could not march to join Edward's army. This was a huge disappointment for Edward and seemed to kill all resolve he had to fight the French.[10]

The king was only 33 years old at the time but was growing increasingly indifferent and gluttonous in his middle age. After spending the last fifteen years fighting, Edward was now focused on enjoying the spoils of his wealth, including lots of drinking and whoring with his closest mates, Hastings and Woodville.[11] To avoid fighting King Louis XI alone, Edward proposed a peace treaty which the French readily accepted. In the Treaty of Amiens, King Louis promised to pay King Edward 50,000 crowns per year. In return, Edward promised to leave France and marry his eldest child, Elizabeth of York, to Louis' son, the dauphin.[12]

Edward and his huge fleet returned to England in September 1475 with virtually nothing accomplished. It was an utter disappointment. Richard was completely against the treaty and urged his brother to do what he promised and expend the money he had raised to fight the French, win back lands, and bring glory to England.[13] But Edward did not have the will to fight. This was certainly a breaking point in the relationship of Richard and Edward. Richard was supremely disappointed in his brother Edward, who was not living up to the shining, glorious young king he had once been. Being an open opponent of the king's treaty with France earned Richard much praise and esteem from the people back in England, especially in the north where Richard was the preeminent noble. Disgusted by his brother's actions in France, Richard left Edward's court and retired to Middleham Castle for nearly two years.[14] He didn't return to London until the spring of 1477 when the king sent him an urgent summons to help deal with George who was stirring up trouble again.

The unravelling of George, Duke of Clarence, began with the death of his wife Isabel on 12 December 1476, after giving birth to their first living son. Days later, the baby boy also died. Whether George mourned the loss of his wife and son is not recorded, but judging by his actions, he wasn't too torn up about it. In fact, just weeks after the deaths George put forth a marriage proposal to Mary of Burgundy, heiress to Duke Charles, who had died just three weeks after Isabel. George saw this as a way to finally get revenge on Richard because it would make George richer and more powerful than his brother. Edward, however, quashed the idea right away. Instead, Edward put forth the queen's brother, Anthony Woodville, Earl Rivers, as a candidate for Duchess Mary's future husband. George then put forward a proposed match between himself and a Scottish princess to which Edward again refused.[15] The king did not want his back-stabbing brother to have more power than he already did because George was a dangerous man. He had proved it many times before and it was likely that he would betray Edward again if he got the chance.

George found the entire situation with the blocked marriages and the Woodville interference intolerable so he made his resentment felt all around court. He refused to eat or drink at Edward's court and openly accused the king of trying to poison him.[16] He started spreading rumours that Edward was a bastard and had no right to the throne, then attempted to stoke uprisings in East Anglia.

In April 1477, George decided to take the law in his own hands by arresting and executing one of the queen's maids for poisoning his wife, when it was most likely that she died innocently from childbirth complications, not by Woodville malice. Edward retaliated by hanging a member of George's household for casting horoscopes predicting the king's death. When George found out what Edward had done, he burst into the king's council meeting and accused Edward of using witchcraft and poison to bring about his downfall.[17] George then reasserted that Edward was a bastard and should not be sitting on the English throne. He left the king's presence and called his men to arms, managing to stir some small uprisings in Cambridgeshire and Huntingdonshire.

At this point Edward finally had enough of George and his egotistical behaviour. In June 1477, Edward summoned George to appear before him at Westminster. When George arrived, he was accused by Edward of 'subverting the laws of the realm and presuming to take justice into his own hands'.[18] George was arrested and placed in the Tower of London. Edward convened parliament in January 1478 to try the case against George. On 7 February 1478, the sentence of death was announced. Even though Richard had his own trouble with George, he pleaded with Edward to spare their brother's life.[19] It took eleven days before King Edward could bring himself to order the execution, and even then, George didn't suffer the public execution of a traitor. Instead, he was privately executed. As the story goes, George was allowed to choose the manner of his death, and being a great lover of drink, he chose to be drowned in a butt of malmsey wine.[20]

This shocking turn of events caused Richard to retreat north again, away from politics and the intrigues of court. He had always been loyal to his brother Edward but he found the execution of their brother George to be intolerable. Richard blamed the Woodvilles for George's death and hated them for corrupting his beloved brother Edward.[21] Richard stayed away from Edward's court for two years, returning to London only briefly in the summer of 1480 to be appointed Lieutenant-General in the North and to receive authorisation to raise men for the defence of the Scottish borderlands. Richard spent the vast majority of 1480–82 fighting the Scots. Edward was supposed to lead an army into Scotland but pawned off the responsibility on Richard so he could continue his pleasure-loving, gluttonous ways. Alone, Richard achieved victory against the Scots on 24 August 1482, when Berwick Castle to fell to him.

After Richard's great victory over the Scots, he made a trip to London over Christmas 1482 to receive thanks from the king and to attend a meeting of parliament in January. Richard was shocked at the state of court of which he had been absent for the past four years. Edward had continued his downward spiral into lasciviousness and the Woodvilles were in complete control of government. Richard saw what he perceived as a monumental waste as his brother could have been a great and glorious king. He was now an overweight, apathetic, former shell of himself.[22] After parliament ended, a disappointed Richard rode north again to the safe, comfortable surroundings of Middleham Castle. Unbeknownst to him, that was the last time he was to see his brother Edward alive.[23]

29

The Road to the Throne

The sudden and unexpected cause of King Edward's death is not entirely known. Some chroniclers say he was struck by apoplexy (a stroke or cerebral haemorrhage) while others believe that his fever and chills indicated an ague (malaria).[1] The consensus is that the king suddenly fell ill and collapsed while on a fishing trip on Good Friday, 30 March 1483. He took to his bed at Westminster Palace and lingered in a weakened state for several days. The king knew he was dying so he summoned his councillors to hear his last wishes. He bade them to honour and protect his eldest son Edward and see that he is placed on the throne as King Edward V. He told those gathered around his bedside that he wanted his brother Richard to be lord protector.[2] Edward deemed Richard to be the best choice to oversee his son's minority reign and to teach him the principles of good kingship.

King Edward IV's death on 9 April 1483 set off a shocking chain of events as all the major players rushed in to fill the power vacuum left by King Edward IV. Immediately after Edward's death, messengers rode out of London in every direction to spread the news. Richard, Duke of Gloucester, was in northern England at Middleham Castle when he received the unexpected news of his brother's death in mid-April. The messenger, sent by William Hastings, Edward IV's lord chamberlain, also informed Richard that Edward had named him protector for young Edward's minority reign.[3] Richard would have no choice now but to be pulled back into London politics, far away from the peace and safety of Middleham Castle with his wife and son in the North.

Before leaving Middleham, Richard dispatched two messengers. The first message was sent to young Edward's uncle and governor, Anthony Woodville, Earl Rivers who resided at Ludlow Castle on the Welsh March with Prince Edward.[3] In his cordial letter, Richard asked to meet up with them so they may enter London together. Earl Rivers agreed and told Richard to meet them on 29 April at Northampton. Secondly, Richard sent a letter to Queen Elizabeth assuring her of his loyalty to her sons.[4] Then on 20 April 1483, Richard departed Middleham with a small retinue and began down the road that would lead to his final destiny.

As Richard made his way south, he received several updates from long-time Yorkist ally Lord Hastings. Hastings was in the heart of the drama at London trying to deal with the aftermath of Edward IV's death. Hastings began sending alarming messages to Richard claiming that the queen and her family were trying to supplant him as protector so they alone could rule through the 12-year-old Prince Edward. In fact, the queen was running council meetings as if she were the ruler, and her brother, Thomas Grey, Marquess of Dorset, was issuing orders in his own name as 'Brother Uterine to the king'.[5]

The Woodvilles argued strongly that the council should oversee Edward's minority reign instead of Richard. They insisted that no one man should have the power of the protectorate and things would be better left to the council to govern England.[6] Additionally, the Woodvilles took possession of the royal treasury in the Tower and appointed the queen's brother, Sir Edward Woodville, to the title of Captain of the king's Ships which authorised him to raise a fleet against their perceived enemies. Lastly, the Woodville council rushed to get King Edward crowned before Richard could reach London by scheduling his coronation date for 4 May 1483.[7]

On 29 April 1483, Richard and his retinue arrived at Northampton, about 100 kilometres northwest of London, where they were supposed to rendezvous with Earl Rivers and Prince Edward. But when Richard arrived, he learned that young Edward and his Woodville escort had already passed through the town and gone fourteen kilometres south to Stony Stafford. Richard stayed in Northampton for the night rather than moving on to Stony Stafford because he was awaiting the arrival of his ally Henry Stafford, Duke of Buckingham. Buckingham was second in line to the throne on the Lancastrian side after young Henry Tudor, and he absolutely hated the Woodvilles. Buckingham was from the old nobility while the Woodvilles were new upstarts. Buckingham especially resented Edward IV for making him marry one of the queen's sisters when he was only 11 years old.[8]

As soon as Buckingham heard of Edward's death, he rushed a messenger to Richard at Middleham pledging to help him fight the Woodvilles. Buckingham arrived at Northampton that afternoon, as did young Edward's uncle Earl Rivers who made the trip with a small retinue to explain they had moved on south only due to scanty accommodations in Northampton.[9] Richard, Buckingham, and Rivers dined together that night and by all accounts had a convivial evening. The three men agreed to ride together to Stony Stafford the next morning to meet up with young Edward to escort him to London.[10]

But on the morning of 30 April 1483, the men did not saddle up and ride out together to join the new king as they had planned. It seems Richard and Buckingham stayed up talking late into the night and came up with a different plan.[11] The next morning, Earl Rivers awoke to find his quarters surrounded by armed men wearing Richard's livery.[12] When the earl inquired as to why he was being confined to his lodgings, Richard and Buckingham said he was under arrest for trying to turn the young king against them.

With the most powerful member of the Woodville family safely under lock and key, Richard and Buckingham rode hard to Stony Stafford to take possession of Prince Edward. When they arrived, they kneeled before the young boy and pledged their loyalty. They explained to him that his father had been ill-counseled by those around him and those same people encouraged the vices which caused his bad health. They told him he could not trust his Woodville relations, he could only trust his uncle Richard. Richard explained how he had always been loyal to King Edward, therefore, young Edward should follow his father's lead and keep Richard as his chief councillor. The frightened child had little choice but to consent.[13] He was taken back to Northampton and put in Richard's custody and all of Prince Edward's household servants were dismissed and replaced with Richard's staff. Richard then ordered the arrest of Prince Edward's half-brother, Sir Richard Grey, and his treasurer, Sir Thomas Vaughan. Along with Earl Rivers, Grey and Vaughan were taken to Pontefract Castle and beheaded less than two months later.

Richard would have to explain himself for this drastic turn of events, so he dispatched a message to the capital city to explain his actions. His message arrived just before midnight on 1 May, its contents sending the queen and her Woodville kin into a tizzy when they learned her son was in her enemy's control. The queen and her children rushed to the safety of sanctuary at Westminster Abbey while their servants did their best to haul all the royal possessions into the abbey. Clearly, they feared for their lives now that Richard had control of Prince Edward and had always hated the Woodvilles for the negative effect on his brother Edward.

On 4 May 1483, Richard and Prince Edward made their grand entry into London, accompanied by Buckingham and their large Yorkist retinue. Contemporary chroniclers reported that they were welcomed into the city with cheers from the citizens, happy to be rid of the hated Woodvilles.[14] Edward was escorted to his lodgings at the bishop of London's palace and Richard went to his London town house called Crosby's Place. A few weeks later Edward was moved to the royal apartments in the Tower of London where he would be safer, according to Richard.[15]

Richard immediately set about making his protectorate and the Woodville ousting permanent. He first called together all the lords spiritual and temporal and they were made to pledge an oath of fealty to Prince Edward. Then Richard summoned his first council meeting where he was unanimously proclaimed Protector and Defensor of the Realm. The council also decided that Edward's coronation would be held on 22 June 1483 and called parliament to assemble three days later.[16]

The council convened again on 13 June with the purpose of discussing the final details of Edward's coronation but instead, a visibly angry Richard accused his long-time allies Lord Hastings and Thomas Rotherham of plotting with the Woodvilles to stop his protectorship.[17] Rotherham was taken to the Tower but Hastings was promptly dragged to the Tower green and beheaded on the spot. Richard circulated a letter around a panicked and confused London explaining that Hastings had been plotting his death.[18] He may have been aware that rumours were starting to circulate the city questioning his intentions towards the throne. People were accusing him of acting like he thought he was to be the next king of England, parading through the city in regal fashion and executing noblemen and clergy alike without so much as a trial.

The council also discussed what to do with the queen and her children who were holding out in sanctuary. Most importantly, they wanted to secure Edward's younger brother Richard of Shrewsbury, Duke of York, as next in line to the throne of England. The archbishop of Canterbury, Thomas Bourchier was sent to speak to the queen on 16 June. Although she refused at first to turn over her son to their custody, Bourchier let her know she could do it willingly or they could take her son by force.[19] She chose the former and her 9-year-old son Richard was escorted to the Tower to join his brother Edward under the guise of joining him for his coronation. But shortly after receiving Prince Richard into the Tower, the council delayed Prince Edward's coronation.

On 22 June 1483, the day that should have been Prince Edward's coronation, a shocking revelation was put forth that was game-changing. On that day, Richard, Buckingham, and a large number of nobles attended Sunday services at St Paul's Cross which was led by Friar Ralph Shaa. In an obviously pre-arranged sermon, the friar spoke of Richard's virtues and then made the bold announcement that Richard was the true king of England. The friar revealed that he had witnessed a marriage pre-contract between Edward IV and Lady Eleanor Butler many years before Edward was king. The revelation meant Edward's marriage to Elizabeth Woodville was invalid, making all of their children illegitimate.[20] Conveniently, Eleanor

Butler had died fifteen years prior so she obviously could not corroborate Friar Shaa's claim.

What was the friar's excuse for not bringing this up earlier? Supposedly he had been too afraid to reveal the secret while Edward IV was alive, but now that Edward IV was dead, the friar wanted to make sure the truth came out and the rightful king of England was sitting on the throne. Richard readily supported the friar's claim without demanding any evidence or formal inquiry into the matter. Whether he really believed it or not is debatable. It certainly was a convenient way for him to step in and oust the Woodvilles.

Over the next two days, Buckingham, a talented orator, spread the friar's message across London, and succeeded in gaining enough support for Richard to gain full control of the kingdom. On 25 June 1483, an informal gathering of the lords and Commons took place at Westminster and they put forth a petition to make Richard the new king of England. The following day, 26 June 1483, the lords and Commons rode to Baynard's Castle and formally asked Richard to become the next king of England. Richard then rode in procession to Westminster Hall and took his seat upon the king's Bench which was a formal indication that he was taking possession of the crown. His coronation took place on Sunday, 6 July 1483, followed by an enormous celebration feast for 3,000 people.[21] His reign had certainly started out in grand fashion, but could he maintain control over his shaky foundation?

30

Unsteady Crown

Soon after his coronation, King Richard III set about establishing his authority throughout the kingdom. He needed to show himself as an upright, well-intentioned monarch, not as a usurping king who set aside his nephews for his own gain. The best way for a king to establish his authority and show his majesty was by going on a royal progress across his country. Richard and his wife Queen Anne left London on 19 July 1483 on their first royal progress.[1] The huge royal train meandered north through England for several weeks, finally arriving at Pontefract Castle on 24 August where they were reunited with their 10-year-old son, Edward of Middleham, now heir to the throne of England. The little family spent nearly a month together at Pontefract before Richard and Anne departed to make their way back to London, arriving back in the capital city in mid-September 1483.

While the king and queen were on progress, the first stirrings of rebellion began popping up in southern and western England. While it's true many people were shocked when Richard took the throne, the biggest source of discontent among the people was the treatment of Edward IV's sons, who became known as 'the princes in the Tower'. People were used to witnessing brutality when it came to politics but locking up two innocent boys went beyond the bounds of acceptable behaviour. It was a step too far, even for the brutal world of medieval England.

When in the early fall of 1483, the two boys were no longer seen through the Tower apartment windows or playing in the garden, rumours ran rampant that Richard had killed them. In fact, the idea that they were dead within a few weeks of his coronation was widely believed by contemporary chroniclers.[2] As long as the boys were alive, Richard's reign would be in danger. He had the motive, he had the opportunity and obviously, the English believed it was within Richard's personality to get rid of the princes.

When the Marquess of Dorset and the Woodvilles got word of the insurrections, they threw their lot in with the rebels and worked together with the aim of rescuing the princes from the Tower.[3] The biggest jolt of lifeblood to the rebellion was when Richard's closest friend and ally Henry

Stafford, Duke of Buckingham, sent word to the rebels that he would join them. Why did the powerful duke turn against the king when he had helped Richard defeat the hated Woodvilles? Buckingham likely couldn't stomach Richard's usurpation. His purpose for helping Richard get control of Prince Edward at Stony Stratford was to secure the protectorship for Richard, not the crown. There is also a possibility that Buckingham had inside knowledge of the fates of the princes. It was in September that chroniclers first started reporting that the princes were no longer being seen at the Tower.[4] Tudor writers all date the murder of the princes as occurring days after Buckingham had reached Brecon which would have placed the murders in late July or early August 1483 while King Richard III was on progress.[5] It's certainly possible that their murders would have been Buckingham's breaking point, enough to risk his own lands and even his life to take out the king he had unwittingly helped seat on the throne.

The duke of Buckingham wasn't the only noble getting involved in the rebellion, so too was Margaret Beaufort, the wealthiest woman in England. Margaret's son, Henry Tudor, was the next Lancastrian in line for the throne after Henry VI. The grumblings against Richard were so strong that she decided now was her chance to try to move her son closer to the throne. Henry's strongest chance of winning English support in his bid for the crown was to promise to marry Edward IV's oldest daughter, Elizabeth of York, thus uniting the Houses of York and Lancaster. Margaret and Buckingham knew how tired the English people were after thirty years of fighting and how most everyone would welcome the reconciliation of the two Houses so there could finally be peace throughout the kingdom. Margaret and Buckingham sent secret messages to the dowager queen Elizabeth Woodville in sanctuary and she agreed to the marriage for her daughter Elizabeth or York.[6] Clearly, the queen believed her two sons were dead at this point, otherwise she would not have married her daughter to a Lancastrian rival.

By the end of September, plans for a major rebellion were well underway and Buckingham sent secret messages to Henry Tudor in Brittany to keep him apprised of the plan.[7] Henry was getting his ships ready to sail to England on 18 October 1483 which was the chosen date for the coordinated uprising. Buckingham had nobles and commoners stationed at various strategic points around England which ended up being part of the problem: it was too large an enterprise to keep secret for long. On 8 October 1483, the men of Kent started their uprising prematurely which totally blew Buckingham's cover. When Richard arrived at Lincoln on 11 October, he got word of Buckingham's plans to betray him and immediately began mustering the royal army. Then on 15 October, Richard issued a public proclamation naming Buckingham as a traitor, put a price of £1,000 on his head, and ordered his English subjects to take up arms against the rebels.[8]

When 18 October rolled around, Buckingham unfurled his banner and the uprisings began in earnest. Richard's ally, the duke of Norfolk, quickly put down the rebellions in Kent and Surrey, thus protecting the all-important capital city of London. Richard marched south with his army to face Buckingham but in the end, there was no need. Buckingham's rebellion fizzled out all by itself. He hadn't been able to draw the number of supporters that he expected, storms had washed out the roads and bridges in his path, and the man who had helped him plan the rebellion, John Morton, Bishop of Ely, had betrayed him and escaped.[9] To add to Buckingham's troubles, Henry Tudor had not arrived with his fleet because bad weather prevented his sailing. The entire plan had fallen apart and now Buckingham, fearful of Richard's vengeance, fled for his life. He was captured hiding at one of his servant's homes and sent to Richard at Salisbury where he confessed his part in the rebellion, hoping against all odds that Richard might have pity on him and spare his life. But alas he did not. Buckingham was tried, found guilty, and beheaded as a traitor in the public marketplace of Salisbury on 2 November 1483. The day after Buckingham's execution, Richard received news that Henry Tudor had attempted to make a landing near Plymouth but quickly sailed away when he learned of the collapse of Buckingham's rebellion.

Richard returned victorious to London, making his grand entry on 25 November 1483. He doled out punishments for the rebels, including the execution of ten captains and an attainder of treason for ninety-six men.[10] Margaret Beaufort was stripped of her titles, although her lands were given to her husband. Had she not been a woman, she probably would have gone to the block along with the other plotters.

Richard did not stop at punishing Margaret but also set out determinedly to get possession of her son, Henry Tudor, who was still in exile in Brittany. Richard tried unsuccessfully to bribe the duke of Brittany to hand over Henry Tudor and he also issued several public proclamations naming Henry Tudor as a usurper and a traitor.[11] Much to Richard's dismay, on Christmas Day 1483 in Brittany, Henry Tudor swore an oath in front of all his followers that if he overthrew Richard III, he would marry Elizabeth of York, thus uniting the Houses of Lancaster and York in peace. Henry was gaining momentum as the disaffected English rebels who could not condone Richard's behaviour flocked to Henry's quasi-royal court in Brittany.[12]

In early 1484, a troubled Richard worried about the stability of his reign and set about building a net of protection. He built up an arsenal of weapons and ammunition in the Tower of London to protect the city from invasion. He personally took a trip to Kent to dispense law and subdue the locals who had instigated a recent uprising. Then King Richard summoned parliament to meet in January 1484 to again confirm him as rightful king. At this parliamentary session he also had his son, Prince Edward, confirmed as the heir to the throne.[13]

Lastly, Richard succeeded at the enormous task of getting the dowager queen Elizabeth Woodville and her five daughters out of sanctuary where they had spent the last ten months. On 1 March 1484, King Richard took an oath in front of parliament promising that he would not harm the Woodvilles if they came out of sanctuary. He promised to welcome them back to court and to arrange advantageous marriages for the queen's daughters.[14] Despite his promise, Elizabeth Woodville didn't trust Richard and was hesitant to leave sanctuary but seeing no other options, the dowager queen and her daughters exited Westminster Abbey in mid-March. It was a huge coup for Richard, completely remarkable that he was able to pull it off, but this would be the last of his last successes. From this point forward, things started to go terribly wrong for Richard. Shortly after their exit from sanctuary, Elizabeth petitioned Richard for her own residence away from court and he consented, but the dowager queen's daughters stayed on at court as Queen Anne's ladies-in-waiting.[15] Soon the presence of his young nieces at court stirred up so much drama that his own reign was put in serious jeopardy.

Richard may have been riding high after wooing the Woodvilles out of sanctuary, but his world was about to come crashing down. After the close of parliament, King Richard and Queen Anne made the long journey north to Nottingham Castle where he set up his defensive headquarters. Richard felt he was in a better position to deal with rebels from all directions, including the Scots who were now starting to threaten England, if he were more centrally located in his country. In mid-April 1484, a messenger rode into Nottingham with devastating news: Richard and Anne's only child, Prince Edward, had died from a sudden illness on 9 April 1484.[16] Prince Edward had always been reported to be a sickly child, but his death was not expected, otherwise his devoted parents would have been with him at Middleham Castle. The loss of their son shook them both to the core. Richard's insecurity was on high alert now that he lacked an heir and he wondered if his son's death was his own fault. He started to wonder if God was punishing him for taking the crown and causing the deaths of his nephews.

Queen Anne's grief at the loss of her son had an enormous negative effect on her health. By this time, it was clear that she was already seriously ill, but the death of her son would hasten her end. She had slowly been declining from 'consumption', what we in modern times call tuberculosis.[17] The disease is contagious and to contract it during medieval times was certainly a death warrant.

Richard dealt with his sorrow by turning his attention to his enemies. First, he had to deal with the pesky Scots and their continual border raids which he was determined to put an end to. From May to July 1484, King Richard issued commission of arrays to recruit men for the northern fighting forces and he oversaw the outfitting of the fleet of ships at Scarborough. Richard won a decisive naval battle over the Scots and he negotiated a three-year truce with King James III, king of the Scots.

Next Richard turned his attention to Henry Tudor who was still in Brittany with his uncle, Jasper Tudor. Although Richard's first attempt at bribing the duke of Brittany to hand over Henry Tudor was unsuccessful, Richard's luck in the summer of 1484 was much better. Fortunately for Richard, the duke of Brittany was very ill and his chief treasurer, Pierre Landois, was running the government in his absence. The duke had provided an almost fatherly protection for Henry and Jasper, but Pierre had no such attachment to the English exiles. On 8 June 1484, Pierre signed a treaty with Richard in which he promised to return Henry Tudor to England and deliver him to Richard.[18]

Richard wasn't the only one who had spies – so did Henry Tudor. His ally John Morton, the bishop of Ely who had recently betrayed the duke of Buckingham, received word of Richard's plans and tipped off Henry Tudor just in the nick of time.[19] Henry discreetly rode out of Vannes, Brittany, under the guise of visiting some friends for the day but as soon as he was safely away from Pierre Landois' reach, he ducked in the woods, disguised himself in servants' clothes, and rode hard for the border of France where he could count on the protection of King Louis. If not for his speed, he likely would have been caught because Landois' men arrived at the French border less than an hour after Henry has passed.[20] When the duke of Brittany found out about Landois' agreement with Richard, he was outraged. To make up to his Tudor friends, the duke sent Henry assurances that he would support the exiles financially, even though they were in France now, and paid for Henry's followers to move their court to France.[21] Henry Tudor had slipped through Richard's hands once again.

King Richard finally left the relative safety and comfort of Nottingham Castle in November 1484 for the venomous intrigues of London. In addition to holding his Christmas court at Westminster Palace, he had also come to London to deal with Henry Tudor whose popularity had only grown in the past months. Richard started taking the threat of invasion from Tudor seriously in late November when he learned that the old Lancastrian leader

John de Vere had escaped imprisonment and joined Henry Tudor's court in France.[22] On 3 December 1484, King Richard issued his first proclamation against Henry Tudor and his followers as traitors. Days later Richard issued commissions of array across the kingdom, especially for the coastal towns to ready their defences for Tudor's impending invasion. Richard really jumped the gun here. December was well past the campaigning season when fleets could sail the Channel safely and armies could supply themselves with fresh crops.[23] From this point forward Richard was on high alert, driven by his own paranoia and expecting every day that Henry Tudor and the Lancastrians would arrive try to overthrow him.

Richard's Christmas 1484 celebrations were magnificent by any royal standards, perhaps even grotesquely over the top as if he had to prove the point of his regality and his right to the throne of England. The Twelve Days revels at his Christmas celebrations included masques, pageants, feasts, dancing, singing, jugglers, acrobats, and games. The food was rich and the garments worn by Richard and his courtiers were sumptuous.[24] The impending fear of invasion from Henry Tudor may have dampened the mood, as did the constant appearance of the sickly Queen Anne. But the strangest thing about that Christmas was Richard's peculiar treatment of his niece, Elizabeth of York. She was outfitted in clothes just as rich and luxurious as Queen Anne and Richard was giving her an inordinate amount of attention. Those who witnessed the king's behaviour at the Christmas court of 1484 grew suspicious that Richard might be preparing Elizabeth of York to be the new queen after Anne's inevitable death.[25] Henry Tudor wanted to marry Elizabeth to bring together the two rival houses. In order to stop Henry Tudor from doing so, Richard may have considered marrying Elizabeth himself.

Just after Christmas, widespread rumours began circulating that King Richard III was, indeed, planning to marry his niece Elizabeth as soon as Anne died. There were even rumours Richard poisoned Anne in order to hasten her death so he could marry Elizabeth sooner.[26] Apparently, Anne was barren so Richard must have been eager to remarry and sire a new heir, but marrying his own niece was a step too far for the nobles and commoners alike. Richard need not hasten his wife's death because she took to her sickbed shortly after Christmas and passed away on 16 March 1485.

The queen's death further stoked rumours of Richard's intention to marry Elizabeth of York, so much so that Richard's councillors insisted he make a public denial just two weeks after the queen's death. At St Johns church in Clerkenwell, in front of the mayor of London, nobles and commoners, Richard was forced to make a clear denial that he had no intention of marrying his niece. Furthermore, he announced that anyone caught spreading such rumours would immediately be imprisoned.[27] His public statement wasn't enough and the council then made him put into writing a formal denial on 19 April 1485. It was the greatest humiliation of his reign, so far.

Elizabeth was packed off to Sheriff Hutton which was very near Richard's castle in York. Richard deemed her to be safest at Sheriff Hutton's fortress in case anyone from Henry Tudor's party should try to abduct her. Elizabeth was not alone at Sheriff Hutton, in fact, this is where Richard kept all the young royals, including Elizabeth's sisters and George's son, Edward, Earl of Warwick, and daughter Margaret.[28] Twenty-five-year-old John de la Pole, the earl of Lincoln, was also in safe-keeping at Sheriff Hutton. John was the son of Richard's sister Elizabeth, Duchess of Suffolk, and Richard planned to name him as his heir. Although it may sound like a captivity situation, it was far from that. All the children were very well treated, and Sheriff Hutton was like their own little royal court where no expense was spared for the young nobles.

In the spring of 1485, Richard was feeling utterly defeated and he suffered greatly from an uneasy conscience. He felt as if he was losing control of his kingdom, or maybe he never really had control of it in the first place. He was racked with anxiety over the current state of affairs and worried that it was divine retribution for usurping the throne from his nephews. He became increasing isolated, keeping only a small group of friends at his court. The dual betrayals of Lord Hastings and the duke of Buckingham had taught Richard how fast allegiances could change and that no one could be trusted. These last few months of Richard III's reign were the most unhappy and lonely.[29] He had lost his family and he was being prevented from remarrying his choice of bride, which meant no possibility of an heir anytime soon. His rule was already unsteady, and the threat of Henry Tudor's invasion plagued his mind. But he had no time to sulk. With the spring came a new campaigning season which meant it was time to prepare for the arrival of Henry Tudor and his rebel army.

31

Fall of the Last Plantagenet King

For Richard, the summer of 1485 would not be spent pursuing the leisurely outdoor activities kings were known to do, like hunting, hawking, archery, and playing bowls. Instead, Richard was actively preparing for an invasion from his nemesis Henry Tudor. Richard's treasury was dangerously low and he had no time to assemble parliament to ask for a war tax, so he set about raising loans from his nobles in order to fund his defensive effort.[1]

In mid-May, Richard left London and rode to his summer headquarters at Nottingham Castle in central England. Richard believed this location would put him in a good position to meet his enemy no matter which coast the rebel Tudor chose to land his fleet. Richard expected Henry to arrive in southeast England near Kent, the area of so many previous insurrections. Landing there had a huge strategic advantage for Henry, not just for the numbers of Kentish men who would readily join his cause against Richard, but also for the close proximity to London itself, for to hold the capital city was to hold the entire kingdom. Richard dispatched his own fleets to patrol the English Channel off the southwest and southeast coasts of England's shores looking for any sign of Henry Tudor.

As soon as King Richard arrived at Nottingham in mid-June, his informants brought him the news he had been anticipating for so long: Henry Tudor was assembling a large fleet near Rouen just across the English Channel and would sail soon. Richard wasted no time responding to the news. He immediately issued a second royal proclamation against Henry Tudor and his followers, this one much more alarming in tone than the first one issued in December 1484. In the new proclamation, Richard tried to frighten his English subjects into submission, threatening the total breakdown of law and order, including robberies, murders, and even worse atrocities if Henry Tudor and his followers were allowed to gain a foothold in England. Richard's proclamation falsely accused the Breton exiles of committing 'the most cruel murders, slaughters and robberies and disherisons that ever were seen in any Christian realm'.[2] The following day Richard issued a commission of array for citizens to arm themselves and be ready to fight at a moment's notice.

Richard was still at Nottingham Castle on 11 August 1485 when a messenger arrived with news that Henry Tudor had made his landing at Pembrokeshire in southwest Wales four days earlier.[3] This was a big surprise to Richard as he had expected Henry to invade in southeast England, but for Henry it was essential to march through Wales to gather up more men for his modest army. His uncle Jasper Tudor was well-respected in Wales and Henry claimed to be descended from seventh-century King Cadwaladr of Wales.[4] He even displayed the red dragon of Cadwaladr on his standard which helped recruit the wild Welshmen to his side to fight against King Richard III of England.

On the same day Richard got news of Henry Tudor's landing, he dispatched urgent letters to his closest noble supporters ordering them to come in all haste and bring as many men as they could muster quickly. The duke of Norfolk and the earl of Northumberland planned to rendezvous with Richard at Leicester. Suspiciously enough, Lord Thomas Stanley asked permission to stay at home because he had the sweating sickness (he did not). Richard hesitantly granted his request but kept Lord Thomas' son George, Lord Strange, as hostage for his father's good behaviour. Just days later, Lord Strange tried to escape from Nottingham Castle but was captured and interrogated by Richard's men. He confessed that he and his uncle Sir William Stanley had conspired to help Henry Tudor's cause, but insisted that his father, Lord Thomas Stanley, was entirely loyal to Richard.[5] Richard believed him. The Stanleys had a track record of switching loyalties according to whichever side was likely to prevail, so Richard was quite naive to accept the Stanleys' promises of loyalty.[6]

While Richard anxiously waited for military reinforcements to arrive at Nottingham, Henry Tudor's army was making its way through Wales, gaining even more Yorkist defectors by every passing day. Popular support for Richard had reduced greatly since his coronation, where thirty-three nobles had attended him. Now he only had a dozen still on his side and three of them would betray him in the end, including the Stanleys and Henry Percy, the earl of Northumberland. Northumberland commanded the rearguard of Richard's army but didn't join the battle. In fact, Northumberland had a plan to ensure Richard met his death during the impending battle with Henry Tudor so that he could place his cousin the young Warwick on the throne and rule through him.[7]

On 19 August 1485, Richard was finally comfortable enough with the numbers in his army to leave Nottingham and begin his fateful march towards his destiny with Henry Tudor. Richard's retinue travelled over thirty kilometres that day and spent the night at Leicester where Richard joined armies with the duke of Norfolk and the earl of Northumberland. Chroniclers were notoriously bad at estimating the number of soldiers involved in medieval battles but for the Battle of Bosworth, the consensus is that Richard had about 8,000 men in his army and Henry Tudor had around 5,000 men.[8]

With Richard's army in full order, he led them out of Leicester on 21 August and proceeded down the old Roman Road towards Atherstone. When Richard arrived at Sutton Cheney, about ten kilometres east of Atherstone, his scouts reported that Henry Tudor's army was a mere five kilometres to the west. Richard decided to stop his march and let his men rest there for the evening before battling the following day. Richard didn't get much rest that night because he was troubled by terrible dreams in which he was allegedly tormented by demons. When he emerged from his tent, he was apparently pale and shaken from whatever vision he had in his dreams that night.[9]

For such an epic and consequential battle as the Battle of Bosworth, we have very little idea of what exactly happened. There were no detailed accounts left behind, only second-hand stories documented through various chroniclers. The best description we have is from Polydore Vergil who was Henry VII's historian. Vergil would have been told firsthand accounts of the battle from Henry and others that were present.[10] Despite the lack of comprehensive documentation, we can piece together major milestones within that battle to determine what happened.

Early in the morning of 22 August 1485 on the high ground of Ambion Hill King Richard III lined up his army into three primary lines of defence. The duke of Norfolk commanded the vanguard (the advance guard), Richard led the centre guard, and the earl of Northumberland led the rear guard. As every great warrior king did before battle, Richard gave a motivational speech to his troops giving them courage and stoking their bloodlust. Then Richard donned his coronation crown, which in hindsight really wasn't a good idea because it made him an easy target on the battlefield.[11] Richard watched from the hill as Henry Tudor's army moved into battle formation at the bottom of Ambion Hill. Henry had managed to raise a respectable 5,000 strong army but was clearly outnumbered by Richard. Sir William Stanley had a force of 3,000 men stationed north of the battlefield while his uncle Lord Thomas Stanley had 5,000 men to the south. The fickle Stanleys held back their men so they can watch the drama unfold and decide which side to join.[12]

After a brief exchange of cannon fire, the two armies advanced on each other simultaneously. The two vanguards battled each other for an hour in fierce hand-to-hand combat.[13] The next account we have of the battle is the decisive moment when Richard spotted Henry Tudor on the battlefield. Richard decided to seize the opportunity and end Henry Tudor for good. Richard gathered a mounted force of 700 men and charged down the hill toward Henry. Henry's pikemen jumped into action, surrounding their leader and deploying very long pikes with metal spears, forming a nearly impenetrable wall of protection. As Richard's men crashed into the wall of pikes, chaos ensued and Richard's men were scattered.[14] It was at this moment when Sir William Stanley finally decided to commit himself, throwing in his lot with Henry Tudor. Seeing that he was betrayed by Stanley, Richard nonetheless bravely fought on, making it near enough to Henry that he was able to cut down his standard and kill the standard bearer, William Brandon. But soon enough Richard and the few men he had left were overtaken by the enemy. Richard was killed and his crown was placed on Henry Tudor's head by Sir William Stanley.[15] Despite a rather dubious royal bloodline, Henry Tudor, was proclaimed King of England by right of conquest.

Once Richard was seen being killed on the battlefield and his royal standard fell, his host broke apart. The last Plantagenet king was dead and a new dynasty had begun. As a final humiliation, Richard's body was stripped naked, slung across a horse, and paraded through Leicester where it would remain on display for two days so the public could see he was really dead.[16] His bones were unceremoniously buried without any stone or marker to identify him, as if he was a mere pauper. Astonishingly, in 2012 Richard's bones were discovered in Leicester buried under a parking lot. Researchers knew it was Richard when they saw the curved spine which was reported by several contemporary chroniclers and wildly over-exaggerated by Shakespeare. Archaeologists studied Richard's skeleton and determined that he died from a massive blow to the head, probably caused by a halberd or some other sharp-edged weapon.[17] In the spring of 2015, Leicester held several days of celebration leading up to a proper funeral and burial at Leicester Cathedral for the misfortunate King Richard III.

32

Was Richard III a Usurper?

Given the chance and under better circumstances, Richard III had the potential to be a good king. During his brother Edward's reign, he had shown himself to excel at diplomatic relationships as well as military leadership. By all accounts, Richard III was a loyal and obedient servant to his brother, King Edward IV, even after their fallout in 1478 after George's execution. Richard never showed any signs of disloyalty to Edward until after his death. That's when Richard made the colossal mistake of setting aside Edward's sons just so he could prevent the Woodvilles from taking control of government. If Edward's children were found to be illegitimate, that would place Richard next in line to the throne, giving him much more power than the Woodvilles. The consequences of this move were not well thought out by Richard. His reputation went down the drain and popular support for his cause dried up. Even his closest allies pulled away from him and flipped to Henry Tudor's side.

Was Richard III really a usurper? Of all the famous usurpers throughout history, this is the easiest one to analyse. To be considered a usurper, one would have to win the throne either by conquest or by illegal means. Although Richard was placed on the throne legally by parliament he never ordered an investigation into Edward's marriage contract to Eleanor Butler, and therefore the truth of the rumour was never sought.[1] For Richard to press on with his coronation without finding the truth stank of desperation. He obviously lacked the evidence to prove it and that's why he rushed through his own coronation as King Richard III of England.

The non-investigation of Edward's marriage contract combined with the murder of two royal princes can certainly be classified as criminal. Murder was illegal during medieval times, and even if Richard hadn't killed the boys with his own hands, their deaths were most likely carried out on Richard's command.[2] Some writers have put forth other theories as to the two princes' disappearance, including the idea that they were secretly smuggled out of the Tower and raised abroad, but there is no evidence for that whatsoever.[3] It is much more likely that the newly crowned Richard began viewing his nephews as rivals to his throne. It is not far-fetched to imagine Richard decided to snuff them out, just as he and Edward had put Henry VI to his death on the night of Edward's second coronation. Although the Ricardian Society aims to restore Richard's reputation as a goodly king, there is no doubt that Richard III was a usurper who illegally stole the crown from his two young innocent nephews in the worst possible way.

Part VI

Henry VII (1485–1509)

33

The Tudors and Beauforts

The ascension of a little-known English exile named Henry Tudor to the throne of England is one of the most improbable underdog stories in the history of medieval Europe. Henry spent most of his life exiled in France before he became king, making him a virtual stranger to the people in England. Even his mother, the rich heiress Margaret Beaufort, had only seen him a few times in the first twenty-eight years of his life. Henry's claim to the throne of England wasn't ironclad by any means.[1] Although he had old royal blood from his mother's side of the family, Henry's grandfather was a minor Welshman who had managed to charm his way into the bed of Queen Catherine de Valois, queen consort and widow of King Henry V. It is from their secret marriage that the House of Tudor was founded.

Catherine de Valois was a young, beautiful French princess, and youngest daughter of the mad king, Charles VI. At the age of 18, Catherine was married to the great warrior king Henry V, making her queen of England. When Henry V died suddenly of dysentery on the battlefields of France in 1422, Catherine was left a widow at only 20 years of age. Their 9-month-old son Henry was suddenly the new king of England, even though he was still a babe in arms. For the first few years of his life, Henry was raised at court with his mother but around the age of 4 he was moved out of her house so he could begin his kingly training.[2]

Naturally, a young, beautiful dowager queen might be interested in pursuing a romantic life of her own, especially now that she had fulfilled her duty by marrying a man of her father's choosing and siring a male heir on her first try. In fact, rumours were ripe around court that Catherine was having an affair with Edmund Beaufort, Duke of Somerset,[3] which really ruffled the feathers of Humphrey, Duke of Gloucester. Humphrey was the brother of Henry V and held the highest position in government next to his brother John, the duke of Bedford. Humphrey feared that a marriage between the dowager queen and Edmund Beaufort would tip the balance of power too far in the Beaufort's direction so he laboured to put an end to that relationship.

With Humphrey's encouragement, parliament passed a law in 1427 declaring that a dowager queen must have the permission of the king before she could remarry. On top of that, the law stated that the king could not give such permission until he had reached his majority, somewhere between 16 and 18 years of age.[4] If a dowager queen became married without the king's approval, her new husband would be stripped of all his lands and titles, plus he would be put to death as a traitor. Since Catherine's son, Henry VI, was only 6 years old at the time, she would have had to wait at least ten years before she could marry. Catherine was unwilling to wait that long. Instead, she began a secret relationship with a member of her household: Owen Tudor.

Owen Tudor came from the Welsh Tewdwrs, one of the most rich and powerful families in Wales during the thirteenth and fourteenth centuries. The Tewdwrs claimed direct descent from Ednyfed Fychan, the seneschal of Llywelyn ap Iorwerth and his son and successor, Dafydd ab Iorwerth, princes of the kingdom of Gwynedd in the early and mid-thirteenth century and were eventually considered Welsh royalty.[5] Owen was born around 1400 and by 1407 he was living in London at the court of King Henry IV where he served as a page to the king's steward.[6] In 1415, Owen sailed to France and fought for King Henry V at the battles of Alençon and Agincourt when he was only 15 years old. As a reward for his faithful service, he was raised to squire which allowed him to carry arms and shields for knights.

Owen became keeper of the queen's wardrobe sometime after the 1427 which gave him intimate access to the young and beautiful dowager Catherine.[7] Sparks flew between the two and a romantic relationship blossomed. At first, they kept the relationship under cover to avoid trouble for themselves since Catherine's actions were in defiance of parliament. Although there is no record of the union, the couple were probably married in secret.[8] Soon it became difficult to keep the relationship a secret because Catherine became pregnant. She gave birth to their first child, Edmund Tudor, in 1430 at the royal manor of Hadham in Hertfordshire, followed shortly thereafter by the birth of another son, Jasper, in 1431 at a manor house in Hatfield.

For the most part, the queen stayed away from court except when she was needed to attend important occasions with her son Henry, but only when she was not pregnant. Catherine became pregnant at least two more times between 1431 and 1436, making it quite impossible for people to deny that she had a defied parliament's order. King Henry VI tolerated their secret relationship and even bestowed lands and titles upon Owen, probably more due to his allegiance to his mother than Owen himself. In 1432, King Henry even granted Owen 'English rights' which meant he was exempt from the 1402 law forbidding Welshmen to own property or hold any royal office in England.[9]

The marriage of Owen and Catherine came to full light in January 1437, when the dowager queen died after a 'long, grievous malady'.[10] Soon after Catherine's death, Owen was summoned to appear before the Privy Council to explain himself and his relationship with the dowager queen. Now that his wife was no longer there to protect him, Owen felt his life was in danger so he packed what he could and quickly fled to Wales. When Humphrey found out that Owen was on the run, he sent a servant to intercept Owen and haul him back to London. Once in London, Owen slipped into sanctuary at Westminster where he would be safe from arrest. After three days, he was coaxed out of sanctuary and appeared before the king at the Privy Council on 15 July 1437. The 16-year-old Henry VI was kind-hearted and decided to fully pardon his stepfather on the condition that he appear whenever summoned by the king or the privy council to which Owen agreed. Henry in return promised Owen a safe conduct back to his native Wales.[11]

Humphrey was not at all pleased with King Henry's pardon and felt justified in breaking the king's promise of a safe conduct. Humphrey dispatched his men to arrest Owen before he could reach Wales and confiscated Owen's considerable possessions. Owen, along with his priest and servant, were taken to Newgate Prison in London and locked up. About six months into their captivity, they attempted to escape but were captured and thrown back in prison. In July 1438, Owen was transferred to Windsor Castle where he could be better watched by the constable, Edmund Beaufort.[12] After one year of imprisonment at Windsor, King Henry VI granted Owen a full pardon. Henry felt that Owen was very badly treated by Humphrey and sought to correct the situation since he was now 18 years old and assuming more responsibility in his government. From that point on, Owen was an accepted member of the court and lived the life of a nobleman.[13] He served King Henry on various occasions, including the escort of Henry's future bride, Margaret of Anjou, from France to England in 1445.

Edmund and Jasper were only 6 and 7 years old when their mother died and their father was imprisoned. King Henry sent his young half-brothers to Barking Abbey and placed them under the care of the abbess, Katherine de la Pole.[14] It was quite normal for well-to-do boys to be educated at a monastery and it was there that the Tudor brothers were taught religion, Latin, French, English, philosophy, and classic literature from the abbey's expansive library. Their education and lodging was funded by King Henry who is said to have taken great pains to see that Edmund and Jasper received not only a top-notch education but also protection, both physically and morally.

Edmund and Jasper spent five years at Barking Abbey and then were called to London by the king in 1442 to live at court.[15] Now aged 12 and

11 years old, the boys had never even met their half-brother. One of Henry VI's greatest virtues was his charity and he felt sympathy for his half-brothers who had lost their mother and been separated from their father at such an early age. Henry could probably sympathise since he never even met his own father and was separated from his mother at an early age himself. Most of all, Edmund and Jasper were his only close relatives and he probably craved the familial atmosphere he had always been missing.

Unfortunately, there are no records as to the exact whereabouts or activities of the Tudor boys from the time they moved to court in 1442 until their rise to prominence ten years later in 1452. We can only assume that their education continued, probably with more of an emphasis placed on military training since the boys were approaching their teenage years and would be expected to serve the king who had so generously paid for their upbringing. There is no evidence of a personal relationship between King Henry and the Tudor boys, but it is possible that their paths crossed many times at court over those ten years.

The first few years at court would have been an exciting place for young Edmund and Jasper, a time of peace, hope, and gratitude that the infant king had lived to reach his majority. The peace and stability wouldn't last long though. Things started going downhill for Henry VI not long after his majority began. His choice of a French bride, Margaret of Anjou, turned out to be highly unpopular.[16] There were high hopes that she could bring peace between France and England but the war dragged on and England lost more French territories in the late 1440s and early 1450s. This combined with rebellions from the Yorkist faction in the early 1450s all led to Henry VI's mental collapse in August 1453. Edmund and Jasper were too young to be intimately involved in government during this time, but they certainly would have been aware of the current state of affairs and that their half-brother, the king, was in serious danger of losing his crown. Living in London during this period meant they would have witnessed more than one attempt at a coup, including Jack Cade's Rebellion and the duke of York's panic-inducing visit in the fall of 1450. If there was one lesson to take away it was that over-empowered noblemen and a weak king did not mix. In fact, it was a recipe for disaster.

From 1452 onwards, Edmund and Jasper appeared more frequently in the records as they started to take on more of an official role in their half-brother's fragile government. At this time, King Henry VI had been married to Margaret of Anjou for over seven years but had failed to produce an heir. It was absolutely imperative that the king have an heir, not only to secure the peaceful succession for the kingdom, but to also ward off possible rivals to the throne. The Tudor brothers were King Henry's nearest relatives and since Edmund was older than Jasper, he would naturally be first in line to the throne if Henry VI should die without fathering an heir. It was at this time Henry started taking legal steps to set up Edmund up as his heir. On 23 November 1452, he declared Edmund and Jasper to be his legitimate half-brothers and raised them both to the peerage by making Edmund, the earl of Richmond, one of the most valuable duchies in England, and Jasper was made Earl of Pembroke.[17] Both Tudor brothers would spend a considerable amount of time in Wales working to quell rebellions and establish law and order in the king's name.

Wales had been a trouble spot for English kings over the years because of its isolated nature and the people's fierce sense of independence. King Henry IV rarely showed himself in Wales and didn't even bother trying to keep law and order. The Welsh resented this lack of authority and rebelled against King Henry IV in the early 1400s. The rebellion was led by Owain Glyndŵr and among his prominent partners were Owen Tudor's father, Maredudd ap Tudur and his uncles Rhys ap Tudur and Gwilym ap Tudur. Their rebellion failed and most of their lands were confiscated by the king. Rhys was captured and executed. The other Tudurs presented themselves at Henry IV's court, pledged their obedience to the king, and were mercifully forgiven. Their rebellion may have failed but the Tudors would always be remembered in the hearts of Welshman and Henry was right to place Jasper in Wales to keep law and order. Jasper showed himself a strong but fair leader who did much to fortify the castles and towns in his realm. He earned the respect of the Welsh through his hard work and fairness in business and personal dealings.[18] Jasper's relationship with the people of Wales was enduring. It was one of the key components in Henry Tudor's victory over Richard III, in 1485.

With Edmund and Jasper Tudor legitimised and raised to the peerage, the next natural step for King Henry would be to secure his half-brothers with prestigious marriages, bringing them more lands, titles, power, and money. If Edmund were to be king someday, he must have a bride with a strong Lancastrian bloodline to help legitimise his own claim. King Henry had the perfect candidate: 10-year-old Margaret Beaufort, the richest heiress in England.[19]

On 24 March 1453, 10-year-old Margaret Beaufort and her mother were summoned to appear before King Henry VI in London. During the visit, Henry dissolved young Margaret's previous marriage contract to John de la Pole and granted her wardship to Edmund and Jasper. Even though Margaret was already wealthy, King Henry showed his generosity by providing 100 marks for new clothes befitting her new status as the future Duchess of Richmond.[20] Beyond that, she could hope to become queen consort one day if she were to marry Edmund Tudor and King Henry VI was to die childless. Henry made similar grants of money to Edmund and Jasper shortly after they were raised to the peerage. Clothing was extremely important in displaying rank so Edmund's and Jasper's new clothing would have included velvet, cloth of gold, furs, and even elaborate saddles and trappings for their horses.

As Margaret Beaufort's new wardens, Edmund and Jasper were responsible for overseeing her territories and finances, as well as her upbringing and well-being, until she became old enough to be married off. Wardships may sound harsh to us today but they were typical for noble children in the middle ages. They were so incredibly profitable that many noblemen paid for the right to possess a ward, not only to reap the profits of their inherited lands but also to marry these wealthy wards to their own children. Other nobles received wards as a thank you for faithful service or for an exceptional deed performed for the crown.

It was not typical, however, for a young ward to remain in his or her parents' care during a wardship but that's exactly what Margaret Beaufort did. Perhaps due to her young age, Margaret Beaufort was allowed to remain in the care of her mother, Margaret Beauchamp.[21] Mother and daughter split their time between two manors owned by Beauchamp, Bletsoe Castle in Bedfordshire and Maxey Castle in Cambridgeshire, both about eighty kilometres north of London. Young Margaret was given an excellent education. Margaret was a great student, she was especially good at French, and later in life involved herself in the printing of books once the printing press reached England.[22] She also learned from her mother's example that a woman was perfectly capable of handling her own household affairs and she grew to be a very shrewd businesswoman because of it.

While the duke of York and Queen Margaret of Anjou wrestled for power, Margaret Beaufort was preparing for her wedding. To no one's surprise, she was to marry the keeper of her wardship, Edmund Tudor. The wedding ceremony took place on 1 November 1455, at Bletsoe Castle, the childhood home of Margaret Beaufort. Edmund was 25 years old and Margaret was only 12 years old, young even by medieval standards.[23] This was a very advantageous marriage for Edmund because at that time Margaret Beaufort was the richest heiress in England. She was the only legitimate child of the first Duke of Somerset, John Beaufort, who traced his lineage to King Edward III through his third son, John of Gaunt. John was made Duke of Lancaster in 1362, making him one of the preeminent landowners in England and therefore very wealthy and powerful.

Not only was John of Gaunt rich and powerful, was very successful at producing heirs. He had a total of twelve children: eight by his first and second wives, and four children through his mistress, Catherine Swynford. His four illegitimate children were known as the Beaufort line, named after his castle in Champagne, France, which was called the Château de Beaufort.[24] Interestingly, Champagne was the location where Chrétien de Troyes wrote Arthurian romances and created the character of Lancelot, knight of the Round Table. Whether John chose the name Beaufort to create parallels between the legend of King Arthur and his heirs is not known but it is a possibility. Many years later Henry Tudor did just that, going so far as to name is first son Arthur instead of the traditional practice of naming the first-born son after the father.

After John of Gaunt's second wife died, he married his mistress, Catherine Swynford. The couple's four children, including Margaret Beaufort's grandfather John, Duke of Somerset, were legitimised by Richard II in 1397 and again by Henry IV in 1407.[25] Slightly unusual, yes, but John of Gaunt was no ordinary man. He was the father of the current king of England, Henry IV, and had held great sway in government and council matters during the preceding reign of his young nephew Richard II. Although he was successful in getting his children legitimised, meaning they could inherit his estates and titles, there was one crucial stipulation. The Beaufort line was legitimised 'except to the royal dignity' meaning neither they could not claim the throne.[26] But that didn't stop them from holding great wealth and power.

Throughout the years, Margaret Beaufort's ancestors had loyally served the House of Lancaster. Margaret's great-uncle, Cardinal Henry Beaufort, was one of the chief rulers during Henry VI's minority. Her aunt, Joan Beaufort, was the queen of Scotland through her marriage to King James I. Her father John was a trusted soldier to his cousin Henry V and was later raised to the dukedom of Somerset by Henry VI.

Margaret's father John had a disastrous military career. His first military engagement came at the young age of 16. He sailed to France to fight for England in the Hundred Years' War but ended up being captured in the Battle of Baugé in March 1421 and held prisoner by France for seventeen years.[27] The enormous ransom cost him most of his inheritance and land holdings in Holland which nearly ruined him. At this point he was desperate to improve his situation. Upon his return to England he arranged a marriage with the Beauchamp family in 1442 and conceived Margaret shortly thereafter. Margaret's mother was Margaret Beauchamp, who was also her family's sole heiress and as such inherited Bletsoe Castle in Bedfordshire, among other manors in Wiltshire and Dorset, giving John Beaufort land holdings that he so desperately needed.

John Beaufort knew he had to redeem himself on the military field to regain the respect of his fellow noblemen and recoup his losses from the ransom he paid for his freedom so he accepted the leading role in a new expedition to France. This expedition was even more disastrous than the first. He overstepped his bounds by levying illegal taxes on the people for his own personal gain and accomplished nothing for England. Upon his return the king was so angry he stripped him of his property and banished him from court. He died shortly after from an apparent suicide on 27 May 1444.[28]

Shortly after Edmund's and Margaret's November 1455 nuptials, Edmund was called to Wales on the king's business to repress Welsh leader Gruffydd ap Nicolas who had taken possession of several castles in Wales. Edmund made his headquarters at Lamphey Bishop's Palace which was very close to Jasper's own home base of Pembroke Castle in southwest Wales. Margaret's whereabouts during this time are unknown. In the spring of 1456, there is a record of husband and wife lodging together briefly at Jasper's Caldicot Castle, located 150 kilometres from Lamphey in southeast Wales.[29] Edmund returned to his duties soon thereafter and is noted as being 'greatly at war' with Gruffydd ap Nicolas during the summer of 1456.[30]

When Edmund left Margaret to fight Gruffydd ap Nicolas, he was probably unaware that he had successfully made his young bride pregnant. Marriages usually weren't consummated until the bride was 14 years old but Edmund may have been anxious to have a child by Margaret as soon as possible. Doing so would have granted him lifetime rights to her estates upon her death, even if it meant endangering his young bride's health. Margaret was small and underdeveloped for her age so a pregnancy was a very dangerous situation for her.

In August 1456, Gruffydd surrendered Carmarthen Castle to Edmund Tudor and pledged obedience to his new overlord. But Edmund's job was not over. Since he was ordered to uphold the king's authority in Wales, he also had to deal with an insurgence of Yorkist rebels, led by William Herbert, Walter Devereux, and Roger Vaughan. The three men were trying to get a foothold in Wales for Richard, Duke of York, who had been serving as England's protectorate until he was ousted by Queen Margaret of Anjou.

On 10 August 1456, the Yorkists seized Carmarthen Castle and imprisoned Edmund Tudor. At some point over the next few months they did release him, perhaps because of his declining health, but apparently he didn't make it far. He died at Carmarthen Castle on 1 November 1456, which happened to be his first wedding anniversary. There is no record of his cause of death but it is widely believed he was a victim of the plague.[31]

At the time of Edmund's death, Margaret was 13 years old, seven months pregnant, and alone in Wales, far from her English home. As if being young, widowed, pregnant, and in danger of contracting the plague wasn't enough, she had even bigger worries on her hands. Her husband, a loyalist to Henry VI and the Lancastrians, had just met his end at the hands of the duke of York. It was absolutely inevitable that the Yorkists would go after Jasper next in their attempt to eliminate all of Henry VI's heirs. Margaret Beaufort's unborn child would be next in line after Jasper. She was understandably terrified and decided to flee to Pembroke Castle where Jasper took her under his protection.[32]

On a cold January night just two months later, Margaret gave birth to her first and only child, a son, on 28 January 1457. Jasper wanted to name the baby Owen after the child's grandfather, but Margaret insisted on naming her son Henry after the king. The birth was exceedingly difficult and would scar her for life. For a time during Margaret's labour, her attendants believed that she and her unborn child would perish. Not only was she very young but she was also slight of stature and undeveloped for her age so it's a wonder she even survived childbirth. It was so difficult for her that she never became pregnant again despite marrying two more times. It is widely believed that she was physically damaged during childbirth and was unable to conceive again, but it's also possible she was too traumatised to ever put herself in that situation again.[33] Either way, Margaret devoted herself to her son, calling him 'my dearest and only desired joy in this world'.[34] Henry inherited his late father's title, Earl of Richmond, and Margaret was determined to see that he got what was due to him.

As a young widow, Margaret would be obliged to observe one year of mourning for her husband, as was customary, and during this time she remained at Pembroke under the protection of her brother-in-law Jasper. This was the only period in her life that she was able to spend significant time with her son before he became king. As soon as her mourning period was over, Margaret and Jasper knew that she must find a new husband and they would rather do it on their own terms than have the crown, or in this case the protector Richard of York choose it for her.

Although she was a young, widowed mother, her wealth and royal blood still made her a very desirable bride. Only two months after Henry's birth, Jasper and Margaret were already planning her next marriage. Together they travelled 350 kilometres from Pembroke Castle in Wales to Greenfield in central England to meet and negotiate a marriage to Sir Henry Stafford, the son of the duke of Buckingham.[35] The Staffords, like the Beauforts, were descendants of Edward III and they were loyal Lancastrians. The Staffords held great swaths of land in the Midlands in central England. Margaret agreed to marry Stafford not for money but for the safety his dukedom could provide her and her son. During their visit, they reached an agreement on the marriage, then Jasper and Margaret returned to Pembroke Castle so Margaret could finish her obligatory year of mourning.

Margaret married 32-year-old Henry Stafford on 3 January 1458 at Maxstoke, an enormous castle in Warwickshire that still stands today. Margaret and her new husband went on to live the life of the rich and powerful, setting up homes at Bourne Castle in Lincolnshire and the Woking manor in Surrey, both Margaret's inheritances. Margaret's wealth allowed them to live magnificently and entertain lavishly. They enjoyed each other's company and travelled together regularly, making progresses through their English lands and frequent trips to London. It must have been bittersweet for Margaret because she had achieved an enviable life, but she longed for the one thing she didn't have, her son.

Five days after Margaret's marriage to Henry Stafford, Henry VI granted the wardship of her 1-year-old son, Henry Tudor, to his uncle Jasper Tudor. Young Henry was obviously very valuable to the Lancastrians and King Henry wanted him in the care of his trusted 'uterine brother' Jasper Tudor at the fortified Pembroke Castle in Wales. It was common for people of rank to be raised away from their parents when they were high-born and Margaret Beaufort had to be content that her trusted brother-in-law Jasper would look after her son.

Little is known of the first few years of Henry Tudor's childhood other than a mention that he was educated by the Benedictine monks at Monkton Priory, very near to Pembroke Castle.[36] His peaceful life at Pembroke Castle wouldn't last for long as Henry would be jolted from everything he knew when he was only 4 years old. That's when the Yorkists gained the upper hand and sent the Lancastrians on the run.

34

Henry's Childhood and the Wars of the Roses

enry Tudor was the nephew of King Henry VI, one of the most unsuccessful rulers in all of English history. To be fair, Henry VI had big shoes to fill from his infamous warrior father, King Henry V. Henry VI became king of England when he was only 9 months old, therefore, he didn't grow up with a good example of kingship to follow. Instead, he favoured the religious life of piety, peace, and reconciliation. These were not good traits to have if you were a king or any kind of medieval ruler.

Henry VI's cousin Richard, Duke of York, did have all the traits of a powerful medieval ruler and he was appointed as protector when Henry VI suffered his first mental collapse in 1453. While the king was in his stupor, York threw out Henry's councillors and replaced them with his own trusted friends and relatives. York even managed to arrest and imprison Henry VI's closest ally, the duke of Somerset, which did not sit well with the king when he suddenly awoke on Christmas Day 1454. King Henry immediately ended York's protectorate, stripped him and his allies of some of their titles, and freed Somerset from the Tower.

Shortly thereafter, the tension between York and Henry bubbled over and civil war broke out. The first battle of the Wars of the Roses was the Battle of St Albans on 22 May 1455. York's forces greatly outnumbered the king's army who was largely unprepared for battle. The royal army was set up in a bad position among the city streets instead of open land and York easily overcame them.[1] Not only did York manage to kill many of the king's nobles, including the despised duke of Somerset, he also found Henry VI near the battlefield and took physical possession of him.

For the next five years, the Houses of York and Lancaster would battle each other four more times (Blore Heath, Ludford Bridge, Northampton, and Wakefield). At the Battle of Wakefield on 30 December 1460, Richard, Duke of York, was lured out of his castle and slain by the enemy. Richard had been the figurehead of the House of York and his death would leave a huge power vacuum. Luckily for the Yorkists, Richard had many sons and his eldest surviving son Edward was the perfect candidate to lead their house forward against the Lancastrians.

It was mid-January 1461 when Edward received the disastrous news of the death of his father and his brother Edmund at the Battle of Wakefield. Now Edward at only 19 years of age was the de facto leader of the Yorkist party. Edward mustered his army of mostly Welshmen and prepared to leave Gloucester for London to meet up with his father's main ally, Richard Neville, Earl of Warwick, also known as 'The Kingmaker'. Just as Edward started his march to London, he received news that a Lancastrian army led by Jasper and Owen Tudor was not far away from his location. The Tudors were also on their way to London so they could join forces with the Lancastrian royal army.

Edward decided his best course of action would be to intercept the Tudor army before they could reach London, so Edward led his army north arriving at a town called Mortimer's Cross on 2 February 1461. The Lancastrians were the first to attack causing the Yorkist flank to fracture but then Edward's line turned the battle in the Yorkists' favour, pushing Jasper Tudor's men into a full retreat. Owen Tudor's line was overtaken by Edward's army and his men fled as well.[2] The Yorkists gave chase and caught up to Owen in Hereford where he was taken into custody and immediately beheaded in the market square. Before placing his head in the block, he reportedly said 'That head shall lie in the stock that was wont to lie on Queen Catherine's lap.'[3] The battle was a complete disaster for Jasper Tudor. Not only was his father killed but as many as 4,000 of his soldiers were killed and Jasper found himself on the run.[4]

Two weeks after their loss at Mortimer's Cross, the Lancastrians rallied and won the Second Battle of St. Albans on 17 February 1461. Queen Margaret then attempted to lead the royal army into London but the city council refused her entry. Her army had a terrible reputation for plundering, raping, and similar such atrocities, so Londoners were too afraid to let them in.[5] They did, however, allow Edward and the earl of Warwick to enter the city on 26 February 1461. Just one week later, Edward was crowned King of England as Edward IV on 4 March 1461.

Edward had little time to celebrate before he had to leave for yet another battle. In one of the most infamous battles in the Wars of the Roses, the Yorkist and Lancastrian armies lined up against each other in a virtual snowstorm at Towton on 29 March 1461. This was the largest battle to date with estimates as high as 60,000 men in Henry's army and 48,000 men in King Edward's army. It was an all-day long battle in which Edward emerged victorious. The Yorkists executed every Lancastrian noble they could find but Margaret, Henry, and their young son made it to the safety of Scotland. It is estimated that 28,000 men died on the field that day.[6]

Now that King Edward IV was in complete control of England, he set out to remove all possible rivals to his throne. In the fall of 1461, the king commissioned Sir William Herbert to take control of Wales where Jasper Tudor had managed to keep a strong foothold for the Lancastrians. Jasper went on the run in Wales, trying to avoid capture by Herbert. Four-year-old Henry Tudor was at Pembroke Castle with his mother Margaret and her husband Henry Stafford. Although Pembroke was a fortified castle that was well-stocked for a siege, they did not put up a fight when Herbert arrived. Instead, the castle peacefully surrendered to Herbert on 30 September 1461.[7] Herbert then tracked down Jasper near Caernarvon and the two sides fought at Twt Hill on 16 October 1461. Details of the battle are scarce, but we do know that Herbert won and as a result, Jasper took a ship to Scotland.

Not only did Herbert take possession of Pembroke Castle, he also took custody of Henry Tudor. This must have been a terribly frightening time in young Henry's life, having lost the protection of his uncle Jasper and handed over to a Yorkist enemy. Henry was extremely fortunate that he had become the ward of a kind and generous man. William Herbert and his wife, Anne Devereaux, treated Henry like a member of the family and raised him alongside their own sons at Raglan Castle for the next ten years.[8] He was given an education befitting a child of nobility, including two Oxford graduates for his teachers and military instruction from Sir Hugh Johns. He was even allowed to see his mother Margaret Beaufort, but only for one-week visit in September 1467.[9]

During Henry's time with the Herberts at Raglan, Jasper Tudor and Margaret Beaufort did not sit by idly. Jasper had lost his nephew, his lands, and his titles. He was more determined than ever to restore his half-brother King Henry VI to the throne and get his nephew back from the Yorkists. When Jasper fled England after the loss at Twt Hill, he sailed to Scotland to join Margaret of Anjou and old king Henry in Scotland. Jasper was a well-respected military leader and a skilled negotiator, continually travelling to France, Brittany, and Wales over the years to gain support for Henry VI's cause. Jasper found a willing conspirator in King Louis XI of France. Jasper resided at Louis' court from October 1469 to September 1470 and even received a monthly pension from the French king, who was nicknamed 'The Spider King' for his ability to spin webs of conspiracies between his enemies.[10]

While Jasper led the fight for the Lancastrians, Margaret Beaufort was working in more subtle ways to rescue her son and restore the House of Lancaster. When her husband's nephew, the second duke of Buckingham (also named Henry Stafford), married the new queen's sister, Catherine

Woodville, Margaret saw her opportunity. She worked tirelessly to ingratiate herself with King Edward IV and the Woodville faction. Her efforts finally started paying off in 1466 when King Edward showed his favour by granting them the palatial manor at Woking in Surrey which featured a moat, orchards, gardens, and a deer park.[11] Stafford was invited to attend council meetings and even parliament. King Edward himself showed them a great amount of favour by visiting them at Woking in 1468.

Just as Margaret Beaufort was making inroads into the Yorkist court, her hopes for a Lancastrian resurrection were revived when the earl of Warwick came out in open rebellion against Edward IV in the summer of 1469. Although Warwick had been instrumental in putting Edward on the throne, he had been quickly cast aside in favour of the king's new relatives, the ambitious Woodvilles. And now the infamous 'Kingmaker' was trying to seat another king: Edward's brother, George, Duke of Clarence.

The first military confrontation between Warwick and the king's men happened on 26 July 1469 at the Battle of Edgecote. Present at the battle were William Herbert and his 12-year-old ward, Henry Tudor, who was there to witness his first battle. Herbert fought for King Edward at Edgecote but lost to Warwick's significantly larger army. Herbert was captured and executed. Henry Tudor was suddenly alone and vulnerable. Luckily, a kinsman of Anne Devereaux named Sir Richard Corbet, who was also present at the battle, helped Henry escape unscathed. Richard took Henry to Hereford where he could be reunited with his uncle Jasper.[12]

King Edward had been on the way to join Herbert's army but didn't make it in time for Edgecote. Having learned the news of the Yorkist defeat, Edward's army disintegrated and Warwick took the king into custody. Warwick's plan was to rule through Edward but the earl found that the public was so much against him that he had to let Edward go after just one month.

The second matchup between the former allies unfolded on 12 March 1470 at the Battle of Losecote Field in which Edward was the victor. Due to waning support in England, Warwick and George got on a ship and fled the country. They tried to come ashore at Calais but were turned away, but then they got the support of King Louis XI of France. Not only did Louis put a roof over their heads, as he did for Jasper Tudor the previous year, but he also conspired to build an alliance between Warwick and Margaret of Anjou. The former enemies signed their treaty of alliance at Angers on 30 July 1470 to work towards the restoration of Henry VI as king of England. To reinforce the deal, they agreed to a marriage between Margaret's son, Prince Edward, and Warwick's younger daughter, Anne Neville.

The new allies wasted no time assembling a large invasion fleet of sixty French ships commanded by the admiral of France. The plan was for Warwick and Jasper to sail for England first, then Margaret, Prince Edward, and Anne Neville would sail shortly thereafter. The invasion fleet departed from Normandy on 9 September 1470 and landed in England at Dartmouth and Plymouth four days later. Jasper went to Wales to gather troops and Warwick took the bulk of their French army on a march towards London. King Edward was in northern England at Yorkshire when he heard the news of Warwick's invasion. Realising he could not make it to London before Warwick, and besides he had no army mustered, he boarded a ship and fled to Burgundy on 2 October 1470. Four days later, his former ally Warwick entered the capital city of London with zero opposition.

Warwick's invasion had been a huge success and he now had complete charge of London. He immediately made his way to the Tower of London where he found a rather unkempt King Henry VI. After cleaning him up and fitting him with new clothes, Warwick staged a re-coronation ceremony for Henry at St Paul's Cathedral in London on 13 October 1470 in which Warwick himself carried Henry's train. Warwick may not have been able to rule through Edward but Henry VI was quite a different story. He was happy to hand over the reins to Warwick. Warwick's first move was to have King Henry summon parliament to meet in order to attaint Edward and have him legally declared as a usurper to King Henry VI's crown. Warwick also used this parliament session to designate the line of succession. After Henry VI, Edward's brother George would be the next king, not Henry's son Prince Edward, which would make his daughter Isabel the queen of England someday.

Immediately after the glorious news that Warwick had reinstated Henry VI, Margaret Beaufort made plans to bring her son Henry and his uncle Jasper to London for a family reunion. The three met up in London on 27 October 1470 and went to Westminster for an audience with Henry VI. According to Tudor chronicler Polydore Vergil, King Henry VI was much impressed with 13-year-old Henry Tudor and prophesied that 'This truly, this is he unto whom we and our adversaries must yield and give over the dominion.'[13]

Next, the reunited trio travelled to Margaret's manor in Woking on 28 October 1470 and stayed for an entire week. Then Margaret, her husband Stafford, and Henry Tudor took a week-long journey where they visited Maidenhead, Guildford, and Henley-on-Thames before returning to London and handing Henry back over to Jasper's custody on 11 November 1470.[14] Margaret and Stafford stayed in London to negotiate the return of

Henry Tudor's earldom of Richmond, which was currently held by George. The two parties were close to an agreement when disaster struck for Margaret Beaufort and the Lancastrians.

On 14 March 1471, news reached London that the ousted King Edward IV had landed an invasion force in Ravenspur and was heading straight for London. Warwick was in Coventry when he heard the news and quickly mustered his army to head for London but he didn't make it in time. When Edward and his army made it to London first on 12 April 1471, the city gates were thrown open to him. His first concern was getting possession of Henry VI and locking him back up in the Tower. The very next day, Edward led his army of 9,000 men north out of London to face Warwick's army which was encamped at Barnet. On 14 April 1471, Edward not only beat Warwick's forces at the Battle of Barnet, he captured and executed Warwick himself. Despite Margaret Beaufort's pleas to her husband Henry Stafford to back the Lancastrian army, Stafford fought on Edward's side at Barnet and was fatally wounded. He lingered for six months before expiring on 4 October 1471.

Two days after the victory at Barnet, Edward got word that Queen Margaret had landed her invasion force in Wales and he set off in hot pursuit. He cornered her at Tewkesbury as she was trying to cross into Wales to join up with Jasper Tudor's army. The Battle of Tewksesbury ensued on 4 May 1471 and it was a disastrous loss for the Lancastrians. Prince Edward was killed on the battlefield and Queen Margaret was found hiding in sanctuary and taken prisoner. King Edward made his triumphant re-entry into London on 21 May 1471 and was re-crowned King of England. On the very day he returned to London, Henry VI mysteriously died in the Tower at the hands of King Edward's men. With King Henry VI and his son Prince Edward dead, the Lancastrian cause seemed to be over once again. The last hope was Henry Tudor.

Jasper and Henry Tudor were on their way to join Queen Margaret's army when they got news of their disastrous defeat so they reversed course and headed back to the safety of Pembroke Castle. They were besieged by Yorkists who wanted to put an end to the last two Tudors and thus the Lancastrian cause. Margaret Beaufort wrote to Jasper, warning him not to accept any sort of pardon from Edward as it would likely be a trick. She implored Jasper to take her son Henry out of the dangerous country of England to a place of greater safety.[15] In early September 1471, Jasper heeded Margaret's advice and escaped from Pembroke with young Henry. They travelled to the port town of Tenby and hired a ship to take them to France. They encountered rough weather and were blown off course, finally landing in the small French duchy of Brittany in mid-September 1471. The duke of

Brittany, Francis II, took in the refugees and lodged them at his palace in Vannes called the Château de l'Hermine.

Henry and Jasper would live as refugees in Brittany for the next fourteen years through the generosity of Duke Francis II of Brittany. At first, Francis saw them as important diplomatic weapons in his arsenal against France and England, but over time real affection grew between the men and Francis did his best to protect them. Francis treated him with all the honour due to men of noble blood and they were initially allowed to move about his kingdom freely, but then even that became dangerous.

When King Edward IV found out that the Tudors were in exile in Brittany, he sent English envoys to negotiate their release with the duke of Brittany. Edward's envoys dangled all sorts of carrots in front of Duke Francis, including military, diplomatic and financial support for his little duchy, but turned them all down.

After repeated pressure from both King Edward and King Louis of France, Francis decided to move the Tudors to a more secure location where they would be safer from any attempted abductions by Edward's men. In October 1472, Henry and Jasper were moved to the secluded Château of Suscinio but then a year later they were moved again, this time to Nantes. A year and a half later, in early 1474, the diplomatic pressure was so intense that Francis moved the Tudors yet again. This time he separated the Tudors and replaced all of their English servants with Breton guards. Jasper was taken to the fortress in Josselin and 17-year-old Henry was placed at the Château de Largoët in Elven. There Henry was well treated by the château's owner, Jean IV de Rieux, the marshal of Brittany. Jean had two sons of his own and he welcomed Henry as a member of his family.

But nowhere was safe for the exiled Tudors, not even Brittany. After five years of putting pressure on Francis to turn over Henry Tudor, King Edward finally succeeded in negotiating Henry's release in November 1476.[16] Edward had convinced Francis that no harm would come to Henry if he returned to England. Edward told Francis he would restore Henry's titles and marry him to one of his own daughters if he were to return to England. Duke Francis relented to English demands and agreed to release Henry.

The English envoys took possession of Henry Tudor at Vannes and escorted him to the port of St Malo where they would take a ship home to England. Henry knew this would spell death for him if he got on that ship so he feigned illness to delay their sailing. At about the same time, Duke Francis had second thoughts and sent his treasurer Pierre Landois to St Malo to rescue Henry. While Pierre held the English envoys in deep conversation, Henry slipped away and made it safely into sanctuary at a church in St Malo.[17] When the

English envoys learned of his escape, they went to the church and demanded his release but the townspeople would not let them break the sacred rules of sanctuary. Instead, the English envoys sailed home empty-handed. Henry made his way back to Brittany where Duke Francis apologised profusely and reaffirmed his allegiance to protect the Tudors. Henry and Jasper were reunited at the Chateau L'Hermine in the coastal town of Vannes where they would remain for the rest of their exile in Brittany.

During Henry's harrowing fourteen years of exile in Brittany, his mother Margaret Beaufort still held out hope that she could bring her son back to England safely and restore him to his earldom of Richmond. To do that, she would have to earn the trust of King Edward and his Woodville relatives who ruled the royal court. With her second husband Sir Henry Stafford dead from his wounds at the Battle of Barnet, she looked for a new match which could bring her closer into Edward's inner circle. For her third and final husband, she chose Thomas Stanley who was not only a land magnate in Lancashire but also the steward of the household for King Edward which kept him close to the king at court. Stanley was also related to the Woodvilles through the marriages of his son and his nephew to the queen's kin.

For the entirety of Henry Tudor's exile, his mother Margaret Beaufort worked behind the scenes towards the restoration of her son's earldom. It took years of work before King Edward and Queen Elizabeth began to trust her, but in the mid-1470's she was finally in their favour. Her husband Stanley was honoured to go to France with King Edward in 1475 and negotiated a peace treaty with Louis XI.[18] Then in July 1476, Margaret Beaufort was trusted enough to attend to Queen Elizabeth and her daughters during the extravagant reburial ceremony at Fotheringhay for Edward's father, Richard, Duke of York. She received a huge honour in November 1480 when she was chosen to carry the infant Princess Bridget during her christening.[19]

Obviously, Margaret had won the trust of the king and queen, which put her in a good position to broach the topic of her son's safe return to England. Margaret and her husband Stanley entered negotiations with King Edward and remarkably came to an agreement in the summer of 1482.[20] Edward agreed to grant Henry a large portion of Margaret Beaufort's estates upon her death plus a formal pardon from King Edward, but only on the condition that Henry return to England. A draft document was drawn up by the king which indicates that this was very nearly a done deal.

Margaret was confident she would soon be reunited with her son, but she would be sorely disappointed. All of Margaret's years of hard work to win back Edward's favour so her son could safely return to England suddenly fell apart when Edward unexpectedly died on 9 April 1483.

35

The Rise of Richard III

What peace the kingdom of England was able to enjoy for the past twelve years was now suddenly in danger with sudden, unexpected death of King Edward IV. He died relatively young, aged 40, but no doubt his lascivious lifestyle contributed to the decline in his health and his ultimate downfall.[1] Now Edward IV's eldest son, who was only 12 years old at the time, would take the throne as Edward V. On his deathbed, the king named his brother Richard, Duke of Gloucester, as protectorate for his son Edward's minority reign, but the Woodvilles had other plans.[2] A huge power struggle ensued in which Richard got possession of young King Edward V and thus all the power at court. On 14 May 1483, Richard was named Protector of the Realm until Prince Edward's coming of age.[3]

At first, Richard played the role of the dutiful uncle but soon his plans would turn sinister. Richard cancelled Prince Edward's coronation, which had been scheduled for 22 June 1483. Next, he executed the queen's brother Anthony Woodville and her son Richard Grey for treason.[4] Then his final blow was having Edward IV's and Elizabeth Woodville's children ruled illegitimate. On behalf of Richard, Friar Ralph Shaa put forth the claim that Edward had been pre-contracted in marriage to Lady Eleanor Butler long before he met and married Elizabeth Woodville, thus making the royal marriage invalid.[5] The next legitimate male heir to King Edward IV was conveniently Richard. On 26 June 1483, the Lords and Commons nominated Richard as their next king and he gladly accepted, processing to Westminster Hall and taking his seat on the king's Bench. He was coronated as King Richard III on 6 July 1483.

Now that he was king of England, one of Richard's first priorities was to secure all rivals to his throne, including the now 26-year-old Henry Tudor who was still living in exile in Brittany, France. One of the things that made Henry Tudor so dangerous was that he attracted English exiles to his side, those nobles who were unhappy about Richard's usurpation of the throne. Even Queen Elizabeth's own brother, Sir Edward Woodville, had stolen two ships from the English fleet and made his way to Henry Tudor's court in Brittany.[6]

Very soon after becoming king, Richard set about establishing cordial relations with Brittany. In July 1483, Richard sent one of his clerks to Brittany to negotiate a peace treaty with Duke Francis II. In August 1483, Duke Francis sent his own envoys to England to deliver his terms to Richard. Francis asked Richard for 1,000 archers for the Breton army so it could defend itself against France.[7] No reference to the Tudors was recorded in their negotiations but surely the subject had to have come up.

Peace negotiations with Brittany were put on pause shortly after because Richard had bigger things on his hands to deal with: uprisings were springing up all around his kingdom and he had good reason to believe that his loyal friend, Henry Stafford, Duke of Buckingham, was the instigator. But in fact, there were two factions planning rebellions against Richard: the duke of Buckingham and the Woodvilles. First was the Woodville conspiracy but it didn't go anywhere. They plotted the rescue of the princes in the Tower with King Edward IV's loyal servants who set little fires around London in an effort to distract authorities so they could sneak into the Tower of London. It didn't work.[8]

A much more serious conspiracy was being hatched by Henry Stafford, Duke of Buckingham, a few weeks after the failed Yorkist rising London.[9] Buckingham was one of Richard's closest allies and had been in attendance of Richard throughout his coup and his coronation. On 2 August 1483, Buckingham departed from Richard at Gloucester to return to his estates, specifically Brecon Castle, where John Morton, the bishop of Ely, was being held prisoner for his disloyalty against Richard. It was around this time that wide belief was that the princes in the tower were killed, and this is probably a big reason why Buckingham left Richard and began plotting his own coup.

In 1483, the last Plantagenet men with claims to the throne of England were Richard III, Henry Stafford, and Henry Tudor. Of all these, Buckingham probably had the best claim.[10] Knowing this as a fact fueled his ambitions as he was described by chroniclers as a very high and mighty man. His prisoner, John Morton, the bishop of Ely, fueled his thoughts and encouraged him to rebel against England. Together, the bishop and the duke laid out their plan for rebellion. They would send messages secretly to different pockets around England with the date of 18 October 1483 when everyone should rise together and win back England from Richard.[11]

One of the key players in Buckingham's rebellion would be Margaret Beaufort. The bishop of Ely was a longtime friend of hers and he was thrilled to see Buckingham stepping up to challenge Richard's authority. This would carve a path forward for the Lancastrians, especially Margaret's exiled son, Henry Tudor. The bishop of Ely sent a message to Margaret Beaufort via her servant, Reginald Bray, describing Buckingham's plan for rebellion.[12] Margaret was game and it is at this time that her mind changed from getting her son's earldom restored to ousting Richard and placing Henry Tudor on the throne. Why would Buckingham team up with Margaret Beaufort to put Henry Tudor on the throne when Buckingham himself had a greater claim? Buckingham's thinking may have been this: if Richard III could be ousted before Henry Tudor sailed to England, Buckingham could claim the throne himself since he was the candidate with the most royal blood.[13]

Margaret sent urgent messengers to her son in Brittany to tell him of the rebellion that was afoot. She sent him a large amount of money to raise a ships and troops so he too could participate in the rebellion.[14] Even with his mother's money, Henry needed much more to mount such a large invasion force. Henry begged his long-time benefactor, Duke Francis, for a loan to fund his venture and Francis gladly agreed. Then Henry hurriedly set about preparations with only about six weeks before Buckingham's 18 October resurrection date. With Francis' help, Henry managed to muster fifteen ships and 5,000 soldiers for his leg of the invasion.[15]

Margaret then set about securing a marriage for her son. In order for Henry to be a serious candidate for king, he would need to marry a princess with a lot of royal blood and preferably from the Yorkist family. By marrying a Yorkist, Margaret felt that it would unite the Houses of Lancaster and York, ending nearly thirty years of the civil war known as the Wars of the Roses. Through her physician, Lewis Caerleon, Margaret sent messages to Elizabeth Woodville in sanctuary inviting her into the rebellion and asking her permission for Henry and Elizabeth of York to wed. Elizabeth Woodville not only consented to the plan, she recruited her family and former servants to participate as well.[16]

Surprisingly, Richard was unaware of all the plotting and planning going on behind his back for the last two months. It wasn't until late September 1483 when he started to hear rumours of a rebellion in the works, and when he called his friend Buckingham to account for his recent activity, the duke feigned illness, not once, but twice.[17] Instead, Buckingham stayed on his estates in Wales and continued to assemble his army. Finally, it became clear to Richard that Buckingham was plotting against him when part of the rebels he recruited for his rebellion rose a whole week early in Kent. Richard's suspicions were confirmed and he rapidly raised his only army to confront Buckingham.

When the planned rebellion date of 18 October rolled around, the smaller groups of rebels spread among the kingdom rose simultaneously in an effort to pull King Richard in different directions, but the king was singularly focused on capturing Buckingham. When Richard left Lincoln with his army, he headed directly for Wales to confront his old friend Buckingham. Meanwhile, Buckingham was having a terrible time raising men for his army. It seems he wasn't exactly well-liked or respected by his tenants because many refused to answer his call to arms. As soon as he left Wales with the men he could manage to muster, his tenants went so far as to destroy some of his estates, including the vital bridges across the Severn. Add to that terrible storms and torrential rains that flooded the roads, hampering his progress, Buckingham's venture was doomed.[18]

With Richard's army getting ever closer to Wales, Buckingham decided his best course of action was to flee. He deserted his army and hid in a former servant's home in Woebley, Herefordshire. Even his servant didn't like him enough to save him. The servant turned in Buckingham to Richard for a modest reward.[19] Buckingham was hauled before Richard at Salisbury on 31 October 1483 and executed on 2 November 1483.

On the very day of Buckingham's execution, Henry Tudor's belated invasion party turned up off the coast of England near Dorset. It seems the weather had prevented his sailing any earlier, but his arrival now would be a total waste of time and put him in great danger. He sailed the coast east to Plymouth and sent a small party ashore to assess the situation. Richard's soldiers were waiting and disguised themselves as friends then went on to tell Henry that Buckingham had won and Richard III had been defeated. Henry was either suspicious of the ploy or he was informed by another party of the real state of events.[20] He and set sail back to Brittany.

The fallout from Buckingham's failed rebellion was monumental and hugely consequential for both sides. Richard's paranoia grew at the realisation of all the traitors he had against him, many of those rebels now fleeing his kingdom for Henry Tudor's court in Brittany. Even the powerful Woodvilles were fighting for Henry Tudor's cause, which shouldn't have been much of a surprise since he murdered the two princes and stole the throne. Margaret Beaufort was lucky to escape Buckingham's rebellion with her life, for if she were a man, she probably would have been attainted and given a traitor's death. Instead, her entire estates and properties were given to her husband and she was placed on virtual house arrest.[21] This is the one time in her life that her gender would actually work in her favour, not against her.

The result of Buckingham's rebellion was very favourable to Henry Tudor as English exiles flocked to him in Brittany throughout the fall and winter of 1483.[22] He didn't receive any backlash for his failed invasion attempt, in fact, he became even more popular. Now that Henry was the last male Lancastrian heir in line to the throne and King Richard was so hated by his nobles and the people of England, Henry became the natural choice for the dissidents. He was sort of in the right place at the right time. Plus, he was a magnetic character and was able to charm his new friends easily. He was said to have a very pleasant personality and a positive, cheerful attitude.[23] Apparently, it was not difficult to be drawn into a friendship with this young, jovial man.

Because of the mass defection of English exiles, Henry's following grew to about 300 people, all of whom were living at Duke Francis' expense in Vannes.[24] The exiles had left England with only the possessions they could carry on their backs. Shortly after Buckingham's rebellion, King Richard attainted them and confiscated their estates, so they were virtually penniless. Henry felt a profound sense of obligation to these people who risked all they had to join him and fight for his cause. This is when there became a shift in Henry's manner where he started taking more personal responsibility for his little Breton court and even started presenting himself in a more kingly manner. For example, Henry would lead Mass at Vannes Cathedral, closely accompanied by the leading exiled nobles, most notably Queen Elizabeth Woodville's son Thomas Grey, Marquess of Dorset.[25]

In order to keep all the positive momentum going in Brittany, Henry hosted magnificent Christmastide celebrations at Rennes for his followers. It wasn't all celebrations though as Henry also took the opportunity to meet with his nobles to work up their masterplan to conquer England. Then on Christmas Day 1483, Henry solemnly swore an oath to marry King Edward IV's eldest daughter and Dorset's half-sister, Elizabeth of York, if he were to become king of England.[26]

When news reached King Richard III of Henry Tudor's pledge to marry the York princess, he was deeply troubled, so he formulated a plan. If Richard could gain possession of Elizabeth of York and all the York princesses, Henry Tudor would not be able to marry her which would ruin his plan to unite the Houses of York and Lancaster. There was only one problem with Richard's plan: the dowager queen Elizabeth Woodville and her children were still hiding in sanctuary at Westminster Abbey. They'd been there ever since Richard's coup in the summer of 1483 and clearly they were too terrified of Richard to come out on their own. So, in March 1484, Richard flexed his muscle to convince them it was in their best interests to leave sanctuary and enter unto his protection. With little other choice, Elizabeth Woodville finally gave in to Richard's demands.[27]

Now that he had possession of Elizabeth of York, things looked up for Richard. He would be able to deny Henry Tudor the one thing he needed to legitimise his seizure of the crown with the joining of Lancaster and York.

Things were really coming together for Richard but then suddenly they fell apart again when on 9 April 1484, his only legitimate son, Prince Edward of Middleham, died after a short illness.[28] Now Richard was without an heir which gave even more credence to Henry Tudor's claim. It was at this point when Richard stepped up his attempts to get possession of Henry and he very nearly succeeded.

In the summer of 1484, Richard sent a series of envoys to Brittany to negotiate peace between the two nations and secure the handover of Henry Tudor. The Tudor's biggest ally, Duke Francis, was very ill at the time and so his treasurer, Pierre Landois, conducted the negotiations. Unbeknownst to Francis, Pierre signed an agreement with Richard and secretly agreed to turn over possession of Henry Tudor to the king. Luckily for Henry, his friend Bishop Morton heard about the secret agreement through the grapevine and sent an urgent messenger to Henry begging him to flee Brittany. In early September 1484, Henry and a small retinue rode leisurely out of Vannes with the purpose of visiting friends at a nearby manor, but it was a ploy. Once Henry was a few kilometres out of the city, he ducked into the woods, changed into servant's clothing, and rode as fast as he could to Anjou where Francis was residing. He made it to the French border in the nick of time as Landois' guards were only an hour or two behind him.[29]

When Duke Francis' health recovered, he found out what had happened and was outraged at the treatment of Henry and the English exiles. Francis was very apologetic to Henry and agreed to pay for the entirety of Henry's court to move to Anjou. Shortly thereafter, Duke Francis paid to move Henry's court again, this time to Paris, where Henry would cultivate support from the new king of France, Charles VIII. Charles agreed to lodge Henry's 400 followers at Sens, just south of Paris, and would later help fund Henry Tudor's invasion force in the fall of 1485.[30]

King Richard was enraged when he heard Henry Tudor had been received honourably in Charles VIII's court in Paris. On 7 December 1484, Richard issued his first proclamation against Henry Tudor and his rebel exiles in France. In it, he ordered his English subjects to take up arms against the treacherous rebels who would come to England and commit 'the most cruel murders, slaughters, robberies and disinheritances that were ever seen in any Christian Realm'.[31]

Richard was further troubled in the winter of 1484/1485 at the escape of loyal Lancastrian John de Vere, Earl of Oxford, who had been locked up in Hammes Castle in Calais by Edward IV in 1475. Oxford, as well as the two English officers who were supposed to be looking after him, escaped from the castle and fled to France to join Henry Tudor. Richard sent his men to secure Hammes Castle from the newfound rebels, but the castle contingent held out until Oxford and some of Henry's followers made a daring rescue attempt and helped the rebels hold the castle against Richard's men.[32] Due to the defection of Oxford to Henry's court and the show of Richard's weakness in Calais, even more English exiles flocked to Henry in the spring of 1485.

Everything was going Henry's way. Things were not going so well for Richard though. Not only did he have the embarrassment of Calais and the Tudor rebel who he could not seem to rid himself of, his wife Anne died on 16 March 1485 after a long illness. The rumours that Richard intended to marry his niece, Elizabeth of York – a step too far for nearly everyone – immediately spread. In another humiliating defeat, Richard had to make a public proclamation denying his intention to marry Elizabeth of York.[33] Is it possible that Richard really did plan to marry his niece? There is no way of knowing but perhaps even he understood that they were too closely related to get a dispensation for their marriage. Either way, the damage was done, and it was yet another unsavory aspect of Richard's character that he would marry his own niece, who he himself had declared a bastard when he declared her parents' marriage invalid.

Henry was greatly disturbed by the rumours of Richard's intention to marry his own betrothed wife, Elizabeth of York, saying it 'pinched him by the very stomach'.[34] Henry feared if Richard married Princess Elizabeth, his Yorkists followers would desert him, so he set out in earnest in the spring of 1485 to ready himself for a military confrontation with King Richard III.[35] Henry spent much of the spring raising money to fund his operation. Most of his financial support came from Charles VIII who gave Henry the huge some 40,000 livres, which equates to millions of pounds today. Henry began mustering his forces in the summer of 1485 at Harfleur, just west of Rouen in Normandy.[36]

The news of Henry's muster reached England in mid-June 1485. Richard responded by issuing commissions of array to raise men for his army and to set up beacons along the southern coast to watch for Henry's fleet around the clock. Richard then issued his second proclamation against Henry Tudor and the rebels.[37] Richard was especially brutal in this proclamation, claiming both Henry and Jasper were from bastard blood and that they would overturn all the laws in the kingdom and seize everyone's property if they were to gain a foothold in England. Those who say the Tudors invented propaganda were wrong. Richard III invented propaganda. The Tudors would later use it to blacken Richard's reputation and legacy.

By late July 1485, Henry had completed his muster at Harfleur and felt sufficiently prepared to put the whole operation in motion. All in all, Henry had amassed 4,000 soldiers, mostly French mercenaries and Scottish soldiers. He was also accompanied by approximately 400 English exiles from his Breton court.[38] He moved his large party down to the port of Harfleur where they set sail on 1 August 1485. The time for the life or death showdown had finally come. It was time for Henry Tudor to face his destiny and return to the homeland where he had fled for his life fourteen years prior.

36

Henry Tudor's Invasion

The shortest route for Henry Tudor's invasion fleet would have been to land off the southeast coast of England near Kent, which is exactly what Richard expected. Instead, Henry took a much longer route, sailing west through the English channel around the southeast tip of England, then turning north for Wales. Even though he had 4,000 men in his army, it wasn't nearly enough to face the royal army.[1] His only chance was to pick up more men, mostly Welshmen, for his army. He was counting on Jasper's popularity and his own Welsh roots to reinforce his troops.

Just before sunset on 7 August 1485, Henry Tudor's troops came ashore on the Pembrokeshire peninsula of Wales near the village of Milford Haven. When Henry's feet touched Welsh soil for the first time in fourteen years, he fell to the ground, kissed the sand, and said aloud 'Judge me, O Lord, and plead my cause.'[2] Then Henry rallied his men and set off on their march through Wales in the name of the lord and Saint George, the patron saint of England.

The first mission of the Tudor army was to get control of Dale Castle, twenty-four kilometres to the west, which Henry believed was being held in Richard's name. Henry was pleasantly surprised when the inhabitants handed over the castle to him without a fight. His army spent their first night in Wales at Dale Castle, then headed out early the next morning for the town of Haverfordwest, twenty kilometres to the northeast.[3]

For the next two weeks, Henry and his rebel army trudged north through Wales, hugging the coastline to the west and the Cambrian Mountains to the east. Following the west Wales coastline certainly wasn't the most direct route to get to Richard at Nottingham or to even make a run on London. But Wales was a dangerous place for many reasons. Richard had strong support in southeast Wales so Henry had to avoid that region entirely. Instead, he plotted his march so that it would pass through north Wales where Sir William Stanley held land and northwest England where Lord Stanley held all the power. Henry needed the Stanleys desperately. Without them and their huge armies, Henry would have been doomed. Henry wrote to his mother and both Stanley brothers on 2 August from Aberystwyth in which he told them the route he had decided on to infiltrate England.[4]

On 4 August, Henry Tudor and his rebel army reached Machynlleth, a small town that held special importance for the Welsh people as it was there in 1404 that Owain Glyndŵr was crowned as Prince of Wales.[5] Machynlleth called itself the 'ancient capital of Wales' and the significance was not lost on Henry Tudor. The Welsh were a superstitious people who yearned for freedom to rule themselves instead of their English overlords. For hundreds of years, Welsh prophets foretold the coming of 'Y Mab Darogan', a Welshman who would free Wales from English oppression.[6] Over the previous millennium, many Welshmen had been prophesied as Y Mab Darogan, including Owain Glyndŵr, but they were still waiting for the one to arrive. In Henry Tudor they saw an English noble with Welsh blood, a man bold enough to challenge the sitting king of England. The Welsh had hope that at last the mab darogan had arrived and they threw their support behind him. Henry was hugely relieved when Rhys ap Thomas agreed to join him, bringing about 2,000 men to Henry's army.[7]

In the past seven days, Henry and his army had travelled around 150 kilometres north through Wales and now as they faced the Snowdon mountain range at Machynlleth, they turned due east and began their approach to England. It took Henry's army a three-day march over rough terrain to travel the eighty kilometres from Machynlleth to Shrewsbury which he expected to be friendly to his cause. However, when Henry and his army arrived at Shrewsbury on 17 August 1485, the portcullis was brought down and they were denied entry to the city. This was the first resistance Henry had encountered in the ten days he had been back on the island of Britain. It was only when Sir William Stanley sent the town bailiff an urgent message to admit Henry Tudor that the portcullis was opened and Henry's troops were allowed to pass through the city.[8] Later that day, Sir William Stanley himself arrived in Shrewsbury to treat with Henry. This was their first ever face-to-face meeting and no doubt they measured each other up.[9]

After leaving Shrewsbury, the rebel army continued east into England, gathering more and more supporters with every passing day. To add to the numbers of Welshmen he had picked up on the first part of his march, now Henry was picking up discontented Englishmen who either had connections to the Stanley family or else remained loyal to Edward IV. At Stafford on 19 August, Henry received a further 1,300 armed men for his army courtesy of Sir Gilbert Talbot, son of the earl of Shrewsbury, and Sir Richard Corbet.[10]

20 August 1485 was a momentous day in the lead up to the Battle of Bosworth. On this day, Henry and his enlarged army entered the city Lichfield and was openly received by its people which was a very encouraging sign. Soon after arriving, Henry was visited for a second time by Sir William

Stanley so they could seal their final plans. William informed Henry that Richard was only one to two days' march away at Nottingham and Henry should get going soon before Richard blocked his path to London. Henry heeded Sir William's advice. That day he mobilised his troops and had them marching past nightfall. Henry and his closest advisers were riding at the very back of the army so they could discreetly discuss their plans. At some point Henry's and his entourage became separated from the main Tudor host and spent a frightening night lost in the countryside. It wasn't until the next morning that Henry found his army camped near Tamworth and rejoined the host.[11]

Henry wasn't the only one who had a busy day on 20 August for that is the day Richard finally chose to react to Henry Tudor's invasion. At first it seems Richard didn't take the threat of Henry Tudor very seriously. It was on 11 August that Richard learned of Henry's landing, yet he didn't activate his army until 20 August.[12] Why did he delay? His scouts had reported Henry's army to be rather modest and perhaps Richard believed that his Welsh allies and the Stanleys would put down Henry and his rebels, which was quite naïve. Richard severely underestimated Henry's ability to gain Welsh supporters and he overestimated the loyalty of his own men, specifically the Stanleys. It wasn't until 19 August that the true picture of deceit was painted by Lord Strange's confession.[13] Lord Strange was the son of Lord Stanley and was being held ransom by Richard for his father's good behaviour. Lord Strange attempted to escape from Richard at Nottingham but was captured. Upon interrogation, Lord Strange confessed that his uncle Sir William Stanley was working in concert with Henry Tudor but insisted that his father, Lord Stanley, husband of Margaret Beaufort, was entirely loyal to Richard. Richard naively believed him.

After the shock of Lord Strange's confession on 19 August and the news that Henry Tudor had passed through Shrewsbury untouched, Richard finally decided to take the threat seriously. His supposed allies had not stopped Henry's progress as he had planned, and now the loyalty of all his allies were in doubt. Richard decided to take matters into his own hands. His scouts reported Henry's location in Lichfield and that Henry was on the road east towards London. Richard scrambled together his army at Nottingham and rode forty kilometres south to Leicester, east of Lichfield, to block Henry's path.

On 21 August 1485, the day before the most important battle of their lives, Henry and Richard were busily preparing their men for the showdown. At Leicester, Richard donned his crown and led his troops in procession to Atherstone with great fanfare. He selected a high ridge in proximity of Ambion Hill for his army to camp for the night.[14] Meanwhile, Henry had one final meeting with the Stanleys to firm up their battle plans. To Henry's great disappointment, the Stanleys insisted on keeping their private armies separate from Henry's main army. Instead, Lord Stanley sent Henry four of his best knights to join Henry's host.[15] This was hardly the support Henry expected but if Lord Stanley was to help Henry, he would have to make Richard think he was loyal up until the very last moment. With time running out, Henry ordered his army to camp that night near Atherstone, just a few kilometres west of Richard's camp.

Early on 22 August 1485, King Richard awoke in a foul mood. He reported to his men that he had been disturbed all night with terrible dreams and had not had much sleep. When he tried to get breakfast, his camp was so unorganised that he could not find a cook, nor could he find a chaplain which vexed him greatly.[16] Richard still had the advantage though. Estimates put his army at nearly double that of Henry Tudor's which numbered around 5,000.[17] However, Henry did have some very experienced military leaders on his side, including his uncle Jasper Tudor, John de Vere, Earl of Oxford, Sir Edward Woodville, and Margaret Beaufort's half-brother, Lord Welles. When it was time for the battle to commence, Henry Tudor rode up and down the front line of his army, firing them up for the bloody clash that was about to unfold. Richard likewise gave his troops a similar pep talk, all while wearing his treasured crown of England.

The Battle of Bosworth is very poorly documented, but historians do agree on at least a few aspects. As the two armies lined up across from each other on the battlefield, the action most likely commenced with a brief round of archers and cannons. Then the two vanguards of Henry's and Richard's armies simultaneously moved towards each other. Richard had the better position high on the ridge. Henry's vanguard, led by the earl of Oxford, found itself in a poor position near a marshy area at the bottom of Ambion hill. Oxford quickly swung his line around the bog and met with Richard's army with violent hand-to-hand combat using axes, sword, and pikes.

While the melee was going on, Richard's scouts came to him and reported Henry Tudor's location. It turns out Henry was largely unprotected on the battlefield, only surrounded by a small group of bodyguards. Richard saw this as a golden opportunity to take Henry out. Richard gathered some of his horsemen and charged towards Henry's small group, smashing into them with full force. Richard mercilessly hacked his way through the outer circle of Henry's bodyguards, killing many in his path, including Henry's standard bearer, Sir William Brandon.[18] As he neared closer to Henry, it looked like all hope was lost for the would-be Tudor king. Unless someone came to his rescue, it would only be a matter of minutes before Richard would reach him and cut him down.

That's precisely when the Stanleys decided it was time to join the battle. While Henry and Richard had lined up their men before the battle, the Stanleys stationed their armies about a kilometre away from the battlefield, just near enough to watch the action unfold. It was only when they saw Richard about to overtake Henry that they committed to the battle. Sir William Stanley's army of 3,000 soldiers swooped down onto the battlefield where Richard and Henry were about the come to blows.[19] Richard and his worn-out men were no match for Stanley's fresh soldiers. When they rushed the battlefield, Richard's army scattered in confusion and fear as the Stanleys were supposed to be fighting for the king, not against him. Despite the odds suddenly turning against him, Richard fought on bravely, even refusing a horse to flee to battlefield. He was determined to put an end to Henry Tudor or die trying. And die he did. Richard was quickly overwhelmed by the surge of Stanley's soldiers. Around this time his battle helmet came off, either accidentally or on purpose, and he was killed by several blows to the head.[20]

With Richard now dead, the remainder of his soldiers fled the battlefield and the Tudors proclaimed themselves victorious. The old story goes that Richard's crown was found under a hawthorn bush and brought to Lord Stanley who ceremoniously placed it atop Henry's head. Henry then thanked god and his men for their victory to which they replied 'God save King Henry!' Henry ordered that the wounded be tended to and the dead buried.[21]

The following day, Henry and his victorious party made their way to Leicester where Henry was received as the new king of England with great pomp and circumstance. With him was brought the bruised and battered body of Richard III, his naked corpse slung over the back of a horse. A great amount of abuse was heaped upon his corpse on the journey to Leicester, including dagger stabs to the buttocks so deep that it cracked his pelvis.[22] Richard was unceremoniously buried at church of the Greyfriars or Franciscan Friary in Leicester.

Henry Tudor's party left Leicester and slowly made their way towards London. Along the way, Henry's mother Margaret Beaufort, now released from her house arrest, met up with them and accompanied them to London.[23] This was the first time she had seen her son in fourteen years. It must have been a glorious reunion filled with relief and thanksgiving.

There has been much debate over the years about the Stanley brothers' intentions. Most historians believe that Lord Stanley was on the fence as to whether to support Henry or Richard but I find this very hard to believe.

First of all, Lord Stanley was married to Henry Tudor's own mother who was her son's biggest champion and was determined to see him sit on the throne of England. I think his plan all along was to help Henry, but in order to do so, Lord Stanley would have to stay outwardly loyal to Richard. If Richard found out that Lord Stanley was plotting against him, he would have undoubtedly arrested and beheaded him. That would have left Henry without a champion in England and he desperately needed Lord Stanley for the success of his venture. Lord Stanley was in a very difficult position. To support Henry, he would probably have to sacrifice his son, Lord Strange. So he did his best to try and get both positive outcomes and he actually succeeded. He helped his stepson Henry win the crown of England and kept his son Lord Strange alive. Apparently, Richard ordered the execution of Lord Strange during the Battle of Bosworth but became understandably distracted and did not see that it was carried out.[24]

37

Lambert Simnel and Perkin Warbeck

On Sunday, 30 October 1485, at Westminster Abbey in London, Henry Tudor was officially coronated as King Henry VII of England. In the two months since his victory at Bosworth, Henry, along with his mother Margaret Beaufort, planned a magnificent coronation that would outshine Richard III's own dazzling ceremony. It was the first step in dynasty building: establishing the magnificence of the king and there was no better way to do that than to spend a lot of money.

After all, this was the first time that most Londoners had ever seen Henry Tudor in person. He had to make sure he was bigger than life and thus dressed himself extravagantly in rich purple velvet, cloth of gold, and ermine trimmed robes. Westminster was decorated in nearly 13 metres of expensive scarlet cloth and even Henry's processional horses were adorned with cloth of gold, a fabric which only the truly rich could afford. In the coronation procession, Henry rode in a canopy covered in gold and silk.[1]

On his coronation procession from the Tower of London to Westminster, Henry was accompanied by those who had fought next to him at the Battle of Bosworth. His uncle Jasper Tudor was given the great honour of riding directly behind Henry during the procession and holding the crown during the anointing ceremony.[2] After the coronation ceremony, the huge royal party celebrated at a sumptuous banquet which was usually followed by a couple of weeks of jousting and further celebrations. But the revelry was temporarily delayed so Henry could get started on the business of running the country and laying down the roots of the most infamous dynasty in English history, the Tudors.

Immediately after his victory at Bosworth, Henry Tudor's first thought was on security, both for himself and for his fiancé, Elizabeth of York. For his own security, Henry created a group of bodyguards in the French tradition called the Yeomen of the Guard. This was a group of about 200 soldiers who accompanied his every move, guarding doors and even tasting the king's food in case it had been poisoned.[3] Henry had sent Elizabeth to the fortress castle of Sheriff Hutton for her own safety during his invasion and now that Richard was defeated, Henry sent his trusted friend Sir Robert

Willoughby to fetch Elizabeth and bring her down to London. Elizabeth was to live at Margaret Beaufort's newly granted mansion in London called Coldharbour under her mother-in-law's ever watchful eye. This was the location that the betrothed couple first met in person and it was private enough for the two to get to know each other before taking their marriage vows on 28 January 1486. Some say they may have gotten to know each other a little too well at Coldharbour since Elizabeth gave birth to their first child only eight months after their wedding.[4] It is possible that their son Arthur was born prematurely but it is also very possible that Henry and Elizabeth consummated their relationship before the wedding.

Now that the appropriate measures had been taken to preserve the safety of himself and his future queen, it was time to dole out rewards for the men who had endured the Breton exile and fought with him at Bosworth. His uncle Jasper was created Duke of Bedford and was restored to his Welsh earldom of Pembroke. Henry awarded his father-in-law, Lord Stanley, the earldom of Derby. The greatest reward of all went to his mother Margaret Beaufort. Not only was she granted luxurious palaces and manors by her son, she was also given the very unique legal title of 'femme sole' which meant she could govern her own properties and land holdings independently of her husband.[5] It was around this time that Margaret got the title she always wanted most: 'the king's mother'. Now that she achieved her goal of putting her son on the throne, she was not one to be content and step out of the limelight. If she had been a man, it was very possible that she would be the one sitting on the throne, a point that was not lost on her. She resolved to exert her royal authority through her son and she was a near constant presence at his court.[6]

Henry tapped his most trusted councillors and brothers in exile to head the top positions in his new government. John Morton, Bishop of Ely, was named chancellor, the highest position in Henry's government. Sir William Stanley who had been so instrumental in Henry's victory at Bosworth was named as one of the chamberlains of the Exchequer to oversee the royal treasury. Henry also looked to his circle of friends to maintain the peace throughout his kingdom: his uncle Jasper in Wales, the Stanleys in northwest England, the earl of Oxford in Essex and East Anglia, and finally the earl of Northumberland in Richard's old stronghold of northern England. Henry also trusted in his friends to help teach him how to be king, how to structure his government, and most importantly, how to deal with rebel threats.[7] It wouldn't be long until he had to put that particular lesson to the test.

When any new king came to the throne, one of the first required courses of legal action was to summon parliament to confirm the ascension of the new king. King Henry's first parliament met on 7 November 1485 and they had a lot of work ahead of them. The first order of business was to make Henry's seizure of the throne legal. The petition was put forth by the Commons to proclaim Henry the rightful King of England by God's divine will and Henry's victory in battle, making him and the heirs of his body the legal inheritors of the kingdom of England.[8]

Several other acts were passed and reversed during Henry's first parliament. An Act of Attainder was passed against Richard III and twenty-eight of his leading adherents, declaring them traitors to the crown and stripping those who survived Bosworth of their lands and titles. In the Act, Richard was accused of 'unnatural, mischievous, and great perjuries, treasons, homicides, and murders in shedding of infants' blood' which certainly refers to the disappearance of the princes in the Tower.[9]

All of the acts of attainder Richard III had issued against Henry Tudor and his adherents were reversed. Also reversed was Richard III's *Titulus Regius* which had illegitimised the children of Edward IV and Elizabeth Woodville, thus making Elizabeth of York once again the heir of the House of York. Henry also took care to re-enact the 1397 legislation declaring the Beauforts legitimate heirs of John of Gaunt and the House of Lancaster.[10] The latter two actions were meant to strengthen Henry's claim to the throne, especially emphasising the Beaufort legitimacy since the Yorkists believed royal claims could be passed through a female to her son.

Henry weaved together his three claims to the throne, Beaufort, York, and Wales, in the use of his heraldic badges worn on the clothing of his servants and displayed on his banners. To represent his Beaufort heritage, he included a portcullis on his royal badge and a Dun Cow on his royal standards. For his Welsh ancestry he flew the flag of the red dragon in honour of his Welsh ancestry. To represent the new union of the rival houses was the newly devised Tudor rose, a combination of the white rose of York and red rose of Lancaster. Henry used the Tudor rose throughout his vast kingdom to promote his new joined kingdom.

Henry's first parliamentary session was concluded in March 1486, at which time Henry and his new bride departed on a royal progress. It was important for Henry to show himself throughout his new kingdom to establish not only his majesty but his authority. This was especially important in northern England where Richard had held such a strong grip over the region and where there were loyalists who might try to rise against Henry. The king and queen spent March of 1486 slowly traversing north through England, stopping at cities along the way to be received under great pomp and circumstance.[11] They would participate in public banquets, attend Mass with the locals, and work to address the needs of the poor.

Upon arriving at Nottingham in the Midlands on 11 April 1486, Henry was told of an organised uprising against him in the north at Yorkshire, led by Viscount Lovell and Sir Humphrey Stafford. These two men were the leading supporters of Richard and had been hiding in sanctuary ever since losing at the Battle of Bosworth. Now they had slipped out of sanctuary and were ready to make a move to oust the new king. Lord Lovell was tasked with attacking York while Stafford would simultaneously lead an attack in Worcester.[12] King Henry reacted swiftly by summoning his nearby nobles to raise men and ride out against the rebels in all haste. The first to arrive on the scene was Henry's loyal uncle, Jasper, who had raised as many as 3,000 men to confront Lovell's rebel army.[13] As soon as Lovell heard Jasper was near with a huge force, he deserted his army and fled into hiding. Stafford was not so lucky. Upon hearing of Lovell's desertion, Stafford fled to a nearby abbey and claimed sanctuary, but was dragged out by Henry's men and executed at Tyburn on 8 July 1486.

After the Yorkshire rising had been handily put down by Henry and his nobles, the royal couple finished their progress north, culminating in their arrival at York on 20 April 1486. By early June, they were back in London so Henry could attend to the business of ruling a kingdom and planning for the arrival of his first child, which he hoped was a son and heir. Henry and his mother Margaret went to great efforts to carefully plan out the arrival of the new Tudor heir. Henry carefully selected Winchester as the place where his wife, the queen, would go into confinement and give birth.[14] Not only was Winchester the ancient capital in Anglo-Saxon time, it was also the supposed location of Camelot and King Arthur. By choosing Winchester as the birthplace, he aimed to tie together the legend of King Arthur to his newborn heir. For her part, Margaret literally wrote a book on how royal children should be born and raised. Margaret's *Ordinances* defined protocols for the queen's confinement, the christening, and the churching, the ritual that celebrated the queen's return to court life after recovering from childbirth.[15]

On the evening of 19 September 1486, Elizabeth of York gave birth to the first royal Tudor, a son and heir, whom they named Arthur after the legendary king. There was much rejoicing throughout the city of Winchester as church bells rang out to announce the safe delivery of the prince. Elizabeth would go on to produce seven more children for King Henry, only three of which survived into adulthood: Margaret, born 28 November 1489, Henry (future Henry VIII) born 28 June 1491, and Mary, born 18 March 1496.

The first year of Henry's reign was a huge success. He had easily put down the sole rebellion and he already had a male heir to inherit his kingdom and continue the dynasty he had founded. By November 1486, rumours began circulating through England that another rebellion was afoot.[16] By the spring of 1487, the conspiracy plans were laid clear: the new group of rebels aimed to put forth the young earl of Warwick as the true king of England.

Eleven-year-old Edward, Earl of Warwick, was the last living Yorkist male. His father was George, Duke of Clarence, the brother of Edward IV and Richard III. When Richard III died without a living legitimate son, Warwick was widely considered his heir being the last living male with royal Plantagenet blood. Because of the strength of his claim, Henry knew Warwick would be the focus of a Yorkist uprising, therefore, he imprisoned him in the Tower of London shortly after his victory at Bosworth.

In the spring of 1487, a meddling English priest recruited a boy of Warwick's age and appearance to impersonate him. The priest groomed the young boy in the ways of royalty so he could convincingly play the part, and that he did.[17] The priest took his protégé, whose real name was Lambert Simnel, to Ireland to find supporters. The Irish were loyal Yorkists and were all too happy to welcome a Yorkist claimant to the throne. Simnel was welcomed to court as the earl of Warwick and promptly declared true king of England. Support in Ireland alone would not be enough to make a serious run against King Henry so messengers were sent to Yorkists sympathisers in England as well as the duchy of Burgundy, home of Warwick's aunt, Duchess Margaret, who hated Henry and was more than happy to give her support.

In late March or early April 1487, Simnel and his supporters sailed to Burgundy where Margaret welcomed him to court as her true nephew. She had probably never seen him in her life and therefore couldn't attest to his identity but nevertheless decided to take his word for it. She supplied to Simnel 2,000 highly skilled German mercenaries to fight in his army.[18] Her city of Flanders became the mustering point for Yorkist defectors, including a new, powerful member: John de la Pole, Earl of Lincoln. After the earl of Warwick, Lincoln was the leading Yorkist male in the kingdom of England and was considered by some a better choice of heir for Richard III. After the Battle of Bosworth, Henry had wisely pardoned de la Pole and brought him into his court where he was treated with favour. Apparently, he couldn't stomach the Tudors taking the throne from a Yorkist contender and turned his back on Henry, thus becoming one of the leaders of the 1487 rebellion.[19]

When the news of the rebels' muster reached Henry, he took quick and decisive action. By 7 April 1487, he had beacons watching the shorelines of England, ready to signal at a moment's notice if an invasion fleet was spotted.[20] In what should have put the entire plot to bed, Henry then had the real earl of Warwick taken out of the Tower and paraded through the streets of London to prove that the boy being put forth by the Yorkists was truly an imposter.[21] It wasn't enough to extinguish the flames of rebellion, however.

On 4 June 1487, Lambert Simnel and his fleet landed in Lancashire in northwest England where they joined up with thousands of Irish soldiers and rapidly made their way south, picking up loyal Yorkists along the way to join their rebel army.[22] They arrived in York on 12 June and attempted to sack the city, but their forces were repelled by the army of the earl of Northumberland. Unbeknownst to them, King Henry himself was less than 100 kilometres away with his own army, waiting to block Simnel's path to London. On the evening of 15 June, the king moved his army to Newark where they set up camp and awaited the arrival of the rebel army. Early the next morning, Henry's spies informed him that Simnel's army was nearing the village of Stoke, less than ten kilometres away. The final battle of the Wars of the Roses, the Battle of Stoke, was about to commence.

As the two armies lined up into battle position on 16 June 1487, it was clear that Simnel's army of 8,000 was outnumbered, perhaps as much as two to one.[23] Nevertheless, Simnel chose to fight. The earl of Oxford led the king's vanguard as they crashed into enemy lines. Fierce fighting ensued for at least three hours, the rebels being buoyed by the German and the savage Irishmen but were eventually overcome by the king's artillery. The victors rushed the field and cut down every rebel they could find, including John de la Pole, Earl of Lincoln. Simnel and his mentor-priest were captured and taken to Lincoln to be interrogated by Henry. The king was merciful to both men. The priest was confined to a trusted bishop's residence while Simnel was employed in the royal kitchen as a turnspit.[24] Recognising that this young boy had merely been a puppet, Henry took pity on him.

Henry did not, however, have pity for the grown men who had participated in the Yorkist uprising. He called parliament in November 1487 to dole out punishments, passing an Act of Attainder against twenty-eight of the rebel leaders, stripping them of their lands, titles, and goods.[25] Henry also took the opportunity to request money from parliament for the overall defence of the realm. At this point, there was no further hints of a Yorkist rebellion but there was plenty of trouble with France.

While Henry worked to contain uprisings in his own kingdom, his old friend Duke Francis of Brittany was dealing with threats from King Charles VIII of France. The duchy of Brittany was an independently ruled province separate from the kingdom of France and for many years, French kings had sought to consolidate the entire territory of France into one kingdom, Brittany being a prime target.

In the fall of 1487, the powerful Duke Francis fell ill and the French took the opportunity to exert their authority over the duchy. Henry felt a profound responsibility to help Francis since he had helped Henry through all the years of his exile. In the spring of 1488, Henry sent three ships and a modest number of armed soldiers to help defend Brittany.[26] Even when combined, Breton and English resources could not match the French. On 20 August 1488, the Bretons suffered a crushing loss at the Battle of Sable, resulting in a treaty where the French secured power over Francis' heir, the 11-year-old Duchess Anne. Clearly, the French planned to marry Anne to a Frenchman and then take over the duchy. Two weeks after the treaty was signed, Francis died, leaving Anne unprotected. Henry again tried to help Brittany, undertaking attempts of invasion in the spring of 1489 and again in the winter of 1491, but ultimately relying on diplomatic negotiations to bring about peace. He was not, however, able to rescue Anne and she was married to King Charles VIII of France shortly thereafter.

No doubt the failure in Brittany was an embarrassing failure for Henry but he had no time to sulk on matters as there was another uprising stirring in England by the fall of 1491. Building on the momentum of Lambert Simnel, the Yorkists put forth another Yorkist pretender, this time a young man claiming to be Richard, the younger of the two princes in the Tower. The imposter, named Perkin Warbeck, would menace Henry for the next eight years of his reign.

Perkin Warbeck was a crew member on a Breton merchant ship in the fall of 1491 when he was lured into the conspiracy to impersonate Prince Richard. Like Lambert Simnel, Perkin Warbeck was coached in royal manners and speech to be more believable to the masses.[27] The conspiracy gained traction in Ireland and by the spring of 1492, Charles VIII of France joined the plotters and brought Warbeck to his French court. It was there that Yorkist exiles gathered in France and where he was treated like a royal. Henry, who had already been at odds with France over the usurpation of Brittany, now faced further concerns at the harbouring of this new imposter. He knew he had to take decisive action to put down the threat.

In October 1492, Henry led an invasion force of 700 ships and 14,000 men into France to defend Brittany and press his own claim to the French throne.[28] The threat was enough to force Charles into negotiations and on 3 November 1492, they concluded a treaty of peace at Etaples. In the treaty, Charles had to agree not to support Perkin Warbeck so the imposter was compelled to take refuge elsewhere. He was welcomed with open arms by

Duchess Margaret of Burgundy, the same noblewoman who had support Lambert Simnel's attempt at the throne.

Perkin Warbeck spent a year building a base of supporters in Burgundy, including Yorkist exiles as well as foreign leaders. King James IV of Scotland had thrown in his lot with the pretender and pledged his support to send armed forces for Warbeck's English invasion. Then in November 1493, Warbeck received the support of Maximilian, King of the Romans and son of Holy Roman Emperor Frederick III. Warbeck visited Maximilian's court in Vienna, Austria, and the two men became fast friends. Warbeck accompanied Maximilian to his father's funeral in December 1493 and in the summer of 1494, Maximilian openly declared Warbeck as the rightful king of England. In return, Warbeck proclaimed Maximilian his heir to the kingdom of England. Throughout the spring of 1495, the two men began preparing the invasion attempt by raising money through loans, calling men to arms, and assembling their battle ships for a planned summer invasion.[29]

As early as February 1495, King Henry knew of the impending invasion and placed his kingdom on high alert.[30] It was around this time when Henry learned from his spies the disconcerting news that some of his closest household men were planning to betray him to join the young man pretending to be Prince Richard. The biggest shock was the betrayal of Sir William Stanley, the brother of Henry's own stepfather. Sir William had saved the day for Henry at Bosworth and Henry had rewarded him by making him lord chamberlain, but apparently that wasn't enough for Sir William, or perhaps he truly believed that Perkin Warbeck was Prince Richard. In either case, Henry had Sir William arrested, tried, and executed for being a traitor to the crown.[31]

For all the time and effort spent on Warbeck's English invasion, it turned out to be a miserable failure. His flotilla of battle ships landed in Kent, which being the site of so many rebellions in the past seemed like a good place to raise a rebel army, but the Kentishmen didn't turn out to join Warbeck. In fact, they defended King Henry by beating back Warbeck's soldiers themselves, capturing over 100 of his men and slaying two.[32] When Warbeck saw the slaughter upfolding on land, he abandoned his men and set his sails for friendlier territory. He was rebuffed in Ireland but found a safe haven at the court of King James IV of Scotland.

In mid-September 1496, King James and Warbeck led a raid across the Scottish border into England where they burned down villages and murdered inhabitants. After only four days, James and Warbeck returned to Scotland in haste after they learned there was a large Neville force heading their way.[33] James was stunned and disappointed that no northern Englishmen rose to join 'Prince Edward' in his quest to claim the throne. Having lost hope in Warbeck's conspiracy, James dismissed the pretender from his court and signed a seven-year truce with King Henry in September of 1497.

Around the same time as James and Henry were signing their peace treaty, Warbeck appeared off the coast of Cornwall in southwest England but this time he only had a meager three ships. Cornish leaders had sent him messages imploring him to land in Cornwall. They were ready to rebel against the king, like they had done many times before, over taxes. The Cornishmen stayed true to their promise and came out in the thousands to join Perkin Warbeck on his march to London.[34]

On 17 September 1497, Warbeck's army besieged the castle at Exeter but after a fierce twenty-four hours of fighting, gave up and retreated to Taunton, at which time he was surrounded by the king's forces. Warbeck managed to escape and make it safely to sanctuary at Beaulieu Abbey. The king's men lured him out a week later with promises of a full pardon if he admitted to being an imposter. Warbeck was taken to King Henry at Taunton and he made a full confession, telling Henry that 'against my will they made me learn English and taught me what I should do and say'.[35]

Henry brought Warbeck back to London and made him repeat his confession in public for all to hear. In return, Henry honoured a pardon. He treated this imposter who had caused him so many years of trouble with amazing leniency, even allowing him to travel and lodge with the royal court.[36] Warbeck took advantage of Henry's kindness by making an escape attempt in June 1498 but he was quickly captured and sent to the Tower where he would be less at liberty. A little over a year later, Henry discovered a new escape plan hatched by Warbeck. This time he involved the unfortunate earl of Warwick who was in the Tower in an adjacent room. Henry had them both arrested before they could put their plan into motion. Warbeck was hanged on 23 November 1499 and Warwick was beheaded five days later.[37]

Henry could now feel some level of relief. The imposter he had battled for eight years was finally dead and conveniently for Henry, the last living Yorkist heir, the earl of Warwick, was taken down with him. There were no real rivals left to challenge Henry, especially not after the strength and might Henry had demonstrated in putting down all the rebellions of the 1490's. Now feeling some semblance of safety, Henry turned his attention towards building even more security for his new dynasty by arranging foreign marriages for his many little princes and princesses.

38

Henry's Last Years

Not since Henry VI married Margaret of Anjou in 1445 was there a prestigious royal foreign marriage for England. Edward IV had married widow Elizabeth Woodville and Richard III had married his childhood friend Anne Neville, both English natives. Due to the decisive way in which Henry had defeated his enemies over a fifteen-year period, his power and his profile grew internationally, influencing foreign leaders to ally with him. In medieval times, there was no greater way to tie two countries together in a mutual alliance than with a royal wedding. King Henry shopped around for a marriage for his eldest child Arthur when his son was still an infant and found a taker in Ferdinand and Isabella, parents to Catherine of Aragon.[1]

In 1489, the marriage between Prince Arthur and Princess Catherine was agreed to in the Treaty of Medina del Campo followed shortly thereafter with the required dispensation. Since Arthur and Catherine were both descended from John of Gaunt, the pope had to approve their marriage for it to be deemed legitimate. Several proxy marriage ceremonies were held afterwards as the betrothed couple grew closer to adulthood.[2] Then in 1500 the planning began. Henry wanted their marriage to be the most celebrated, magnificent event in all of Europe so he could display the strength, wealth, and power of the Tudor dynasty. He spared no expense and had the luxury of an entire year to plan his grand extravaganza.

On 2 October 1501, the princess Catherine of Aragon arrived on English soil after surviving a perilous voyage across the Channel through stormy seas. Catherine spent the next month making her way towards London, nearly 300 kilometres away from where she had landed in Plymouth.[3] On 6 November she lodged in the village of Dogmersfield, about seventy kilometres southwest of London when she was surprised by the unexpected arrival of King Henry himself. He had tried to wait patiently for Catherine to make her arrival in London but couldn't contain his excitement at meeting the Spanish princess, showing up unannounced at Dogmersfield. Although it was against the Spanish tradition for the bride to be seen before the wedding, Catherine received the king graciously and then shortly thereafter was introduced to her fiancé Arthur.[4]

Catherine made her official entry into London on 12 November 1501, escorted by Arthur's younger brother Henry and her future-father-in-law, King Henry. At London Bridge they were welcomed by the mayor and then the procession through the city began. The streets and sidewalks were packed with Londoners trying to get a glimpse of the future queen. The conduits flowed freely with wine and there was music and celebrations throughout the city.[5] Along the procession, Catherine stopped to watch six carefully planned pageants before arriving at St Paul's Cathedral where she would lodge in the bishop's palace until the wedding.

On the morning of 14 November 1501, Princess Catherine emerged from bishop's palace and was escorted to St Paul's by Prince Henry. The two cut a fine figure in their white satin and cloth of gold outfits made specially for the occasion. As they arrived at the church, they mounted a platform constructed for the occasion so that the massive crowds could all see their splendor. The platform was covered in red carpet and stretched nearly 200 metres up to the church altar. Henry gave the hand of Catherine to his brother Arthur and the bishops kicked off the three-hour ceremony.[6] Afterwards, a huge celebratory wedding feast was held at Lambeth Palace followed by ten days of further banquets, pageants, jousts, and disguisings. Then the young couple departed London for their permanent resident at Ludlow Castle in Wales.

Henry must have been extremely proud of this achievement, both personally and for the prestige it brought his kingdom. Unfortunately, the royal wedding would be the pinnacle of his reign. From this point forward, King Henry would experience a staggering number of losses in his family and circle of friends. These devastating losses would shape him into the miserly, heartless king for which he is most well-known, not the jovial young Henry from the early days of his reign. He was forever changed by the events that would unfold in the early 1500s.

Less than five months after the grandiose wedding, Henry was riding high but then was promptly brought down by the shocking news that Arthur had died at Ludlow on 2 April 1502. It seems both Arthur and Catherine had contracted a case of the sweating sickness. Catherine recovered but unfortunately Arthur did not.[7] King Henry and Queen Elizabeth were utterly devastated. They took turns consoling each other and resolved that they were young enough to try for more sons. Their only living son, Prince Henry, the former spare heir, would now inherit the throne of England as Henry VIII.

Before he even had time to recover from the devastation of losing his on Arthur, an even worse blow was dealt to Henry when Queen Elizabeth died in childbirth on 11 February 1503, as did the daughter she delivered. The king was inconsolable at the loss of his wife and partner to whom he had been completely loyal. Their marriage may not have started as a love match, but over the years they did indeed grow to love each other quite deeply. The king withdrew in total despair, then fell into an illness so terrible that his attendants feared for his life. It took him an entire month to recover and get back to some sense of normalcy.[8] Never had Henry been one to give up. He knew he had no choice but to pick up the pieces and carry on, for the sake of his kingdom and his children.

First, he settled the situation with the widowed Catherine of Aragon. In August 1503, King Henry and Catherine's father Ferdinand came to the agreement that Catherine should be married to Prince Henry once he came of age (he was only 12 years old at the time).[9] Next, Henry took advantage of his own widowed status to get into the foreign marriage market himself. He entertained the idea of marrying another daughter of Ferdinand's and the prospect of marriage with the duchess of Savoy was a real possibility, but in the end, Henry wasn't interested in a new spouse, he was merely playing the royal matrimonial game and feeling out other foreign leaders.[10]

From about 1504 on, Henry started to retreat from court life and relegate governmental tasks to his advisors, the most notorious of those being Empson and Dudley who were described as 'ravening wolves'.[11] King Henry gave the two men free reign to collect taxes and extort money from his noblemen, charging them exorbitant fines for minor offences and forcing them to pay bonds to reassure their loyalty and good behaviour towards the king. The ruthlessness of these two men had a major effect on King Henry's reputation since he did nothing to stop their predatory methods. Henry lost the love of his people in these later years due to his miserly ways and his refusal to regulate his councillors.

The common perception is that Henry VII was always a greedy, penny-pinching king, but that's simply not the case. Long before the tragedies of the early 1500's, Henry held a magnificent court and spent huge amounts of money impressing his many visitors, both from England and abroad. He spent lavishly on clothing, ceremonies, and festivals as well as entertainers, poets, and scholars who would visit his court. He spoiled his family with gifts, he loved to gamble, and was generous in the wages he paid to his household staff.[12] It was only in the later part of his reign that his personality changed into a withdrawn and apathetic ruler.

For the last few years of his life, Henry VII suffered repeated bouts of illness that would confine him to his bed for weeks at a time.[13] During Easter 1507, he suffered a serious attack of quinsy (a severe sore throat) and was unable to eat or drink for nearly a week. In March 1509, the king again took to his bed, this time with consumption, or tuberculosis. It cruelly took its time ravaging the body, causing uncontrollable weight loss until the victim literally wasted away. By mid-April, it was clear to everyone he was dying. On 21 April 1509, the 53-year-old monarch quietly passed away at Richmond.

Obviously, Margaret Beaufort was devastated at the loss of her only son but took it upon herself to fulfill one last duty: ensure the safe succession of her grandson, Prince Henry. From Henry VII's death to Henry VIII's coronation two months later, she acted as a regent for her grandson, planning the coronation and choosing the councillors who would advise him.[14] King Henry VIII and Queen Catherine were jointly coronated in London on 24 June 1509. Margaret watched the ceremony from a private viewing gallery, just as she had done for her son when he took the throne almost twenty-five years prior.[15] Having fulfilled her final duty, Margaret took to her bed and died on 29 June 1509, just five days after Henry VIII's coronation.

39

Was Henry VII a Usurper?

Henry Tudor overcame extreme challenges throughout his life and unexpectedly rose to the throne of England after defeating King Richard III at the Battle of Bosworth in 1485. With his ascension, he became the first king from the House of Tudor who would go on to have such infamous monarchs as King Henry VIII, Queen Mary I, and Queen Elizabeth I. Were the Tudors the rightful monarchs or was Henry VII a usurper?

With Henry VII, it's not as clear cut as simply answering the question 'Was he a usurper?' because there are so many other questions to consider. If the Yorkists had usurped the crown from the Lancastrians, is it considered usurpation for the Lancastrians to take it back? Was Henry Tudor even the rightful heir of Lancaster? Is it conscionable to overthrow a king whose subjects viewed as extremely dangerous, even murderous as most people believed King Richard III killed his two young nephews so he could claim the throne for himself?

The last reigning Lancastrian king was the pitiful Henry VI, who was overthrown twice by Yorkists. As a result, Edward IV and Richard III from the House of York ruled over England for twenty-four years, depriving the princes of the House of Lancaster their right to rule. The crux of the Yorkists claim was that succession should be allowed to pass through females, for example, the daughter of a king could pass along the right of succession to her eldest living son and he could become king. This, of course, is how the House of York came about. Traditionally in England, the precedent had been set that succession would only flow through the male line but there was no legal statute defining the rules of succession.

Previously, we judged that Henry IV was not a usurper because he ascended the throne legally and without violence, therefore, the House of Lancaster were the rightful rulers of England. Between Henry IV, his son Henry V, and his grandson Henry VI, the House of Lancaster ruled over England for nearly 100 years. It was only when Richard of York, then his son Edward IV, ousted King Henry VI by force, locked him up in the Tower, and took over the kingdom that the House of York came to the throne.

When Henry VI died in May 1471, it was unclear who would carry the torch for the House of Lancaster. There was no clear front runner but there were three strong candidates. Edward, the earl of Warwick, son of the deceased George, Duke of Clarence, could trace his lineage to Edward III through the king's second son, Lionel of Antwerp. The problem with this line is that it passes through Lionel's daughter Philippa, when England was more accustomed to succession passing through a male line.

Henry Tudor traced his descent to Edward III through John of Gaunt and his Beaufort children and grandchildren, including the formidable Margaret Beaufort. Margaret was the chief source of Henry's English royal blood, although he did have French royal blood through his grandmother Catherine de Valois.

The third candidate to lead the House of Lancaster was Sir Henry Stafford, Duke of Buckingham, who traced his connection to Edward III through the king's youngest son, Thomas of Woodstock. Once again, succession would have passed through a woman, Thomas of Woodstock's daughter Anne, therefore his line of succession wasn't clear cut either.

No matter the rightful claimant of the House of Lancaster, did Richard deserve to be deposed? Many of his subjects and nobles would have answered yes. After usurping the throne from his nephews, his reputation as a trustworthy, loyal leader was completely undone. He was hated, distrusted, and many wanted to take vengeance upon him for his treatment of the young, innocent princes in the Tower. But that does not justify facing a reigning king on the battlefield and slaying him. Even though it was vengeance against Richard III and the House of York, a usurpation is still a usurpation. Henry Tudor had no legal precedence over the crown and he came to power through violence, therefore, Henry VII is a usurper.

Conclusion

Being a medieval king was no easy feat. Despite being the wealthiest and most powerful man in the kingdom, it was not a given that a reigning king could hold on to his crown. A successful medieval king had to be able to juggle the multiple needs of his kingdom, and even then, success was not guaranteed. Kings had to be able to defend and protect their countries from foreign adversaries which often involved leading armies and waging wars. Kings had to demonstrate their ability to maintain law and order which was difficult to do with such vast territories. Kings also had to master the delicate balancing act of making sure their nobles were happy, but their ambitions kept in check. As history has shown many times, when a nobleman got too much power, the whole balance of government could be toppled.

The hardest thing of all about being a medieval king was holding onto the crown. England set itself up for hundreds of years of challenges to the throne by having no formal or legal statutes defining the line of succession. This opened the door to a whole string of challengers to the throne, including a number who ultimately succeeded and were thus labeled as usurpers.

The goal of this book has been to reevaluate the stories of six medieval kings who have been traditionally labeled as usurpers and then make a judgement as to whether or not they were deserving of that title. The definition of the word 'usurp' is very clear – to usurp is to gain power by force or by illegal means. It's not enough to just look at the end product of a supposed usurpation. One must instead understand each king's backstory and the circumstances which brought them the throne. Only then can we truly assess whether a king deserved his crown or if he usurped it.

The first king we examined was William the Conqueror who has the unique distinction of being the only foreign usurper among the group. William already held the dukedom of Normandy in France and when his cousin Edward the Confessor, King of England, died childless in 1066, William saw his opportunity to add England to his domain. Although the Witan selected Harold Godwin as Edward the Confessor's successor, William demonstrated his military prowess by invading England and quickly overthrowing King Harold. William would go on to reign for twenty-one years from 1066 to 1087. No other king has left such an indelible mark on

England as William did. He brought with him the Norman way of doing things, which revolutionised England's culture and laid the foundation for its rise as a major foreign entity in the later Middle Ages. Despite all his successes, that does not remove the fact that William the Conqueror did usurp his throne, both illegally and by force.

King Stephen's reign from 1135 to 1154 was far less successful than William the Conqueror. Stephen's usurpation of his cousin Matilda's crown ignited the English civil war known as 'The Anarchy' which raged throughout the entirety of his reign. Stephen was not a strong leader like William the Conqueror. His lackadaisical approach to law and order ignited the ire of his people and his inability to put down rebellions from Matilda and her adherents damaged any confidence his people had in his kingly abilities. Not only was he lacking the skills to lead a kingdom, but he also was not closest in line of succession to the previous king. Robert Curthose and William Clito were the closest living male relatives to King Henry I but Stephen bypassed them when he claimed the throne for himself. In the case of King Stephen, he was most definitely a usurper since he came to the throne illegally and then used force against Matilda and her supporters for nearly twenty years in order to keep the throne for himself.

The final four kings in this book all have something in common: the impetus for their seizures of the throne came from the feeling that they were being denied their rightful places in government. All four kings were princes of royal blood and therefore expected to hold lofty roles in government. However, rivals and favourites who had the ears of kings sought to push them entirely out of government and they felt they had no other choice than to fight back.

No other king is a greater example of this than Henry IV who reigned from 1399 to 1413. Henry and his father John of Gaunt were next in line to the throne after Richard II yet the king continually endeavored to push them out of government, instead preferring the counsel of his favourites. When John of Gaunt died, Richard maliciously exiled Henry for life in an effort to remove him from state affairs permanently. Richard did not expect Henry to fight back, in fact the king was away in Ireland at the time of Henry's invasion. Although Henry raised an army, he never engaged his forces against Richard. Instead, he sought Parliament's approval to remove the despised king and restore Edward III's Act of Entail in which Henry was in fact the heir to Richard's throne. For these reasons, Henry IV did not usurp Richard II's throne.

Richard, Duke of York, came to challenge King Henry VI's throne in the 1450's because he was being continually excluded from the king's court. As next in line to the throne, Richard wanted a bigger say in governmental matters but Henry's favourites wouldn't allow it. When Richard died in 1460, his eldest son Edward took over as the new leader of the House of York. Young Edward brought about a reinvigoration of the Yorkist party. Edward was handsome, charming, charismatic, a capable military leader, and a fierce warrior. He demonstrated his military prowess at the Battle of Mortimer's Cross where he and the Yorkists massacred Jasper Tudor's Welsh army and beheaded his father Owen Tudor. Although the Yorkists lost the next battle in the Wars of the Roses, the Second Battle of St. Albans, the citizens of London rejected Margaret of Anjou and instead implored Edward to take the throne. Edward spent the next ten years fighting off the Lancastrians until he won the decisive Battle of Tewkesbury in 1471. He spent the remaining twelve years of his reign in relative peace up until his unexpected death in 1483. Edward was indeed the lawful heir of Henry VI, however, Edward repeatedly used military force against Henry VI to win the throne, making him a usurper.

Richard III is one of the most notorious usurpers of all time. Immortalised in Shakespeare's work as an evil hunchback, Richard made the decision to take possession of Edward IV's heir because he feared the Woodvilles would completely shut him out of his rightful place in government. Therefore Richard made the fateful decision to depose his two young nephews in order to make himself king of England. Subjects were shocked at Richard's actions and enraged over the treatment of the two boys popularly known as 'the princes in the tower'. Although Richard used legal means to have the boys declared illegitimate, making himself next in line to the throne, he also used force when he took physical possession of the boys, not to mention the criminal act of murder.

Only two years after Richard III's usurpation of the throne, a challenger came along by the name of Henry Tudor. The son of Margaret Beaufort and a close relation of Henry VI, Henry Tudor spent half his life in exile and only decided to mount an invasion after the people of London raised rebellions against Richard III in the fall of 1483. Henry's mother would have been next in line to Henry VI had she not been born a woman. In her son she saw the opportunity to gain the power she felt was rightfully hers. Henry sailed to England in 1485 and won the crown by defeating King Richard at the Battle of Bosworth. Since Henry was taking over the crown from a usurper, was he himself a usurper? Like Henry IV, Henry Tudor felt he was ridding the kingdom of a horrible, dangerous, and murderous king. Nevertheless, he had no legal right to the throne and he took it by force. Henry's reign, therefore, closed out the Middle Ages in England, much as they began: with a usurper on the throne.

Acknowledgements

This book would never have been written without the love and support of my friends and family, including my husband Mark, children Thomas and Julia, mother Kathy, sister Melissa, and brother-in-law Shawn. Thank you for making me believe this book was possible and for cheering me on throughout the writing process.

I would also like to give a sincere thanks to Eleri Pipien and Claire Hopkins from Pen and Sword Books for helping this first-time author become published, as well as Heidi Malagisi for being a beta reader and providing excellent feedback on the early manuscript.

Last but not least, I'd like to thank all my favourite historical authors to whom I am indebted, all of which you'll find in the bibliography. My work is only possible because of all those who came before me and for that I am eternally grateful.

Notes

Part I: William the Conqueror (1066–1087)

1: The Anglo-Saxons
1. For a detailed account of foreign invasions from 410 AD to 1066: Ackroyd, Peter, *A History of England, Volume 1, Foundation*, (MacMillan, 2011).
2. West, Ed, *1066 and Before All That: The Battle of Hastings, Anglo-Saxon and Norman England*, (Skyhorse, 2017), 8.
3. Ackroyd, *A History of England*, 69.
4. Ackroyd, *A History of England*, 67.
5. Morris, Marc, *The Norman Conquest: The Battle of Hastings and the Fall of Anglo-Saxon England*, (Pegasus Books, 2013), 12.
6. Craig, G., 'Alfred the Great: A Diagnosis', *Journal of the Royal Society of Medicine*, Vol. 84, May 1991, https://journals.sagepub.com/doi/pdf/10.1177/014107689108400518.
7. Ackroyd, *A History of England*, 83.
8. West, *1066 and Before All That*, 40.
9. West, *1066 and Before All That*, 25.
10. West, *1066 and Before All That*, 16.
11. Barlow, Frank, *Edward the Confessor*, (University of California Press, 1970), 42.
12. Marvin, Julia, *The Oldest Anglo-Norman Prose Brut Chronicle, An Edition and Translation*, (Boydell Press, 2006).
13. West, *1066 and Before All That*, 43.
14. Morris, *The Norman Conquest*, 35.

2: William the Bastard
1. West, *1066 and Before All That*, 48.
2. Morris, *The Norman Conquest*, 38.
3. West, *1066 and Before All That*, 52.
4. Morris, *The Norman Conquest*, 38.
5. Morris, *The Norman Conquest*, 41.
6. West, *1066 and Before All That*, 56.
7. Morris, *The Norman Conquest*, 72.
8. Borman, Tracy Joanne, *Queen of the Conqueror: The Life of Matilda, Wife of William*, (Bantam, 2012), 24.
9. Morris, *The Norman Conquest*, 51.
10. Ackroyd, *A History of England*, 86.
11. Ackroyd, *A History of England*, 85.
12. West, *1066 and Before All That*, 41.
13. Borman, *Queen of the Conqueror*, 29.

14. West, *1066 and Before All That*, 73.
15. Morris, *The Norman Conquest*, 113.
16. Howarth, David Armine, *1066: The Year of the Conquest*, (Dorset Press, 1993), 48.
17. Morris, *The Norman Conquest*, 140.

3: The Norman Invasion

1. Douglas, David C, *William the Conqueror*, (University of California Press, 1964), 187.
2. Howarth, *1066*, 120-121.
3. West, *1066 and Before All That*, 89.
4. Morris, *The Norman Conquest*, 149.
5. Howarth, *1066*, 154.
6. Howarth, *1066*, 152-153.
7. Howarth, *1066*, 157.
8. Howarth, *1066*, 159.
9. Howarth, *1066*, 169.
10. Douglas, *William the Conqueror*, 201.
11. Morrillo, Stephen, *The Battle of Hastings: Sources and Interpretations*, (Boydell Press, 1996), 147.
12. Morris, *The Norman Conquest*, 182.
13. Howarth, *1066*, 186-187.

4: The Subjugation of England and Normandy

1. Douglas, *William the Conqueror*, 218-219.
2. Rex, Peter, *The English Resistance: The Underground War Against the Normans*, (Amberley Publishing, 2014), 815 (Kindle).
3. Douglas, *William the Conqueror*, 232-234.

5: Family Betrayal

1. Douglas, *William the Conqueror*, 237.
2. Douglas, *William the Conqueror*, 239.
3. Morris, *The Norman Conquest*, 298-302.
4. Borman, *Queen of the Conqueror*, 214.

6: The Domesday Book

1. Douglas, *William the Conqueror*, 280.
2. Morris, *The Norman Conquest*, 309.
3. Morris, *The Norman Conquest*, 327.
4. Douglas, *William the Conqueror*, 358-360.

7: Was William the Conqueror a usurper?

1. Peers, Chris, *King Stephen and The Anarchy: Civil War and Military Tactics in Twelfth-Century Britain*, (Pen & Sword Books, 2018), 457 (Kindle).
2. Morris, *The Norman Conquest*, 8.
3. Morris, *The Norman Conquest*, 51.
4. 'usurp', Dictionary.com 2020: https://www.dictionary.com/browse/usurp?s=t.
5. West, *1066 and Before All That*, 41.

Part II: King Stephen (1135–1154)

8: The Empress Matilda
1. Gillingham, John, *William II*, (Penguin Monarchs, 2019), 19.
2. Douglas, *William the Conqueror*, 371.
3. Gillingham, *William II*, 21.
4. Hollister, C. Warren, *Henry I*, (Yale University Press, 2001), 46.
5. Orderic Vitalis, *Historia ecclesiastic* (*Ecclesiastical History*), edited and translated by Margorie Chibnall, 6 vols, (Oxford University Press, 1969–1980), 4:94.
6. Gillingham, *William II*, 21.
7. Gillingham, *William II*, 48.
8. Gillingham, *William II*, 49-50.
9. Hollister, *Henry I*, 103-104.
10. Hollister, *Henry I*, 106.
11. Hollister, *Henry I*, 198-201.
12. Hollister, *Henry I*, 41.
13. Chibnall, Marjorie, *The Empress Matilda: Queen Consort, Queen Mother and Lady of the English*, (Wiley-Blackwell, 1993), 1.
14. Hollister, *Henry I*, 238.
15. Hollister, *Henry I*, 274.
16. Hollister, *Henry I*, 276-277.
17. Chibnall, *The Empress Matilda*, 51-52.
18. Hollister, *Henry I*, 309.
19. Chibnall, *The Empress Matilda*, 12.
20. Hollister, *Henry I*, 312.
21. Hollister, *Henry I*, 317-318.
22. Chibnall, *The Empress Matilda*, 55.
23. Castor, Helen, *She-Wolves: The Women Who Ruled England Before Elizabeth*, (Harper Perennial, 2012), 69.
24. Hollister, *Henry I*, 467-468.
25. Hollister, *Henry I*, 474.

9: Stolen Crown
1. Castor, *She-Wolves*, 75.
2. King, Edmund, *King Stephen*, (Yale University Press, 2011), 9109 (Kindle).
3. Hollister, *Henry I*, 477.
4. King, *King Stephen*, 9199 (Kindle).
5. King, *King Stephen*, 1588 (Kindle).
6. Chibnall, *The Empress Matilda*, 64.
7. Chibnall, *The Empress Matilda*, 66.
8. Peers, *King Stephen and The Anarchy*, 1409 (Kindle).
9. King, *King Stephen*, 1758 (Kindle).
10. Castor, *She-Wolves*, 80.
11. King, *King Stephen*, 1845 (Kindle).
12. Peers, *King Stephen and The Anarchy*, 356-409 (Kindle).
13. Chibnall, *The Empress Matilda*, 72-73.
14. King, *King Stephen*, 2064 (Kindle).
15. King, *King Stephen*, 2095 (Kindle).

16. Hanley, Catherine, *Matilda: Empress, Queen, Warrior*, (Yale University Press, 2019), 1851 (Kindle).
17. Hanley, *Matilda*, 1874 (Kindle).

10: Almost Queen of England
1. Chibnall, *The Empress Matilda*, 79-80.
2. Hanley, *Matilda*, 1920 (Kindle).
3. Castor, *She-Wolves*, 89-91.
4. Hanley, *Matilda*, 2161 (Kindle).
5. Hanley, *Matilda*, 2184 (Kindle).
6. Peers, *King Stephen and The Anarchy*, 1883 (Kindle).
7. Hanley, *Matilda*, 2387 (Kindle).
8. Peers, *King Stephen and The Anarchy*, 2018 (Kindle).
9. Hanley, *Matilda*, 2548-2571 (Kindle).
10. Hanley, *Matilda*, 2704 (Kindle).
11. Chibnall, *The Empress Matilda*, 98.
12. Hanley, *Matilda*, 155.
13. Hanley, *Matilda*, 2902 (Kindle).

11: The Anarchy Continues
1. Castor, *She-Wolves*, 104-105.
2. Hanley, *Matilda*, 2970 (Kindle).
3. Peers, *King Stephen and The Anarchy*, 2115 (Kindle).
4. King, *King Stephen*, 5014-5047 (Kindle).
5. Peers, *King Stephen and The Anarchy*, 2170 (Kindle).
6. King, *King Stephen*, 5661 (Kindle).
7. Hanley, *Matilda*, 3355 (Kindle).
8. Hanley, *Matilda*, 3380 (Kindle).
9. Hanley, *Matilda*, 3404 (Kindle).
10. Peers, *King Stephen and The Anarchy*, 2225 (Kindle).
11. Warren, Wilfred Lewis, *Henry II*, (University of California Press, 1973), 34.

12: Changing of the Guard
1. Chibnall, *The Empress Matilda*, 153.
2. Hanley, *Matilda*, 3679 (Kindle).
3. King, *King Stephen*, 7821 (Kindle).
4. Chibnall, *The Empress Matilda*, 155-156.
5. Warren, *Henry II*, 41.
6. King, *King Stephen*, 9180 (Kindle).

13: Henry's Final Invasion
1. Warren, *Henry II*, 48-49.
2. Warren, *Henry II*, 50.
3. King, *King Stephen*, 8473 (Kindle).
4. King, *King Stephen*, 8772 (Kindle).
5. Peers, *King Stephen and The Anarchy*, 2878 (Kindle).
6. Hanley, *Matilda*, 3989 (Kindle).

14: Was King Stephen a usurper?
1. Warren, *Henry II*, 258.
2. 'usurper', Dictionary.com. 2020: https://www.dictionary.com/browse/usurp.
3. Hollister, *Henry I*, 105.
4. Castor, *She-Wolves*, 66-67.

Part III: King Henry IV (1399–1415)

15: Edward III and the Succession Problem
1. Given-Wilson, Chris, *Henry IV*, (Yale University Press, 2016), 11.
2. Ormrod, W. Mark, *Edward III*, (Yale University Press, 2012), 10.
3. Jones, Dan, *The Plantagenets: The Warrior Kings and Queens Who Made England*, (Viking, 2013), 303.
4. Jones, *The Plantagenets*, 350.
5. Given-Wilson, *Henry IV*, 15-18.
6. Jones, *The Plantagenets*, 365-366.
7. Ormrod, *Edward III*, 22.
8. Jones, *The Plantagenets*, 380.
9. Saul, Nigel, *Richard II*, (Yale University Press, 1997), 8.
10. Jones, *The Plantagenets*, 437.
11. Abernathy, Susan, 'Philippa of Hainault, Queen of England', *The Freelance History Writer*, November 2012, https://thefreelancehistorywriter.com/2012/11/07/philippa-of-hainault-queen-of-england/.
12. MacEwen, Terry, 'Edward the Black Prince', *Historic UK*, https://www.historic-uk.com/HistoryUK/HistoryofEngland/Edward-The-Black-Prince/.
13. Jones, Michael, *The Black Prince: England's Greatest Medieval Warrior*, (Pegasus Books, 2018), 5478-5503 (Kindle).
14. Jones, *The Black Prince*, 5560-5583 (Kindle).
15. Goodman, Anthony, *The Wars of the Roses: Military Activity and English Society, 1452-97*, (Dorset Press, 1990), 354.
16. Jones, *The Plantagenets*, 442-443.
17. Mortimer, Ian, *Medieval Intrigue: Decoding Royal Conspiracies*, (Continuum, 2010), 259.
18. Mortimer, *Medieval Intrigue*, 260.
19. Saul, *Richard II*, 396-397.

16: Rival Cousins
1. Mortimer, Ian, *The Fears of Henry IV: The Life of England's Self-Made King*, (Jonathan Cape, 2007), 27-28.
2. Given-Wilson, *Henry IV*, 64-76.
3. Kirby, J.L., *Henry IV of England*, (Constable, 1970), 22.
4. Jones, *The Plantagenets*, 442.
5. Given-Wilson, *Henry IV*, 93.
6. Jones, Dan, *Summer of Blood: England's First Revolution*, (Penguin Books, 2016), 54.
7. Jones, *Summer of Blood*, 79.
8. Jones, *Summer of Blood*, 78.
9. Jones, *Summer of Blood*, 95.
10. Jones, *Summer of Blood*, 101.
11. Jones, *Summer of Blood*, 108-110.

12. Jones, *Summer of Blood*, 131-134.
13. Mortimer, *The Fears of Henry IV*, 18-19.
14. Jones, *Summer of Blood*, 171.

17: The Lords Appellant

1. Given-Wilson, *Henry IV*, 34-36.
2. Goodman, Anthony, *John of Gaunt: The Exercise of Princely Power in Fourteenth-Century Europe*, (Routledge, 2016), 102.
3. Mortimer, *The Fears of Henry IV*, 57.
4. Given-Wilson, *Henry IV*, 38.
5. Mortimer, *The Fears of Henry IV*, 67.
6. Mortimer, *The Fears of Henry IV*, 69.
7. Mortimer, *The Fears of Henry IV*, 51.
8. Mortimer, *The Fears of Henry IV*, 72.
9. Jones, *The Plantagenets*, 66-69.
10. Given-Wilson, *Henry IV*, 61-62.
11. Given-Wilson, *Henry IV*, 64-71.
12. Given-Wilson, *Henry IV*, 72-76.
13. Warner, Kathryn, *Richard II: A True King's Fall*, (Amberley Publishing, 2018), 4169 (Kindle).

18: Henry's Invasion

1. Jones, *The Plantagenets*, 478-482.
2. Jones, *The Plantagenets*, 483-484.
3. Saul, *Richard II*, 399.
4. Jones, *The Plantagenets*, 484.
5. Jones, *The Plantagenets*, 485.
6. Jones, *The Plantagenets*, 487.
7. Jones, *The Plantagenets*, 489.
8. Jones, *The Plantagenets*, 490.
9. Jones, *The Plantagenets*, 490.
10. Saul, *Richard II*, 408.
11. Given-Wilson, *Henry IV*, 127.
12. Kirby, *Henry IV of England*, 55.
13. Mortimer, *The Fears of Henry IV*, 175-176.
14. Given-Wilson, *Henry IV*, 131-132.
15. Saul, *Richard II*, 414.
16. Saul, *Richard II*, 415.
17. Jones, *The Plantagenets*, 491-492.
18. Given-Wilson, *Henry IV*, 140.
19. Saul, *Richard II*, 420-421.
20. Jones, *The Plantagenets*, 495.

Part IV: King Edward IV (1461–1470 & 1471–1483)

20: The Inept King Henry VI

1. Johnson, Lauren, *The Shadow King: The Life and Death of Henry VI*, (Pegasus Books, 2019), 142.
2. Johnson, *The Shadow King*, 555-556.

3. Lewis, Matthew, *Richard, Duke of York: King by Right*, (Amberley Publishing, 2016), 43.
4. Johnson, *The Shadow King*, 71.
5. Griffiths, Ralph and Thomas, Roger S., *The Making of the Tudor Dynasty*, (Wren Publishers, 1998), 454.
6. Lewis, *Richard, Duke of York*, 67-69.
7. Johnson, *The Shadow King*, 187.
8. Amin, Nathen, *The House of Beaufort: The Bastard Line that Captured the Crown*, (Amberley Publishing, 2017), 4359-4386 (Kindle).
9. Maurer, Helen E., *Margaret of Anjou: Queenship and Power in Late Medieval England*, (Boydell Press, 2003), 27.
10. Grummitt, David, *Henry VI*, (Routledge, 2015), 129-130.
11. Jones, Dan, *The Wars of the Roses: The Fall of the Plantagenets and the Rise of the Tudors*, (Viking, 2014), 95-96.
12. Lewis, *Richard, Duke of York*, 132-134.
13. Johnson, *The Shadow King*, 252-253.
14. Griffiths and Thomas, *The Making of the Tudor Dynasty*, 520.
15. Jones, *The Wars of the Roses*, 109-110.
16. Johnson, *The Shadow King*, 256.
17. Jones, *The Wars of the Roses*, 113.
18. Jones, *The Wars of the Roses*, 114.
19. Jones, *The Wars of the Roses*, 115.

21: The Wars of the Roses
1. Lewis, *Richard, Duke of York*, 169.
2. Johnson, *The Shadow King*, 273.
3. Jones, *The Wars of the Roses*, 127.
4. Lewis, *Richard, Duke of York*, 207-208.
5. Jones, *The Wars of the Roses*, 129-131.
6. Johnson, *The Shadow King*, 308-312.
7. Lewis, *Richard, Duke of York*, 224.
8. Johnson, *The Shadow King*, 322.
9. Johnson, *The Shadow King*, 325.
10. Maurer, *Margaret of Anjou*, 116.
11. 'The First Battle of St Albans', BritishBattles.com, https://www.britishbattles.com/wars-of-the-roses/first-battle-of-st-albans/.
12. Johnson, *The Shadow King*, 344-345.
13. Johnson, *The Shadow King*, 349.
14. Maurer, *Margaret of Anjou*, 156.
15. Kendall, Paul Murray, *Warwick the Kingmaker*, (Norton, 1957), 41-2.
16. Kendall, *Warwick the Kingmaker*, 50.
17. Ross, Charles Derek, *Edward IV*, (University of California Press, 1975), 20.
18. Pollard, A.J., *Warwick the Kingmaker: Politics, Power and Fame*, (Bloomsbury Academic, 2007), 40.
19. Jones, *The Wars of the Roses*, 158.
20. Jones, *The Wars of the Roses*, 159.
21. Jones, *The Wars of the Roses*, 159.

22: The Rose of Rouen

1. Ross, *Edward IV*, 22.
2. Ross, *Edward IV*, 26.
3. Johnson, *The Shadow King*, 398.
4. Johnson, *The Shadow King*, 400.
5. Ross, *Edward IV*, 27.
6. Ingram, Mike, *Richard III and the Battle of Bosworth*, (Helion and Company, 2019), 95.
7. Johnson, *The Shadow King*, 408.
8. Lewis, *Richard, Duke of York*, 300.
9. Licence, Amy, *Henry VI and Margaret of Anjou: A Marriage of Unequals*, (Pen & Sword Books, 2018), 116.
10. Lewis, *Richard, Duke of York*, 300.
11. Lewis, *Richard, Duke of York*, 302.
12. Licence, *Henry VI and Margaret of Anjou*, 118-119.
13. Lewis, *Richard, Duke of York*, 304.
14. Johnson, *The Shadow King*, 242-243.
15. Johnson, *The Shadow King*, 417.
16. Licence, *Henry VI and Margaret of Anjou*, 121.
17. Seward, Desmond, *Wars of the Roses*, (Viking, 1995), 62.
18. Lewis, *Richard, Duke of York*, 307.
19. Johnson, *The Shadow King*, 427.
20. Higginbotham, Susan, 'The Death of Edmund, Earl of Rutland', *History Refreshed by Susan Higginbotham*, https://www.susanhigginbotham.com/posts/the-death-of-edmund-earl-of-rutland/.
21. Johnson, *The Shadow King*, 451-452.
22. Johnson, *The Shadow King*, 431.
23. Breverton, Terry, *Jasper Tudor: Tudor Dynasty*, (Amberley Publishing, 2014), 118.
24. Breverton, *Jasper Tudor*, 118.
25. Kendall, *Warwick the Kingmaker*, 82.
26. Johnson, *The Shadow King*, 430.
27. Breverton, *Jasper Tudor*, 121.
28. Breverton, *Jasper Tudor*, 122.
29. Santiuste, David, *Edward IV and the Wars of the Roses*, (Pen & Sword Books, 2010), 43.

23: The First Reign of Edward IV

1. Ross, *Edward IV*, 36.
2. Seward, *Wars of the Roses*, 81.
3. Breverton, *Jasper Tudor*, 127.
4. Lewis, Matthew, *The Wars of the Roses: The Key Players in the Struggle for Supremacy*, (Amberley Publishing, 2015), 134.
5. Johnson, *The Shadow King*, 446.
6. Ross, *Edward IV*, 37.
7. Ridgway, Claire, 'Coronation of Edward IV', *Tudor Society*, https://www.tudorsociety.com/28-june-1461-coronation-of-edward-iv/.
8. Johnson, *The Shadow King*, 452.
9. Ross, *Edward IV*, 48-49.
10. Breverton, *Jasper Tudor*, 133-134.
11. Johnson, *The Shadow King*, 463-464.

12. Licence, *Henry VI and Margaret of Anjou*, 140.
13. Licence, *Henry VI and Margaret of Anjou*, 140.
14. Kendall, *Warwick the Kingmaker*, 106.
15. Johnson, *The Shadow King*, 472-474.

24: Warwick's Rebellion
 1. Johnson, *The Shadow King*, 481.
 2. Ross, *Edward IV*, 54-55.
 3. Ross, *Edward IV*, 59.
 4. Ross, *Edward IV*, 59-60.
 5. Haigh, Philip A, *The Military Campaigns of the Wars of the Roses*, (Sutton, 1995), 80.
 6. Johnson, *The Shadow King*, 484-485.
 7. Grummitt, *Henry VI*, 213-214.
 8. Johnson, *The Shadow King*, 488.
 9. Ross, *Edward IV*, 91.
10. Ross, *Edward IV*, 85.
11. Seward, *Wars of the Roses*, 120.
12. Seward, *Wars of the Roses*, 122-123.
13. Kendall, *Warwick the Kingmaker*, 206.
14. Kendall, *Warwick the Kingmaker*, 212.
15. Lewis, *The Wars of the Roses*, 159-160.
16. Haigh, *The Military Campaigns of the Wars of the Roses*, 102.
17. Haigh, *The Military Campaigns of the Wars of the Roses*, 102-103.
18. Haigh, *The Military Campaigns of the Wars of the Roses*, 104-105.
19. Kendall, *Warwick the Kingmaker*, 255-256.
20. Santiuste, *Edward IV and the Wars of the Roses*, 96.
21. Lewis, *The Wars of the Roses*, 164.

25: The Second Reign of Edward IV
 1. Lewis, *The Wars of the Roses*, 165.
 2. Kendall, *Warwick the Kingmaker*, 276.
 3. Seward, *Wars of the Roses*, 160-170.
 4. Johnson, *The Shadow King*, 521-522.
 5. Seward, *Wars of the Roses*, 179.
 6. Haigh, *The Military Campaigns of the Wars of the Roses*, 119.

26: Was Edward IV a usurper?
 1. Johnson, *The Shadow King*, 451-452.
 2. Ross, *Edward IV*, 315.
 3. Ross, *Edward IV*, 415.

Part V: Richard III (1483–1485)

27: Loyalty Binds Me
 1. Kendall, *Warwick the Kingmaker*, 45.
 2. Kendall, *Warwick the Kingmaker*, 50.
 3. Kendall, *Warwick the Kingmaker*, 60, 65.
 4. Lewis, *The Wars of the Roses*, 159-160.
 5. Haigh, *The Military Campaigns of the Wars of the Roses*, 104-105.

6. Seward, Desmond, *Richard III: England's Black Legend*, (Franklin Watts, 1984), 32-54.
7. Lewis, *The Wars of the Roses*, 164.
8. Lewis, *The Wars of the Roses*, 165.
9. Kendall, Paul Murray, *Richard the Third*, (Norton, 1996), 96.
10. Ross, *Edward IV*, 152.
11. Kendall, *Richard the Third*, 99.
12. Kendall, *Richard the Third*, 275-276.
13. Ross, *Edward IV*, 160.
14. Kendall, *Richard the Third*, 101.
15. Ross, *Edward IV*, 166-167.
16. Ross, *Edward IV*, 167.
17. Haigh, *The Military Campaigns of the Wars of the Roses*, 122.
18. Kendall, *Richard the Third*, 322.
19. Haigh, *The Military Campaigns of the Wars of the Roses*, 125-126.
20. Haigh, *The Military Campaigns of the Wars of the Roses*, 128.
21. Santiuste, *Edward IV and the Wars of the Roses*, 136.
22. Santiuste, *Edward IV and the Wars of the Roses*, 136.

28: 'False, fleeting, perjured Clarence'

1. Johnson, *The Shadow King*, 537.
2. Ross, *Edward IV*, 175.
3. Ross, *Edward IV*, 186-190.
4. Carroll, Leslie, 'Richard III & Anne Neville: A Love Story?', *History Hoydens*, November 2009, http://historyhoydens.blogspot.com/2009/11/richard-iii-anne-neville-love-story.html.
5. Kendall, *Richard the Third*, 160.
6. Kendall, *Richard the Third*, 130.
7. Ross, *Edward IV*, 191-193.
8. Kendall, *Richard the Third*, 132.
9. Kendall, *Richard the Third*, 133.
10. Santiuste, *Edward IV and the Wars of the Roses*, 142-145.
11. Ross, *Edward IV*, 316-317.
12. Seward, *Wars of the Roses*, 222.
13. Lewis, *The Wars of the Roses*, 216.
14. Ross, *Edward IV*, 140.
15. Ross, *Edward IV*, 240.
16. Ross, *Edward IV*, 240.
17. Kendall, *Richard the Third*, 144.
18. Kendall, *Richard the Third*, 146.
19. Kendall, *Richard the Third*, 146.
20. Ross, *Edward IV*, 243.
21. Lewis, *The Wars of the Roses*, 219-220.
22. Kendall, *Richard the Third*, 168-172.
23. Kendall, *Richard the Third*, 175.

29: The Road to the Throne

1. Kendall, *Richard the Third*, 181.
2. Lewis, *The Wars of the Roses*, 223.

3. Kendall, *Richard the Third*, 191-193.
4. Kendall, *Richard the Third*, 193.
5. Kendall, *Richard the Third*, 201.
6. Jones, *The Wars of the Roses*, 268.
7. Kendall, *Richard the Third*, 204.
8. Fields, Bertram, *Royal Blood: King Richard III and the Mystery of the Princes*, (Sutton Publishing, 2000), 72-73.
9. Fields, *Royal Blood*, 74.
10. Jones, *The Wars of the Roses*, 269.
11. Fields, *Royal Blood*, 74.
12. Ross, Charles Derek, *Richard III*, (University of California Press, 1982), 72.
13. Lewis, *The Wars of the Roses*, 226.
14. Fields, *Royal Blood*, 79.
15. Fields, *Royal Blood*, 78.
16. Jones, *The Wars of the Roses*, 274.
17. Seward, *Wars of the Roses*, 266.
18. Kendall, *Richard the Third*, 209.
19. Kendall, *Richard the Third*, 251.
20. Kendall, *Richard the Third*, 263.
21. Seward, *Richard III*, 115.

30: Unsteady Crown

1. Kendall, *Richard the Third*, 300.
2. Seward, *Richard III*, 120-127.
3. Jones, *The Wars of the Roses*, 281.
4. Fields, *Royal Blood*, 149-151.
5. Jones, *The Wars of the Roses*, 280.
6. Seward, *Wars of the Roses*, 246.
7. Jones, *The Wars of the Roses*, 282-283.
8. Jones, *The Wars of the Roses*, 284.
9. Kendall, *Richard the Third*, 327-329.
10. Kendall, *Richard the Third*, 330.
11. Jones, *The Wars of the Roses*, 289-290.
12. Seward, *Wars of the Roses*, 255.
13. Seward, *Wars of the Roses*, 292.
14. Kendall, *Richard the Third*, 344.
15. Kendall, *Richard the Third*, 344.
16. Seward, *Richard III*, 155-156.
17. Seward, *Wars of the Roses*, 252-253.
18. Seward, *Richard III*, 158.
19. Kendall, *Royal Blood*, 168
20. Seward, *Richard III*, 159.
21. Kendall, *Richard the Third*, 359.
22. Kendall, *Richard the Third*, 361-363.
23. Kendall, *Richard the Third*, 363.
24. Seward, *Richard III*, 167.
25. Lewis, *The Wars of the Roses*, 253.
26. Seward, *Richard III*, 168-169.

27. Kendall, *Richard the Third*, 363.
28. Kendall, *Richard the Third*, 399-400.
29. Seward, *Richard III*, 170.

31: Fall of the Last Plantagenet King
1. Seward, *Richard III*, 175.
2. Seward, *Richard III*, 181.
3. Ross, *Richard III*, 210.
4. Amin, *The House of Beaufort*, 113 (Kindle).
5. Seward, *Richard III*, 185.
6. Jones, Michael, *Bosworth 1485*, (Hodder & Stoughton, 2014), 166-167.
7. Seward, *Richard III*, 187.
8. Ross, *Richard III*, 215.
9. Jones, *The Wars of the Roses*, 296.
10. Seward, *Richard III*, 216.
11. Seward, *Richard III*, 188.
12. Jones, *The Wars of the Roses*, 298.
13. Haigh, *The Military Campaigns of the Wars of the Roses*, 161.
14. Jones, *Bosworth 1485*, 195-197.
15. Lewis, *The Wars of the Roses*, 259.
16. Jones, *The Wars of the Roses*, 299.
17. 'How Richard III Died', University of Leicester, https://www.le.ac.uk/richardiii/science/osteology-6-howR3died.html#:~:text=On%2022%20August%2C%201485%2C%20at,him%20and%20end%20the%20conflict.&text=One%20massive%2C%20fatal%20blow%20to,the%20rest%20of%20his%20body.

32: Was Richard III a Usurper?
1. Fields, *Royal Blood*, 115.
2. Seward, *Richard III*, 123.
3. Fields, *Royal Blood*, 144-145.

Part VI: Henry VII (1485–1509)

33: The Tudors and Beauforts
1. Cunningham, Sean, *Henry VII*, (Routledge, 2007), 47.
2. Johnson, *The Shadow King*, 40.
3. Amin, *The House of Beaufort*, 3379 (Kindle).
4. Jones, *The Wars of the Roses*, 61-62.
5. Breverton, *Jasper Tudor*, 22-23.
6. Jones, *The Wars of the Roses*, 62.
7. Breverton, *Jasper Tudor*, 35-36.
8. Jones, *The Wars of the Roses*, 63.
9. Roberts, Sara Elin, *Jasper: The Tudor Kingmaker*, (Fonthill Media, 2015), 378 (Kindle).
10. Jones, *The Wars of the Roses*, 64.
11. Jones, *The Wars of the Roses*, 65.
12. Jones, *The Wars of the Roses*, 66.
13. Breverton, *Jasper Tudor*, 49-50.

14. Jones, *The Wars of the Roses*, 67-68.
15. Cunningham, *Henry VII*, 10.
16. Jones, *The Wars of the Roses*, 83-84.
17. Cunningham, *Henry VII*, 11.
18. Breverton, *Jasper Tudor*, 213.
19. Norton, Elizabeth, *Margaret Beaufort: Mother of the Tudor Dynasty*, (Amberley Publishing, 2011), 18.
20. Norton, *Margaret Beaufort*, 3.
21. Norton, *Margaret Beaufort*, 36.
22. Jones, Michael K, and Underwood, Malcolm G, *The King's Mother: Lady Margaret Beaufort, Countess of Richmond and Derby*, (Cambridge University Press, 1992), 180-187.
23. Jones and Underwood, *The King's Mother*, 95.
24. Jones and Underwood, *The King's Mother*, 17.
25. Amin, *The House of Beaufort*, 608-645, 1669 (Kindle).
26. Amin, *The House of Beaufort*, 1672 (Kindle).
27. Jones and Underwood, *The King's Mother*, 27.
28. Norton, *Margaret Beaufort*, 18.
29. Bayani, Debra, *Jasper Tudor: Godfather of the Tudor Dynasty*, (MadeGlobal Publishing, 2015), 765 (Kindle).
30. Breverton, *Jasper Tudor*, 80.
31. Roberts, *Jasper*, 880 (Kindle).
32. Breverton, *Jasper Tudor*, 82.
33. Breverton, *Jasper Tudor*, 84.
34. Norton, *Margaret Beaufort*, 42.
35. Roberts, *Jasper*, 931 (Kindle).
36. Breverton, *Jasper Tudor*, 84.

34: Henry's Childhood and the Wars of the Roses

1. 'The First Battle of St Albans', BritishBattles.com, https://www.britishbattles.com/wars-of-the-roses/first-battle-of-st-albans/.
 2. Breverton, *Jasper Tudor*, 118.
 3. Breverton, *Jasper Tudor*, 118.
 4. Breverton, *Jasper Tudor*, 118.
 5. Jones, *The Wars of the Roses*, 183.
 6. Seward, *Wars of the Roses*, 81.
 7. Norton, *Margaret Beaufort*, 59.
 8. Norton, *Margaret Beaufort*, 60-72.
 9. Norton, *Margaret Beaufort*, 73.
10. Roberts, *Jasper*, 1239 (Kindle).
11. Norton, *Margaret Beaufort*, 76.
12. Norton, *Margaret Beaufort*, 86.
13. Jones and Underwood, *The King's Mother*, 52.
14. Jones and Underwood, *The King's Mother*, 52.
15. Jones and Underwood, *The King's Mother*, 58.
16. Griffiths and Thomas, *The Making of the Tudor Dynasty*, 92-93.
17. Roberts, *Jasper*, 1478-1500 (Kindle).
18. Jones and Underwood, *The King's Mother*, 59.

19. Norton, *Margaret Beaufort*, 106.
20. Norton, *Margaret Beaufort*, 107.

35: The Rise of Richard III

 1. Jones, *The Wars of the Roses*, 193.
 2. Lewis, *The Wars of the Roses*, 223
 3. Kendall, *Richard the Third*, 218.
 4. Kendall, *Richard the Third*, 215.
 5. Kendall, *Richard the Third*, 263.
 6. Griffiths and Thomas, *The Making of the Tudor Dynasty*, 115.
 7. Norton, *Margaret Beaufort*, 125.
 8. Griffiths and Thomas, *The Making of the Tudor Dynasty*, 102-105.
 9. Kendall, *Richard the Third*, 327-329.
10. Kendall, *Richard the Third*, 320.
11. Kendall, *Richard the Third*, 321.
12. Cunningham, *Henry VII*, 21-22.
13. Cunningham, *Henry VII*, 24.
14. Griffiths and Thomas, *The Making of the Tudor Dynasty*, 104-105.
15. Cunningham, *Henry VII*, 24.
16. Jones, *The Wars of the Roses*, 282-283.
17. Norton, *Margaret Beaufort*, 116.
18. Kendall, *Richard the Third*, 327-329.
19. Jones, *The Wars of the Roses*, 284.
20. Kendall, *Richard the Third*, 329.
21. Kendall, *Richard the Third*, 330.
22. Seward, *Wars of the Roses*, 255.
23. Seward, *Wars of the Roses*, 292-293.
24. Seward, *Wars of the Roses*, 255.
25. Cunningham, *Henry VII*, 24.
26. Kendall, *Richard the Third*, 334.
27. Kendall, *Richard the Third*, 344.
28. Seward, *Richard III*, 155-156.
29. Seward, *Richard III*, 159.
30. Kendall, *Richard III*, 359.
31. Jones, *The Wars of the Roses*, 290.
32. Griffiths and Thomas, *The Making of the Tudor Dynasty*, 136-137.
33. Lewis, *The Wars of the Roses*, 253.
34. Chrimes, S.B., *Henry VII*, (Eyre Methuen, 1972), 1007 (Kindle).
35. Chrimes, *Henry VII*, 135 (Kindle).
36. Griffiths and Thomas, *The Making of the Tudor Dynasty*, 142.
37. Seward, *Richard III*, 181.
38. Griffiths and Thomas, *The Making of the Tudor Dynasty*, 143-144.

36: Henry Tudor's Invasion

 1. Jones, *The Wars of the Roses*, 291-292.
 2. Penn, Thomas, *Winter King: Henry VII and the Dawn of Tudor England*, (Simon & Schuster, 1994), 1.
 3. Griffiths and Thomas, *The Making of the Tudor Dynasty*, 160.

4. Seward, *Wars of the Roses*, 303.
5. 'Welsh Parliament: The Crowning of Owain Glyndwr in Machynlleth', *BBC News*, June 2017, https://www.bbc.com/news/uk-wales-politics-40264766.
6. Breverton, *Jasper Tudor*, 217.
7. Griffiths and Thomas, *The Making of the Tudor Dynasty*, 166.
8. Cunningham, *Henry VII*, 33.
9. Cunningham, *Henry VII*, 33.
10. Griffiths and Thomas, *The Making of the Tudor Dynasty*, 170.
11. Cunningham, *Henry VII*, 34.
12. Cunningham, *Henry VII*, 36.
13. Seward, *Wars of the Roses*, 303-304.
14. Griffiths and Thomas, *The Making of the Tudor Dynasty*, 178-179.
15. Norton, *Margaret Beaufort*, 137-138.
16. Jones, *The Wars of the Roses*, 296.
17. Ross, *Richard III*, 215.
18. Ross, *Richard III*, 222-225.
19. Seward, *Wars of the Roses*, 307.
20. Jones, *The Wars of the Roses*, 298-299.
21. Seward, *Wars of the Roses*, 307.
22. Jones, *The Wars of the Roses*, 299.
23. Norton, *Margaret Beaufort*, 140.
24. Seward, *Richard III*, 192.

37: Lambert Simnel and Perkin Warbeck

1. Breverton, *Jasper Tudor*, 258.
2. Griffiths and Thomas, *The Making of the Tudor Dynasty*, 206.
3. Chrimes, *Henry VII*, 2050 (Kindle).
4. Norton, *Margaret Beaufort*, 158.
5. Jones, *The Wars of the Roses*, 301-302.
6. Jones and Underwood, *The King's Mother*, 73-74.
7. Griffiths and Thomas, *The Making of the Tudor Dynasty*, 189.
8. Chrimes, *Henry VII*, 1573, 1768 (Kindle).
9. Corbet, Anthony, *Edward IV: England's Forgotten Warrior King*, (Stratton Press, 2018), 181.
10. Jones and Underwood, *The King's Mother*, 68.
11. Jones, *The Wars of the Roses*, 303.
12. Hicks, Michael, *The Wars of the Roses*, (Yale University Press, 2012), 241.
13. Breverton, *Jasper Tudor*, 264.
14. Jones, *The Wars of the Roses*, 304.
15. Norton, *Margaret Beaufort*, 159-162.
16. Storey, R.L., *Reign of Henry VII (Problems of History)*, (Blandford Press, 1968), 74.
17. Jones, *The Wars of the Roses*, 307-308.
18. Breverton, *Jasper Tudor*, 267.
19. Lewis, *The Wars of the Roses*, 261.
20. Haigh, *The Military Campaigns of the Wars of the Roses*, 170.
21. Chrimes, *Henry VII*, 2126 (Kindle).
22. Breverton, *Jasper Tudor*, 268.
23. Lewis, *The Wars of the Roses*, 261.

24. Jones, *The Wars of the Roses*, 311.
25. Chrimes, *Henry VII*, 2206 (Kindle).
26. Griffiths and Thomas, *The Making of the Tudor Dynasty*, 195.
27. Jones, *The Wars of the Roses*, 312.
28. Griffiths and Thomas, *The Making of the Tudor Dynasty*, 195-196.
29. Temperley, Gladys, *Henry VII*, (Palala Press, 2015), 1339-1416 (Kindle).
30. Jones, *The Wars of the Roses*, 315.
31. Jones, *The Wars of the Roses*, 316.
32. Temperley, *Henry VII*, 1403-1422 (Kindle).
33. Jones, *The Wars of the Roses*, 317.
34. Chrimes, *Henry VII*, 2451 (Kindle).
35. Boffey, *Henry VII's London in the Great Chronicle*, (Medieval Institute Publications, 2019), 83.
36. Jones, *The Wars of the Roses*, 317.
37. Chrimes, *Henry VII*, 2451 (Kindle).

38: Henry's Tragic Last Years

1. Chrimes, *Henry VII*, 6909 (Kindle).
2. Chrimes, *Henry VII*, 2249 (Kindle).
3. Jones, *The Wars of the Roses*, 319-320.
4. Penn, *Winter King*, 54-55.
5. Penn, *Winter King*, 62.
6. Penn, *Winter King*, 61-62.
7. Norton, *Margaret Beaufort*, 180.
8. Cunningham, *Henry VII*, 107.
9. Chrimes, *Henry VII*, 7028 (Kindle).
10. Chrimes, *Henry VII*, 7052-7073 (Kindle).
11. Temperley, *Henry VII*, 3048 (Kindle).
12. Norton, *Margaret Beaufort*, 145-146.
13. Chrimes, *Henry VII*, 9973 (Kindle).
14. Seward, *Wars of the Roses*, 332.
15. Jones and Underwood, *The King's Mother*, 236.

Bibliography

Abernathy, Susan, 'Philippa of Hainault, Queen of England', *The Freelance History Writer*, November 2012, https://thefreelancehistorywriter.com/2012/11/07/philippa-of-hainault-queen-of-england/

Ackroyd, Peter, *A History of England, Volume 1: Foundation*, (MacMillan, 2011)

Aird, William M., *Robert Curthose: Duke of Normandy*, (Boydell Press, 2008)

Amin, Nathen, *The House of Beaufort: The Bastard Line that Captured the Crown*, (Amberley Publishing, 2017)

Bacon, Francis, *The History of the Reign of King Henry the Seventh*, (Cornell University Press, 1996)

Barlow, Frank, *Edward the Confessor*, (University of California Press, 1970)

Barlow, Frank, *The Godwins: The Rise and Fall of a Noble Dynasty*, (Routledge, 2015)

Bates, David, *William the Conqueror*, (Yale University Press, 2009)

Bayani, Debra, *Jasper Tudor: Godfather of the Tudor Dynasty*, (MadeGlobal Publishing, 2015)

Bevan, Bryan, *Henry VII: The First Tudor King*, (Rubicon Press, 2000)

Blacman, John, *Henry the Sixth*, (Cambridge University Press, 1919)

Boardman, Andrew, *The First Battle of St Albans*, (NPI Media Group, 2006)

Boffey, Julia, *Henry VII's London in the Great Chronicle*, (Medieval Institute Publications, 2019)

Borman, Tracy Joanne, *Queen of the Conqueror: The Life of Matilda, Wife of William*, (Bantam, 2012)

Breverton, Terry, *Henry VII: The Maligned Tudor King*, (Amberley Publishing, 2016)

Breverton, Terry, *Jasper Tudor: Tudor Dynasty*, (Amberley Publishing, 2014)

Carroll, Leslie, 'Richard III & Anne Neville: A Love Story?', *History Hoydens*, November 2009, http://historyhoydens.blogspot.com/2009/11/richard-iii-anne-neville-love-story.html

Carson, Annette, *Richard III: The Maligned King*, (Sutton Publishing, 2008)

Castor, Helen, *She-Wolves: The Women Who Ruled England Before Elizabeth*, (Harper Perennial, 2012)

Chibnall, Marjorie, *The Empress Matilda: Queen Consort, Queen Mother and Lady of the English*, (Wiley-Blackwell, 1993)

Chrimes, S.B., *Henry VII*, (Eyre Methuen, 1972)

Cole, Teresa, *After the Conquest: The Family of William of Normandy Struggle for the Crown*, Amberley Publishing, 2018)

Cole, Teresa, *The Norman Conquest: William the Conqueror's Subjugation of England*, (Amberley Publishing, 2016)

Cox, Helen R., *Battle of Wakefield Revisited*, (Helen Cox, Herstory Writing, 2010)

Craig, G., 'Alfred the Great: A Diagnosis', *Journal of the Royal Society of Medicine*, Vol. 84, May 1991, https://journals.sagepub.com/doi/pdf/10.1177/014107689108400518

Cunningham, Sean, *Henry VII*, (Routledge, 2007)

Cunningham, Sean, *Prince Arthur: The Tudor King Who Never Was*, (Amberley Publishing, 2016)

Dockray, Keith, *Edward IV: From Contemporary Chronicles, Letters and Records*, (Fonthill Media, 2015)

Douglas, David C., *William the Conqueror*, (University of California Press, 1964)

Fields, Bertram, *Royal Blood: King Richard III and the Mystery of the Princes*, (Sutton Publishing, 2000)

Gairdner, James, *Henry the Seventh*, (Macmillan, 1889)

Gairdner, James, *Letters and Papers Illustrative of the Reigns of Richard III and Henry VIII*, (Adamant Media, 2004)

Gillingham, John, *William II*, (Penguin Monarchs, 2019)

Given-Wilson, Chris, *Henry IV*, (Yale University Press, 2016)

Goodman, Anthony, *John of Gaunt: The Exercise of Princely Power in Fourteenth-Century Europe*, (Routledge, 2016)

Goodman, Anthony, *The Wars of the Roses: Military Activity and English Society, 1452–97*, (Dorset Press, 1990)

Goodwin, George, *Fatal Colours: Towton 1461: England's Most Brutal Battle*, (W.W. Norton & Company, 2012)

Griffith, Mari, *Root of the Tudor Rose*, (Accent Press, 2015)

Griffiths, Ralph and Roger S. Thomas, *The Making of the Tudor Dynasty*, (Wren Publishers, 1998)

Griffiths, Ralph A., *The Reign of King Henry VI*, (Sutton Publishing, 1998)

Grummitt, David, *Henry VI*, (Routledge, 2015)

Haigh, Philip A., *The Military Campaigns of the Wars of the Roses*, (Sutton, 1995)

Hammond, P.W., *The Battles of Barnet and Tewkesbury*, (St Martin's Press, 1990)

Hanley, Catherine, *Matilda: Empress, Queen, Warrior*, (Yale University Press, 2019)

Harvey, Nancy Lenz, *Elizabeth of York, the Mother of Henry VIII*, (MacMillan Publishing, 1973)

Hicks, Michael, *The Wars of the Roses*, (Yale University Press, 2012)

Hicks, Michael, *Warwick the Kingmaker*, (Wiley-Blackwell, 1991)

Higginbotham, Susan, 'The Death of Edmund, Earl of Rutland', *History Refreshed* by Susan Higginbotham, https://www.susanhigginbotham.com/posts/the-death-of-edmund-earl-of-rutland/

Higginbotham, Susan, *The Woodvilles: The Wars of the Roses and England's Most Infamous Family*, (The History Press, 2014)

Hollister, C. Warren, *Henry I*, (Yale University Press, 2001)

Howarth, David Armine, *1066: The Year of the Conquest*, (Dorset Press, 1993)

Hunt, Jocelyn, and Towle, Carolyn, *Henry VII*, (Pearson Education, 1998)

Ingram, Mike, *Richard III and the Battle of Bosworth*, (Helion and Company, 2019)

James, Jeffrey, *Edward IV: Glorious Son of York*, (Amberley Publishing, 2015)

Johnson, Lauren, *The Shadow King: The Life and Death of Henry VI*, (Pegasus Books, 2019)

Jones, Dan, *The Plantagenets: The Warrior Kings and Queens Who Made England*, (Viking, 2013)

Jones, Dan, *Summer of Blood: England's First Revolution*, (Penguin Books, 2016)

Jones, Dan, *The Wars of the Roses: The Fall of the Plantagenets and the Rise of the Tudors*, (Viking, 2014)

Jones, Michael, *The Black Prince: England's Greatest Medieval Warrior*, (Pegasus Books, 2018)

Jones, Michael, *Bosworth 1485*, (Hodder & Stoughton, 2014)

Jones, Michael K., and Malcolm G. Underwood, *The King's Mother: Lady Margaret Beaufort, Countess of Richmond and Derby*, (Cambridge University Press, 1992)

Kendall, Paul Murray, *Richard the Third*, (Norton, 1996)

Kendall, Paul Murray, *Warwick the Kingmaker*, (Norton, 1957)

Kendall, Paul Murray, *The Yorkist Age: Daily Life During the Wars of the Roses*, (Norton, 1962)

King, Edmund, *King Stephen*, (Yale University Press, 2011)

Kirby, J.L., *Henry IV of England*, (Constable, 1970)

Lack, Katherine, *The Conqueror's Son: Duke Robert Curthose: Thwarted King*, (Sutton, 2008)

Lewis, Matthew, *Richard, Duke of York: King by Right*, (Amberley Publishing, 2016)

Lewis, Matthew, *The Wars of the Roses: The Key Players in the Struggle for Supremacy*, (Amberley Publishing, 2015)

Licence, Amy, *Edward IV & Elizabeth Woodville: A True Romance*, (Amberley Publishing, 2016)

Licence, Amy, *Elizabeth of York: The Forgotten Tudor Queen*, (Amberley Publishing, 2013)

Licence, Amy, *Henry VI and Margaret of Anjou: A Marriage of Unequals*, (Pen & Sword Books, 2018)

MacEwen, Terry, 'Edward the Black Prince', *Historic UK*, https://www.historic-uk.com/HistoryUK/HistoryofEngland/Edward-The-Black-Prince/

Markham, Sir Clements Robert, *Richard III: His Life and Character: Reviewed in the Light of Recent Research*, (Sagwan Press, 2015)

Marren, Peter, *1066: The Battles of York, Stamford Bridge and Hastings*, (Pen & Sword Books, 2004)

Maurer, Helen E., *Margaret of Anjou: Queenship and Power in Late Medieval England*, (Boydel Press, 2003)

Morrillo, Stephen, *The Battle of Hastings: Sources and Interpretations*, (Boydell Press, 1996)

Morris, Marc, *The Norman Conquest: The Battle of Hastings and the Fall of Anglo-Saxon England*, (Pegasus Books, 2013)

Mortimer, Ian, *1415: Henry V's Year of Glory*, (Bodley Head, 2009)

Mortimer, Ian, *The Fears of Henry IV: The Life of England's Self-Made King*, (Jonathan Cape, 2007)

Mortimer, Ian, *Medieval Intrigue: Decoding Royal Conspiracies*, (Continuum, 2010)

Mowat, R.B., *Henry V*, (Wentworth Press, 2019)

Norton, Elizabeth, *Margaret Beaufort: Mother of the Tudor Dynasty*, (Amberley Publishing, 2011)

Okerlund, Arlene Naylor, *Elizabeth of Power (Queen and Power)*, (Palgrave Macmillan, 2009)

Oman, Charles, *Warwick, The Kingmaker*, (Macmillan Publishers, 1891)

Ormrod, W. Mark, *Edward III*, (Yale University Press, 2012)

Peers, Chris, *King Stephen and The Anarchy: Civil War and Military Tactics in Twelfth-Century Britain*, (Pen & Sword Books, 2018)

Penn, Thomas, *Winter King: Henry VII and the Dawn of Tudor England*, (Simon & Schuster, 1994)

Pollard, A.J., *Edward IV*, (Penguin, 2019)

Pollard, A.J., *Richard III and the Princes in the Tower*, (Palgrave MacMillan, 1991)

Pollard, A.J., *The Wars of the Roses*, (Palgrave Macmillan, 1995)

Pollard, A.J., *Warwick the Kingmaker: Politics, Power and Fame*, (Bloomsbury Academic, 2007)

Rees, David, *The Son of Prophecy: Henry Tudor's Road to Bosworth*, (Black Raven Printing, 1985)

Rex, Peter, *The English Resistance: The Underground War Against the Normans*, (Amberley Publishing, 2014)

Ridgway, Claire, 'Coronation of Edward IV', *Tudor Society*, https://www.tudorsociety.com/28-june-1461-coronation-of-edward-iv/.

Roberts, Sara Elin, *Jasper: The Tudor Kingmaker*, (Fonthill Media, 2015)

Ross, Charles Derek, *Edward IV*, (University of California Press, 1975)

Ross, Charles Derek, *Richard III*, (University of California Press, 1982)

Royle, Trevor, *Lancaster Against York: The Wars of the Roses and the Foundation of Modern Britain*, (Palgrave MacMillan, 2008)

Santiuste, David, *Edward IV and the Wars of the Roses*, (Pen & Sword Books, 2010)

Saul, Nigel, *Richard II*, (Yale University Press, 1997)

Scofield, Cora L, *The Life and Reign of Edward the Fourth, King of England and of France and Lord of Ireland, Volumes 1 & 2*, (Longmans, Green and Company, 1923)

Seward, Desmond, *The Demon's Brood*, (Pegasus Books, 2014)

Seward, Desmond, *Henry V: The Scourge of God*, (Viking, 1988)

Seward, Desmond, *The Hundred Years War: The English in France 1337-1453*, (Atheneum, 1978)

Seward, Desmond, *The Last White Rose: The Secret Wars of the Tudors*, (Constable, 2011)

Seward, Desmond, *Richard III: England's Black Legend*, (Franklin Watts, 1984)

Seward, Desmond, *Wars of the Roses*, (Viking, 1995)

Storey, R.L., *The End of the House of Lancaster*, (Sutton Publishing, 1999)

Storey, R.L., *Reign of Henry VII (Problems of History)*, (Blandford Press, 1968)

Temperley, Gladys, *Henry VII*, (Palala Press, 2015)

Warner, Kathryn, *Richard II: A True King's Fall*, (Amberley Publishing, 2018)

Warren, Wilfred Lewis, *Henry II*, (University of California Press, 1973)

Weird, Alison, *Elizabeth of York: A Tudor Queen and Her World*, (Ballantine Books, 2013)

Weir, Alison, *The Princes in the Tower*, (Ballantine Books, 1994)

Weir, Alison, *Queens of the Conquest: England's Medieval Queens*, (Ballantine Books, 2017)

West, Ed, *1066 and Before All That: The Battle of Hastings, Anglo-Saxon and Norman England*, (Skyhorse, 2017)

Williams, Neville, *The Life and Times of Henry VII*, (Weidenfeld and Nicolson, 1973)

Wright, Arthur Colin, *Decoding the Bayeux Tapestry: The Secrets of History's Most Famous Embroidery Hidden in Plain Sight*, (Frontline Books, 2019)

Index